Y̶ou can view this as a recipe book and use it as such, but I hope this book will inspire you to walk the path of the Hearth Witch, which is so much more. While you may begin to learn how to work with natural resources from books like this one, the true teaching only comes when you start listening to the land and its plants and animals.

When the sacred within you recognises the sacred that surrounds you everywhere, a deeper spiritual reality opens up in which all space becomes sacred space, all time becomes sacred time, and all acts become sacred acts.

This is the true path of the Hearth Witch. Walk it in beauty.

Anna Franklin

THE
HEARTH
Witch's
GARDEN
HERBAL

Anna Franklin is a third-degree witch and high priestess of the Hearth of Arianrhod, and she has been a practicing Pagan for more than forty years. She is the author of over thirty books and the creator of the *Sacred Circle Tarot*, *Fairy Ring Oracle*, and the *Pagan Ways Tarot* (Schiffer, 2015). Her books have been translated into nine languages.

Anna has contributed hundreds of articles to Pagan magazines and has appeared on radio and TV. She lives and works in a village in the English Midlands, where she grows her own herbs, fruit, and vegetables, and generally lives the Pagan life. Visit her online at www.AnnaFranklin.co.uk.

THE
HEARTH
Witch's
GARDEN
HERBAL

PLANTS, RECIPES & RITUALS FOR
HEALING & MAGICAL SELF-CARE

ANNA FRANKLIN

Llewellyn Publications
WOODBURY, MINNESOTA

FIRST EDITION
First Printing, 2023

Book design by Rebecca Zins
Cover design by Kevin R. Brown
Interior floral background © Dover Publications
Interior floral woodcut © *1167 Decorative Cuts* (New York: Dover Publications, 2007)

Llewellyn is a registered trademark of Llewellyn Worldwide Ltd.

NOTE: The information in this book is provided for educational and entertainment purposes only. It does not constitute a recommendation for use.

Library of Congress Cataloging-in-Publication Data
(Pending)

ISBN 978-0-7387-7230-1

Llewellyn Publications
A Division of Llewellyn Worldwide Ltd.
2143 Wooddale Drive
Woodbury MN 55125-2989

WWW.LLEWELLYN.COM

Printed in the United States of America

Contents

PART 2

· · · · · · · · · · ·

The A-Z Herbal 83

Introduction

Not so long ago, the garden was an essential resource for most families, used to supplement the household's food supply as well as provide medicine, dye plants, and domestic essentials such as soap ingredients and bedding. Only the very rich could afford a garden full of purely decorative flowers, with wide lawns to walk on.

Nowadays most of us tend to see our gardens as a refuge, a place we can escape our hectic lives, reconnect with nature, and rejuvenate our minds and spirits. We have a deep psychological and spiritual need for green spaces; during the Covid lockdowns, I was never more thankful for my garden. The garden is my happy place.

It is not surprising that many of the world's religions think of paradise, the idyllic afterlife, as a garden. The word *paradise* itself comes from the Persian *pairidaeza*, which means "enclosed garden." In Christian lore the Garden of Eden is a perfect lost home from which humankind was expelled. In the Koran paradise is a shady garden with unfailing fountains, neither too hot nor too cold, with fruits hanging down, ready to be picked. In our own gardens, each one of us tries to create our own little bit of earthly paradise.

Our gardens can be many things to us: a haven from the busy world, the place we link with the natural world, somewhere that delights the senses, a place of ritual, or a place of meditation. It can also provide us with food, medicine, and magical ingredients.

Gardening helps us to attune to the ebb and flow of the earth's energy in its seasonal turning. My garden teaches me more about the magic of nature than any book. Season by season, I collect its wealth.

I hope this book helps you understand more about the spiritual aspects of your own garden, as well as share some surprising uses for familiar garden plants. You might find that the flowers you already grow are as magical as any expensive, exotic magical herb you can buy.

A Note on Botanical Names

Many plants have similar names. The only way to be sure you have the right plant is to refer to the official botanical name, usually in Latin or Greek. This normally has two parts, the first referring to the genus the plant belongs to and the second referring to the specific species and usually descriptive, so that *Quercus rubra* translates as "oak red," with *quercus* meaning oak and *rubra* meaning red. The second part of the name can tell you a lot about the plant: *officinalis*, for example, means that it was a medicinal herb listed in the official pharmacopeia, *vulgaris* means "common," *sylvestris* means "of the woods," *sativa* means "cultivated," and so on. Using botanical names isn't entirely foolproof; they are sometimes changed as the plants are reclassified and may appear differently in older books. Throughout this work I've tried to give both old and new botanical names. The older name will appear after the prefix syn., meaning synonym.

Part 1

The Witch's Garden

Witches garden a little differently; for us, the garden is sacred space, and gardening is magic at its most immediate and most raw.

We remember that our gardens don't really belong to us and that we are only looking after them for all the plants and creatures that live there and for the spirits that were there before we came and will be there long after we have gone. No matter how small the garden is, we are caretakers of the land and have a duty to it.

We know that the garden is full of the power of the invisible. It has its own *anima loci*, or "soul of place." We recognise this and the garden's other spirits and try to work in cooperation with them. We honour them and make offerings to them, season by season.

We recognise that plants have spirits too. Each plant is recognised as a living teacher and approached as an individual, which may (or may not) become an ally.

Everything we do in the garden is done with magical intent. Seeds are planted with intent and cared for with love. We open ourselves to communicating with their spirits—a meeting of human and plant spirit that should benefit both.

We look on the garden as belonging as much to the wildlife as it does to us. The creatures who visit are our garden familiars. If we treat them properly, they aid us in our work and may be agents of the spirit world to us.

Gardening teaches us about the magic of hope, growth, and renewal. It requires patience and observation to be in tune with our plants, and there is nothing better to teach us about herb craft. And we remember that there is no garden without weeds! Sometimes they are the most useful plants of all.

. . . . .

MOIST MOTHER EARTH

We recognise Mother Earth as the goddess who gives us life, who supports and nourishes us; without her we would not exist. This means recognising that the land beneath our feet is not merely dirt but sacred space, the body of the Goddess herself.

Mother Earth is known in every part of the world and has had many names. The Greeks called her Gaia, the Romans called her Terra; in Slavic mythology she has a beautifully descriptive name in Russian, Mati Syra Zemlya, which means "moist Mother Earth." She presides over the whole cycle of being: planting, growth, and harvest; birth, growth, decline, death, and rebirth.

Whatever name she is known by, she is the all-encompassing source of life, the spirit flowing throughout the great matrix of nature, a fountain of energy that sustains animals, plants, and people, connecting it into a unified, sacred whole. The old Pagan myths show us a world in which everything is alive and connected.

Offering to Mother Earth

It seems fitting to begin work in a garden with an offering to Mother Earth. You can do this as often as seems fit.

Sit or stand in the garden with a jug of wine. Open your senses to its sights, its smells, and its sounds. Take your time. Now go deeper. Sense the life there—the plants and animals—and how it interconnects. Go deeper. Feel the life stirring in the earth, the source of all things. Feel the energy of the Goddess moving through it. Say:

> Mother Earth, you are life, you are abundance,
> You produce all in nature;
> You produced me, your child.
> You are first in all things, you surround me;
> You are beneath my feet.
> You give me the food I eat, the water I drink.
> From you comes all I see, all that breathes.

Pour the wine on the earth; this is called a libation. Say:

> Mother Earth, I give thanks for this place,
> For the sun and the wind, the rain and the land.
> Mother Earth, I give thanks for all that lives here,
> The winged creatures, the crawling creatures,
> The flying creatures, and the four-legged creatures.

Mother Earth, I give thanks for all that grows here.
Blessed be.

Spend as long as you wish reflecting on this.

Maintaining Balance

For the witch, the relationship between us and Mother Earth is a reciprocal one, a harmony that must be maintained. This was the sacred agreement the old Pagan religions recognised; when something is taken, something else must be given in return. It was both a practical and a ritual task, with goodness returned to the soil and ceremonies performed at certain times of year to honour the gods. This is a covenant that the modern world has broken, where Mother Earth is seen as a commodity, raped and pillaged for her gifts.

In 2019 the UN warned that because of modern agricultural practice and the use of chemical fertilisers and pesticides, soils around the world are heading for exhaustion and depletion, with an estimated sixty harvests left before they are too barren to feed the planet.[1] The excessive use of pesticides has depleted the earth's soil and contributed to a drastic decline in insect numbers that threatens "catastrophic collapse of nature's ecosystems."[2] Furthermore, the nutritional quality of the food we eat has sharply declined, attributable in part to newer varieties of produce grown purely for yield and appearance, and partly to declining soil health. A study from the University of Texas, published in December 2004 in the *Journal of the American College of Nutrition*, showed that fruits and vegetables grown decades ago were far richer in vitamins and minerals than they are now.[3] In Britain a comparable study published in the *British Food Journal* found that in twenty vegetables the average calcium content had declined 19 percent, iron 22 percent, and potassium 14 percent from

---

1   https://www.scientificamerican.com/article/only-60-years-of-farming-left-if-soil-degradation
    -continues.

2   Francisco Sánchez-Bayo and Kris A. G. Wyckhuys, "Worldwide Decline of the Entomofauna:
    A Review of Its Drivers," *Biological Conservation* 232 (2019): 8–27.

3   Donald R. Davis, et al., "Changes in USDA Food Composition Data for 43 Garden Crops, 1950 to
    1999," *Journal of the American College of Nutrition* 23, no. 6 (2004): 669–82, doi:10.1080/07315724.2004
    .10719409.

1930 to 1980.[4] Another concluded that we would have to eat eight oranges today to derive the same amount of vitamin A as our grandparents would have had from one.[5]

All life on earth depends on a six-inch layer of topsoil. That's a sobering thought.

Soil is not just dirt; it is a living thing, with a wide variety of microorganisms, insects, earthworms, and other creatures. Organic farmers and gardeners use composted manure and other organic matter to help improve soil fertility. This enhances the soil's capacity to store and supply essential nutrients to plants and improves soil structure. Microorganisms, earthworms, and insects feed on plant residues and manures for energy and nutrition, and in the process they mix organic matter into the mineral soil and recycle plant nutrients.

We are slowly relearning the old lesson that the relationship between us and the gods, between us and Mother Earth, must be a mutual one. This touches on the core purpose of the witch: maintaining balance. Whenever conflict, disorder, and imbalance manifested in tribal and old village societies, the village wise woman, cunning man, or shaman would be consulted to discover how the pact with the gods/Mother Nature had been broken and what must be done to put it right. Witches are healers, not just of human bodies but of Earth itself.

While it is clear that farmers and big agri-business have to change their ways, we can play our parts on the patches of land we are responsible for (our gardens), and it is fitting that we begin right here, balancing the needs of all that lives in the garden, maintaining the land and its ecosystem in harmony.

How Your Garden Benefits the Environment

If you have been gardening for a couple of decades or more, you will have noticed that the climate is changing. Shifting weather patterns can bring increased rain or increasing levels of drought and higher or lower temperatures for the season. In the future we may not be able to grow the things we do now where we are. Soon many native plants may no longer be able to survive in their historic ranges, and the wildlife they support will be decimated. However, your garden—no matter how big or small—can have a big impact on your local environment and help protect local wildlife by doing the following:

---

4   A. Mayer, "Historical Changes in the Mineral Content of Fruits and Vegetables," *British Food Journal* 99, no. 6 (1997): 207–211, https://doi.org/10.1108/00070709710181540.

5   https://www.scientificamerican.com/article/soil-depletion-and-nutrition-loss.

IMPROVES AIR QUALITY

Plants take in carbon dioxide from the atmosphere through their leaves and expel oxygen, as well as help remove toxins from the air. Your plants help the local atmosphere.

DETOXIFIES THE GROUND

Plants also absorb through their roots, including chemicals and heavy metals in the soil and groundwater, gradually converting it into healthier ground. Naturally, this is not good for the particular plant, but a sick plant can alert you to soil toxicity.

CARBON CAPTURES

All plants capture and lock away carbon dioxide (CO_2), one of the greenhouse gasses driving climate change, releasing it again when they die. A fully grown tree can absorb and store around 21 kilograms (46 pounds) of carbon dioxide a year[6] and keep it sequestered for hundreds of years. A sapling will absorb significantly less, but every tree contributes. There are around 23 million gardens in the UK[7] and 85 million in the USA[8]—think what a difference it would make if every one of those gardeners planted a tree, no matter how small, and imagine the effect if every gardener in the world took part.

PROVIDES NATURAL SHADE

Shade trees planted near your home can reduce energy used for cooling in the summer.

REDUCES YOUR CARBON FOOTPRINT

Growing some of your own food will reduce your carbon footprint: fewer trips to the shops, no food-miles, less waste.

PREVENTS SOIL EROSION

Plant roots bind soils together, making them less likely to wash away.

REPLENISHES NUTRIENTS IN THE SOIL

Topsoil is created by organic materials, such as leaves, that fall from plants. Decaying organic material provides nutrients, and some plants fix nutrients into the ground.

---

6   https://www.co2meter.com/blogs/news/could-global-co2-levels-be-reduced-by-planting-trees.

7   Wildlife Gardening Forum, http://www.wlgf.org/garden_resource.html.

8   https://www.nwf.org/Our-Work/Environmental-Threats/Climate-Change/Greenhouse-Gases/Gardening-for-Climate-Change.

HELPS TO REDUCE NOISE POLLUTION

Vegetation absorbs sound, so hedges, trees, and shrubbery reduce noise pollution.

HELPS WILDLIFE

The more plants and trees you have in the garden, the more you will be encouraging the local wildlife, especially if you include native plants. Birds, insects, and other animals need them to survive. If you live in a built-up area, providing natural spaces for insects, birds, and small mammals is vitally important.

. . . .

While almost every garden helps the environment, you can do even more:

PLANT NATIVE SPECIES

Including native plants in your garden helps maintain important pollinator connections and ensure food sources for wildlife. You can plant shrubs with berries for birds plus bee, insect, and butterfly friendly plants.

REWILD PART OF YOUR GARDEN

This means giving part of your garden back to nature and letting nature do its thing—including letting the native "weeds" (I call them wildflowers) grow, which provide food for the local insects. Remove any non-native plants from this area. Increasingly, over time, it will become a complex established ecosystem.

If you can't do this, avoid large paved areas and artificial grass.

CREATE A WILDLIFE POND

A garden pond, whether large or small, can be a haven for wildlife, and the wildlife will find it pretty quickly. It is vital habitat for wetland creatures such as frogs and dragonflies and great for many species of insects, birds, and mammals. Remember to make one side shallow so that frogs and small mammals can climb out. Have some shade over part of the pond to reduce algae growth, but part should be in full sun. Fill it with rainwater if you can, but if tap water must be used, be sure to let it naturalise for at least a week before adding any forms of life, including plants.

BUILD INSECT HOTELS

Insects pollinate your plants, aerate the soil, and provide food for birds. The beneficial insects in your garden need somewhere to hibernate for the winter, so why not make them their own five-star bug hotel? It is best to do this in the early autumn, when there is plenty of suitable material available, such as dry leaves, twigs, hollow stems, dead grass, pinecones, and bits of bark, and it will give the insects time to settle into their new home before the cold comes. There are some great ideas online for making bug hotels, and kids will love to get involved. Otherwise, you can simply make a log pile in a shady area for centipedes, woodlice, and beetles; a pile of pinecones and leaves is good for ladybirds and lacewings.

HAVE HOLES IN YOUR BOUNDARY WALLS

It is important for wildlife to be able to move around from one place to another. A hedgehog, for example, can travel up to a mile in a single night, looking for food. One of the reasons for declining populations is the high, solid fences that some people have around their gardens. You can help by putting small holes in the bottom of your fences (as long as your neighbour agrees).

RECONSIDER YOUR GARDEN LIGHTING

The blue and white toned lighting often used in gardens is one of the major factors in biodiversity collapse as it confuses insects. Leave areas of your garden in darkness, and don't use your lights all the time. You can buy red-tone lights that don't affect insects as much. Try to use energy efficient products in your garden; replace energy hungry outdoor bulbs with LEDs or, better still, use solar lighting.

REDUCE THE USE OF POWER TOOLS

Avoid using power tools as much as you can. Using a gasoline-powered mower for an hour pollutes ten to twelve times more than the average car.[9] If you can, switch to hand tools and push lawnmowers. The air from leaf blowers kills small creatures, and I would urge you not to use them at all.

INSTALL A RAIN BARREL

Install a rain barrel to collect free rainwater and your plants will like this much better than tap water. You can prevent water loss from your plants by mulching around them.

MAKE A COMPOST HEAP

Building a compost heap (or using a purchased compost bin) is a wonderful way to reduce your impact on the environment and create a great free source of nutrients for your garden. You can add virtually all food waste and organic matter to your compost bin—fruit and

---

9   https://washingtoncitypaper.com/article/222039/straight-dope-how-much-pollution-do-gasoline
     -powered-lawn-mowers.

vegetable peelings, leftovers, twigs, leaves, non-seeding weeds, eggshells, card egg boxes, cardboard, tea bags (if they don't contain plastic), coffee grounds, and even your old wool jumpers, but don't add cooked food or meat. To my compost I also add the sawdust bedding and poo cleaned out from my chickens. You will need to add something to "activate" your compost (i.e., get everything working), and for this you will need to add soft greens, manures, or urine (yes, you can use your own, though male urine is said to work better than female).

DON'T RAKE YOUR LEAVES

While you might need to remove slippery leaves from paths, in the rest of the garden fallen leaves provide a habitat for many overwintering wild creatures. Some beneficial insects lay their eggs in leaf litter, and by raking up the leaves you will be curtailing their life cycle and adding to population decline. If you do rake them up, put them on the compost heap or bag them and save them to use as mulch in the spring. Lay a mulch of fallen leaves around plants (about 3 inches deep) and allow it to rot down into the soil. The earthworms will love it, and you will be adding nutrients and organic matter into the ground. Leaf mulch maintains soil moisture and soil temperature and prevents weeds, soil erosion, and compaction.

NO AUTUMN CLEANUP

Abandon the big autumn cleanup of the garden. Leave the fallen wood, leaves, and seed heads where they are till spring, as birds, insects, and other wildlife need their shelter and food over the winter.

DITCH THE CHEMICALS

In the twentieth century, chemicals were promoted as an easy technical solution to all cultivation problems. Synthetic fertilizers, pesticides, and weedkillers became commonplace not only on farms, but also in domestic gardens. We now know that these products are having a disastrous effect on ecosystems, wildlife, and human health.[10]

Pesticides from treated plants and soil reach surface water through runoff. More than 90 percent of water and fish samples from all streams in the US contain one or more pesticides,[11] and wild salmon are swimming around with dozens of synthetic chemicals in their systems.[12] In the UK half of rivers and freshwaters exceed chronic pollution limits, and

---

10   https://policy.friendsoftheearth.uk/opinion/effects-pesticides-our-wildlife.
11   M. W. Aktar, D. Sengupta, and A. Chowdhury, "Impact of pesticides use in agriculture: their benefits and hazards," *Interdiscip Toxicol.* 2, no. (2009): 1–12, doi:10.2478/v10102-009-0001-7.
12   https://www.scientificamerican.com/article/how-fertilizers-harm-earth.

88 percent of samples showed pesticide contamination.[13] We are now seeing the wholesale pollution of most of our streams, rivers, ponds, and coastal areas from agri-chemicals.

Chemical fertilisers are equally problematic. When the excess nutrients run off into our waterways, they can cause algae blooms that are sometimes big enough to make waterways impassable. When the algae die, they sink to the bottom and decompose in a process that removes oxygen from the water. Fish and other aquatic species can't survive in these dead zones.

It's time to dump the chemicals and look for natural solutions. If you care for your plants well, you won't need them. Choose plants that are suited to the growing conditions you have; native plants will thrive better. Allow them plenty of space, and prune where you need to. Provide good drainage and mulch your plants to keep down weeds and reduce the need for watering. Regularly hand-weed and hoe. Wash off pests with the garden hose or try one of the aphid sprays listed below. Greenfly can be dusted with diatomaceous earth (available online). Investigate companion planting to reduce pest invasion. If you grow vegetables, rotate your crops on an annual basis. Be prepared to accept a low level of pest or disease damage on your organic plants.

Recipes for Garden Care

GARLIC APHID SPRAY

1 TABLESPOON MINERAL OIL

5 CLOVES GARLIC, CHOPPED

2 TEASPOONS WASHING-UP LIQUID (DISH SOAP)

600 ML OR 2½ CUPS WATER

Soak the cloves in the oil overnight. Strain off the oil and add it to the water and soap. Shake and spray on to aphid infestations.

---

13   https://policy.friendsoftheearth.uk/opinion/effects-pesticides-our-wildlife.

Soapy Water Aphid Spray

4 TABLESPOONS WASHING-UP LIQUID (DISH SOAP)

4½ LITRES OR 1 GALLON WATER

Combine and spray onto aphid infestations.

Epsom Salt Aphid Spray

2 TABLESPOONS EPSOM SALT

2 TABLESPOONS WASHING-UP LIQUID (DISH SOAP)

4½ LITRES OR 1 GALLON WATER

Combine and spray onto aphid infestations.

Slug and Snail Protection

If snails are troublesome in your garden, try crushing some eggshells and putting them around your plants as they don't like to cross fine particles. If your plants are in pots, you can put a copper band around the pots, which gives the slugs a slight electric shock. You can try encouraging frogs and toads into your garden, as they will eat slugs. Or you can try a beer trap: half fill a jar with beer and bury it up to its neck in the garden.

Nettle Aphid Spray

HANDFUL OF FRESH STINGING NETTLES

500 ML OR 2½ CUPS BOILING WATER

Pour boiling water over the nettles and infuse for 20 minutes. Strain into a spray bottle. Spray directly onto aphids.

Stinging Nettle Liquid Manure

Gather fresh nettles and put them in a bucket. Cover them with water. After several days the mixture will start to ferment and smell. It is ready to use after 2 weeks. Dilute 1:10 with water and use around the base of your plants.

Nasturtium Aphid Treatment

HANDFUL OF FRESH NASTURTIUM LEAVES

500 ML OR 2½ CUPS BOILING WATER

Pour boiling water over the nasturtium leaves and infuse for 20 minutes. Strain into a bottle. Paint directly onto aphids with a small brush.

Horsetail Spray for Downy Mildew

HANDFUL OF FRESH HORSETAIL (*EQUISETUM ARVENSE*)

500 ML OR 2½ CUPS BOILING WATER

Pour boiling water over the horsetail and infuse for 20 minutes. Strain into a spray bottle. Spray directly onto mildew.

Ant Deterrent

1 TABLESPOON SUGAR

1 TABLESPOON BORAX

2 TABLESPOONS WATER

FEW DROPS ORANGE ESSENTIAL OIL

Combine sugar and borax in a bowl, add water, and mix well. Add the essential oil. Soak cotton balls in the mixture and leave where ants get into your house.

Companion Planting

Nowadays most farms grow plants in a mono-crop system, with acres containing a single crop. Even garden vegetable growers tend to plant multiples of a particular crop in one place. This makes it much easier for pests and diseases to find their favourite plants and spread through them, which is when people generally reach for chemical pesticides. If we look at how Mother Nature manages things, we find a variety of plants in any one place, which makes it harder for pests and diseases to range through. Mother Nature knows how to keep the balance.

We can apply this lesson in our own gardens by utilising companion planting. It works in several ways—strongly scented companion plants can confuse or deter pests looking for their favourite plant (for example, garlic's smell is unappealing to many pests), other companions attract pollinators and beneficial insects that prey on aphids (for example, borage attracts pollinating bees and tiny pest-eating wasps). Some plants attract natural predators such as birds, which eat slugs, or hoverflies, which eat aphids, or entice bees that pollinate your crops.

Perhaps the best-known example of companion planting is the Native American Three Sisters method whereby maize, climbing beans, and winter squash are planted together and help each other grow. The tall maize provides a support for the climbing beans while the low-growing squash shades the ground to prevent moisture loss and its big leaves keep down weeds and discourage pests. Moreover, the beans are nitrogen fixers in the soil, which make nitrogen available to other plants.

Companion planting supports plant diversity and that benefits the plants, the soil, the ecosystem, and the gardener, who doesn't have to work so hard!

Crop	Companion Plants
Asparagus	Calendula deters asparagus beetle.
Brassicas	Nasturtiums attract cabbage white butterflies and stop them laying on your brassicas. Mint deters flea beetles.
Beets	Onions deter borers, mites, slugs, cutworms, and maggots.
Courgette/zucchini	Calendula
Broad beans	Summer savoury repels blackfly.
Carrot	Onion scents deter carrot flies, so plant spring onions (scallions), leeks, or chives nearby. Sage repels carrot fly.
Chrysanthemum	Chives deter aphids.
Cucumber	Nasturtiums repel cucumber beetles.

CROP	COMPANION PLANTS
LETTUCE	GARLIC AND CHIVES DETER APHIDS. POACHED EGGPLANTS (*LIMNANTHES DOUGLASII*) ATTRACT HOVERFLIES, WHICH CONTROL APHIDS.
RUNNER BEANS (CLIMBING BEANS) AND FRENCH BEANS	NASTURTIUMS ATTRACT APHIDS AWAY FROM YOUR CROPS. PLANTING SWEET PEAS NEARBY WILL ATTRACT POLLINATING INSECTS AND INCREASE YOUR CROP YIELD.
ONION	MINT DETERS ONION FLY.
PEAS	CHIVES DETER APHIDS. ALYSSUM BRINGS IN POLLINATORS AND ENCOURAGES GREEN LACEWINGS, WHICH EAT APHIDS.
PEPPERS	BASIL, OREGANO, AND MARJORAM.
RADISH	MINT DETERS FLEA BEETLES.
TOMATOES	MINT OR CHIVES DETER APHIDS, FRENCH MARIGOLDS DETER WHITEFLY. BASIL REPELS WHITEFLIES, MOSQUITOES, SPIDER MITES, AND APHIDS. PARSLEY ATTRACTS INSECTS AWAY FROM TOMATOES. BORAGE ATTRACTS POLLINATING BEES AND TINY PEST-EATING WASPS.
MELON	DILL, FENNEL, AND PARSLEY ATTRACT POLLINATORS
POTATOES	TANSY DETERS CUTWORM. CILANTRO (CORIANDER) PROTECTS AGAINST APHIDS, SPIDER MITES, AND POTATO BEETLES. CALENDULA, TANSY, CATMINT, AND HORSERADISH WARD OFF COLORADO POTATO BEETLES.
SUNFLOWERS	CHIVES DETER APHIDS.
SWISS CHARD	ALYSSUM (*LOBULARIA MARITIMA* SYN. *ALYSSUM MARITIMUM*) ATTRACTS HOVERFLIES, WHICH CONTROL APHIDS.
ROSES	GARLIC, MINT, CHIVES, AND THYME DETER APHIDS.

Moon Gardening

Gardening by the moon can bring a very satisfying unity to your gardening and magical work. It used to be common practice to garden by the moon's phases, with the idea being that when you sow has an effect on the plant: "If a tree be planted in the increase of the moone, it growth to be great; but if it be in the wane, it will be smaller, yet a great deal more lasting."[14]

While the moon is a constant presence in the night sky, it is ever changing. As it waxes and wanes, pulling with it the tides of the sea, the moon influences all that is living. Generally speaking, as the moon waxes, the energy flows upwards into the leaves and stalks of the plant; as it wanes, the virtue travels to the roots. Plants to be harvested for their roots should be planted and gathered at the waning moon, and plants required for their flowers, leaves, and fruits should be planted and gathered at the waxing moon.

WAXING MOON

The waxing moon is a time for new beginnings or things that will grow to fullness in time. As the earth breathes out, sap rises and growth above soil is favoured. A waxing moon is the best time to sow and plant anything that yields a harvest above the soil, including flowers. In the first week following the new moon, sow leafy vegetables and plants whose flowers and seeds are the edible part. Lawns also grow well when planted at the waxing moon. Repot plants during the waxing moon, as they will recover and grow better than if done at the waning moon. Do not prune during the waxing moon, however, as sap is rising in the plants and they will bleed heavily.

FULL MOON

During the full moon, growth above soil reaches its peak. The concentration of active ingredients in herbs and plants is highest at the full moon, when they should be picked. Yule trees that are felled on the traditional day—the third day before the eleventh full moon of the year—will keep their needles for longer than those felled later.

---

14 Quoted in Robin Page, *Gardening the Country Way* (Cambridge: Silent Books, 1991).

WANING MOON

The waning moon is a time of winding down and relinquishing old relationships and situations. It is the time to perform purifications and cleansing magic. Cleaning out the greenhouse and clearing beds is best done at the waning moon. It is also a good time to weed and hoe to banish unwanted plants and pests. Strenuous physical work is easier now than during a waxing moon, and any injuries sustained by overdoing it will heal quicker. This is a good time to prune trees and shrubs—they will bleed less and recover more quickly. The energies of the waning moon are good for root crops; sow root vegetables such as carrots and turnips just after the full moon, along with lettuce. Do not sow flowers at this time. Do not plant anything in the week before the new moon.

THE DARK MOON

During the three days of the dark moon, when the moon is not visible, it is best to do no gardening, if possible. The dark moon is a time of integration and silent transformation. It is wise to rest and allow the work you have done to mature under the hand of Mother Nature.

The Spirits of Your Garden

The spiritual and physical are not separate but indivisible, the one a reflection of the other. Our gods and goddesses represent the diversity of the natural world, the indwelling divinity present in all things, a life force that suffuses the whole of nature. When you stand in your garden, you stand upon the body of Mother Earth—not a commodity but a sentient being who sustains us and nourishes us.

Thinking this way is alien to modern Western materialistic society, but it is nothing new; it has been how humankind has thought and behaved throughout much of its history, and it is how indigenous cultures still think and behave. In these times of ecological crisis, we need to listen to indigenous ways of relating to nature as we begin to recognise the interconnectedness of all life and the need to work with nature rather than against it. Acknowledging the sacred within everything means that we must treat all space as sacred space and all beings as equal.

It is important to build up a relationship with the place that you work and the spirits that inhabit it over time. It will gradually become more and more powerful, and you will gain the trust of its spirits.

Shrines in the Garden

To remind us of the sacred in the garden, it is good to have some small shrines to its deities and spirits. I have a God and Goddess statue in the garden, a representation of a water nymph by the pond, and a place to make offerings to the anima loci. In the spring I put out Green Man masks to represent the spirit of vegetation. Shrines become places to make offerings, connect with the gods, work magic, and meditate.

The Anima Loci

The garden has its own soul, or *anima loci* ("soul of place"), its essential personality. I believe that this evolves from the matrix of all that has lived there—the people, animals, plants, spirits, and events that have happened nearby. It is not fixed but continues to change. When the anima loci is recognised and acknowledged, its power awakens.

Choose a quiet place in the garden and open your heart to its soul. Speak quietly and ask for its help to make the most of your garden as a place of beauty that humans, plants, animals, and spirits can share. When you are planning changes in the garden and when you are planting, weeding, and pruning, ask it to oversee the work.

Ritual to Befriend the Anima Loci

Prepare a garland of flowers, all of which you must pick yourself from your garden. Go into the garden at dawn with some wine (if possible, homemade wine made from garden produce) or fruit juice, a cup, some cakes that you have made yourself, and your garland.

Put on the garland. Say:

> *Soul of this place, I call to you.*
> *Soul of this place, I honour you.*
> *Attend me now and witness my intentions.*

Pour some of the wine into the cup. Pour a few drops on the ground, saying:

> *Soul of this place, I make this offering to you.*

Drink some of the wine yourself.
Take the cakes and crumble one onto the ground, saying:

> *Soul of this place, I make this offering to you.*

Eat one of the cakes. Say:

> *Soul of this place, draw near and listen to my words. I come to honour you,*
> *to pledge to you that I shall honour the sacred earth on which we both live;*

*I shall not pollute nor harm it. I shall honour the wild places and hold sacred the
creatures of the earth, my brothers and sisters of fur and fin, of leaf and bark.
I shall hold sacred the cycles of the seasons and be part of the dance of the earth.*

Like you, I shall take no more than I need, and I will tread softly upon the earth.

*Test my words, and if you find them truthful, spoken from my heart, then
accept me as your friend. If you find them false, then treat me accordingly.*

Sit quietly for a while and listen to the world around you. You may see evidence of spirit
presence or hear voices in the trees, whispering in the wind. When you are ready to leave,
get up, leave the rest of the cakes, pour the remaining wine onto the ground, and say:

*Soul of this place, you have listened to my words and weighed my intentions.
I go now, but I shall hold you in my heart. Soul of this place, hail and farewell.*

GODS OF THE GARDEN

The gods are present everywhere, and there are some that take a special interest in gardening. As well as having a shrine to the archetypal Lord and Lady, depending on what path
you follow, you might like to have a special shrine to one of the gods below (or another
from your heritage):

GREEN MAN: I think of the Green Man as the spirit of vegetation. Many Pagans
have sculptures and masks that represent him, a face surrounded by leaves, and
in the mediaeval period in England they were often an architectural feature on
buildings, including churches. Many mythologies have a vegetation spirit, a god
who represents growth in spring. Every spring I put out my Green Man masks in
the garden to call the spirit of vegetation back to the land and ask for his blessing.

VIRIDIOS: Viridios ("green/fresh/vigorous") is an ancient British god of vegetation,
rebirth, and agriculture in Celtic mythology, a Green Man figure.

VENUS: Venus is a very ancient Italian goddess associated with cultivated fields
and gardens who was only later associated with the Greek goddess of love, Aphrodite. Aptly for a patron deity of gardeners, her statue appears in many gardens to
this day. It is appropriate for Pagan gardeners to honour her in the garden. I have
a small figurine of her where I offer roses, her sacred flower.

CHLORIS: Chloris ("pale green/fresh") is the Greek goddess of flowers, new growth, and spring. She is married to Zephyrus, the god of the west wind, who brings the warm breezes in springtime.

FLORA: Flora ("flower") is a Roman goddess of flowers and of the season of spring. Her festival, the Floralia, was held between April 28 and May 3 and symbolized the renewal of the cycle of life. Flora is married to Favonius, the west wind.

XOCHIQUETZAL: In Aztec mythology, Xochiquetzal ("flower-precious-feather") is a goddess of agriculture and fertility. Depicted as a young woman, her symbols are vegetation and flowers. Worshipers wore flower masks at her festival.

PACHAMAMA: In Inca mythology, Pachamama ("mother earth") is an earth mother goddess who presides over planting and harvesting. She is ever-present and uses her own creative power to sustain life on earth.

DEMETER: Demeter is the Greek goddess of the harvest, crops, the fertility of the earth, grains, and the seasons. Her Roman equivalent is Ceres.

HEGEMONE: In Greek mythology, Hegemone ("mastery") is a Greek goddess of plants, who makes them bloom and bear fruit.

SAINT DOROTHY: In Christian lore, St. Dorothy is the patron saint of gardeners. It was customary to bless fruit trees on St. Dorothy's Day (6 February), which is perhaps why she is the patron saint of gardening.

THE FOUR ELEMENTS

If you are a witch, it is good to have all four elements manifested in your garden. Of course, there is the earth itself (even if it is only in pots), there is the air that blows through it, water in the garden pond or the rain that falls, and fire in bonfires, candles, or firepits. Other representations are up to your imagination.

NATURE SPIRITS, FAIRIES, AND DEVAS

Nature spirits have had a variety of names in different times and places, but they have been acknowledged in every part of the world at one time or another. They are the spirits who inhabit and protect the natural world, causing plants to grow and flocks to multiply. The ancient Greeks, for example, had nymphs who were believed to live in and care for rivers (potamids), running water and streams (naiads), meadows and mountains (orestiads or oreads), oak trees (dryads and hamadryads), ash trees (meliads), flower nymphs (anthousai), and the sea (nereids or oceanides), to name just a few. The belief that everything has spirit is called animism.

In Western Europe, even after the coming of Christianity, these attitudes were not lost but morphed into a belief in fairies. Right into the twentieth century, a connection with the fairies was a very real part of people's lives. An excellent relationship with them was essential for the well-being and prosperity of anyone who depended on the land for their livelihood, since fairies dwelt in every part of it and could bless or curse as they chose. Fairies were given offerings of milk on the old standing stones, bread and salt in the corners of fields, cream in saucers left on the hearth, and were left part of the harvest. Special stones—called dobby stones in the northern counties of England—had shallow depressions for making offerings to them and were placed by field gates or the farmhouse door.

Some modern occultists call nature spirits devas ("shining ones"). The Theosophical Society, an occult group founded in the nineteenth century, believe that devas live in a hidden spiritual realm that co-exists with our own. Their function is to give the material world its pattern and coherence; they hold the blueprint for material form. The term came into popular consciousness in the 1960s when Peter Caddy and Dorothy Maclean established a thriving garden at Findhorn in Scotland, even though the soil was nothing more than sand and gravel and was battered by the bitter climate of the North Sea. Nevertheless, the plants there often grew to twice their normal size, and they harvested 40-pound cabbages. They claimed that they had received instructions for planting and cultivating their garden from nature spirits, which they called devas. Dorothy's first communication happened while she was in a deep meditative state, focusing on her love for the pea plant she was attempting to grow. She felt the essence of the pea plant and received the message that nature spirits would like to collaborate with them in cultivating the garden: "It was not easy for me to go against normality when I could prove nothing to myself or anyone else in a pragmatic way. It is not easy for our souls or for our intuition to surface in a materialistic world."[15] A spiritual community was set up on the site, the Findhorn Foundation, to demonstrate what can be achieved when humans and nature spirits work in harmony.

As we moved away from our close connection to the earth, we lost our link with nature spirits. We forgot how to see them, how to contact them, and how to treat them. Stories of them persisted, but they lost their awesome status; we diminished them, in our imaginations, into the cute Tinkerbell-type fairies of nursery tales. But make no mistake, those fictional creatures that appear in storybooks and cartoons—the tiny, tutu-skirted,

---

15   MacLean, *To Hear the Angels Sing.*

gossamer-winged beings of Victorian fable—are far from the truth; real nature spirits/fairies are natural energies, primal expressions of the life force of the cosmos.

It was once the custom to honour these guardian spirits with offerings and seasonal rituals. As long as this happens, the spirits remain friendly and beneficent. If they are neglected or offended, they might take their revenge. Sometimes, neglected spirits drift away, and when this happens the land becomes spiritually (and sometimes physically) barren.[16]

In order to gain the friendship of your garden spirits, you must take certain steps. You must treat them with respect and prove that you are worthy to have a relationship with them. However, you cannot make them obey you at will. They are not there to teach you as you demand and certainly not to serve you and grant your wishes. They simply exist and have their own objectives and schedules.

They appreciate being treated with consideration. To form a bond with them means to participate in an equal exchange. You can achieve this reciprocity by protecting the environment of your garden, not poisoning it with toxins, leaving the last apples on the tree for them and fallen leaves on the ground. There are ancient ways of making offerings to the spirits that surround us; though in practice the food and drink we leave is often eaten by wild animals, it is understood that the spirits first take nourishment from it.

It is best to leave a small uncultivated area in the garden for the free ranging of the nature spirits. If you can make this private, it is a good place to meditate and contact them.

Libation to the Garden Spirits

A libation is an offering to the spirits that is poured upon the earth. Fairies are particularly fond of rosemary. Take:

A SPRIG OF ROSEMARY OR 2 TEASPOONS ROSEMARY LEAVES

250 ML OR 1 CUP OF BOILING WATER

In a heatproof bowl, pour the water over the leaves. Stand for 15 minutes and strain, discarding the leaves. Take the cooled rosemary infusion and pour it onto the ground, saying:

> Spirits of this place, I give to you this offering of holy rosemary
> In true fellowship and all honour
> As I give to you and pay tribute to you
> So may you know me as fairy friend
> And aid me in my work.

---

16   For more on seasonal rituals, see my *Hearth Witch's Year* (Llewellyn, 2021).

Reflect on this. When you are ready to finish, say:

Blessed be.

Elf Blot

The old Anglo-Saxons left offerings, called *blots*, for the elves. They did this to solicit healing and ask for good harvests. In Sweden, *alfablots* ("sacrifices to the elves") were large community festivities to honour the elves and ask them for blessings.

Go into the garden at twilight, taking with you some milk or wine and fresh bread that you have baked yourself. Lay the bread on the ground and pour the milk or wine around it, saying:

> *People of the otherworld*
> *I bring you this sacrifice*
> *Wholesome bread and the whitest milk/finest wine*
> *In return, grant me your blessings*

Reflect on this. When you are ready to finish, say:

Blessed be.

CONTACT WITH THE SPIRITS

The otherworld has a habit of breaking through into this world to contact us if we only have the eyes to see it and the ears to hear it. If you approach a place with an open heart and heightened awareness, you may be astonished at what you experience. There are many exercises you can follow to help make you more aware, but Nature herself is the greatest teacher in this quest.

While children are often aware of fairy folk, most people lose contact as they get older. The cares and stresses of the everyday world intrude; we get caught up in other things. The otherworld may be trying to communicate with you but cannot get through the babble of *What shall I make for dinner? What shall I wear tonight? I must get my suit from the dry cleaners,* and so on. We must be able to slow down and listen to the rhythms of the otherworld. When you find the still, silent place within, the otherworld can begin to communicate with you. Don't rush; don't try to force it; stop trying to accomplish it; simply learn to be.

DREAMING WITH THE EYES OPEN

If you are merely an observer, you will never make contact with nature spirits; you must knowingly interact with the landscape. Sometimes we call this light trance consciousness "dreaming with the eyes open."

To achieve it, when you first arrive at a place, greet it as you would a living being. Stand or sit quietly for a while. Try to relax your body as you would for a meditation. Still your mind by closing your eyes and concentrating on the sounds around you; perhaps you can hear the birds and the wind or the rolling of the sea on the shore. Be aware of your mind probing around the area, seeking for its ambience, its energies, and its places of interaction with the otherworld.

Then open your eyes. While maintaining this heightened consciousness, you can walk through the garden and explore it with new levels of awareness.

HALLOWING THE EYES

The twelfth-century historian Saxo described how one must first hallow the eyes before being able to see spirits and to be safe in their presence. There are numerous accounts of the eyes being prepared in special ways in order to see the fairies. In reality, it is the third eye that should be anointed with a specially prepared ointment or oil to open the Sight. The third eye is an energy centre, or chakra, whose position corresponds to the centre of the forehead. It is this centre that deals with the psychic senses and enables sight of the otherworld.

OIL TO HALLOW THE EYES

At the first waxing of the moon, take 13 white rose petals and put them in a glass jar. Cover them with almond oil. Place the jar outside each night for three nights. Do not let the light of the sun touch it at any point. Pour off the oil into a clean jar and bury the rose petals beneath an apple tree. Now put into the oil 3 hollyhock flowers, 3 marigold flowers, 9 young leaves from a hazel, and 9 sprigs of thyme. Put the jar in the sun for three days. Do not let the moonlight touch it at any point. Strain, then combine the two prepared oils. Bury the herbs under an oak tree. Dab a little oil onto the third eye position in the centre of your forehead when meditating on the nature spirits or otherwise working with them.

PLANT SPIRITS: THE ROOTED PEOPLE

We're surrounded by plants wherever we go, and we depend on them to provide the oxygen we breathe and the food we eat, but this is only a tiny part of their role in the ecosystem.

Plants are linked to the living earth from which they spring. Each plant is a living teacher and must be approached as an individual spirit, a vital life force that may become your ally if approached with love and respect. Witches utilise plant spirit powers, but to capture these without alienating or dissipating them is not simply a matter of walking three times around a tree, asking, "Can I have a branch?" and leaving a coin in return. When properly approached, they may share something of their life force, their spirit.

Sometimes a plant or tree will call to you, and you should listen and trust your instincts. Every plant has a role, a place within the great pattern. Accept any insight that is given to you, no matter what the circumstances. If the plant is approached with love and trust, its force may harmonise with you and share its secrets. If the plant is taken with force or the wrong motives, if it is mistreated or misused, it may cause discomfort, mislead, or seek to gain control of you.

The life force, or spirit, of the plant is more important than any "active ingredient" in magical work. Spend time with your plants, noting where they live—in sun or shade, on chalky soil or sandy soil and so on—their growth habits, when they flower, and when they set their seeds. Note the shape of the leaves, their texture and colour, and their taste, if edible.

In this way you will begin to learn from the plants themselves. It is a knowledge that cannot be bought and cannot be learned from books, but only by doing. Allow yourself to trust your inner wisdom.

Communicating with Plant Spirits

Choose a plant to try to communicate with, perhaps one you are specifically drawn to. Contemplate its colour and shape. What is it that attracts you? How does it feel to the touch? What is its scent like? Take your time and gently feel your way with this. Be grateful for the time you spend with your plant and come to appreciate it more. Try sensing its aura, its spirit. Try sending it feelings of love and gratitude. If you open your heart, you may find the plant spirit responding and beginning to communicate with you.

Garden Plants

Traditionally the wise woman's garden contained plants for food, herbs for the kitchen and for healing, dye plants, plants to delight the senses with beautiful colours and perfumes, plants to attract insects and feed familiars, plants to contact the spirits, plants for magic, divination, and spells, and trees like rowan and holly for protection. However, what you grow is entirely up to you. You might like to grow beautiful flowers, good things to eat, focus on herbs for healing, plants for vegetable dyes, or plants to help you with your magic. Every plant has many uses and many magical qualities.

What you can grow will depend on several things—where you live and what your climate is, what your soil is like, what you want your plants for, and how much space you have. You can choose plants for their magical attributes, use in ritual, or spell ingredients. You could plant an elemental garden, a zodiac garden, a dye garden, a healing herb garden, a night-blooming moon garden, or a garden with ritual herbs.

However, every plant has its own attributes, and it pays to work with what you already have before dismissing it. In this book you may find that familiar garden plants have qualities and uses you didn't realise.

AN ELEMENTAL GARDEN

A magical way to grow your plants is to create an elemental garden with herbs arranged according to whether they fall under the dominium of earth, air, fire, or water. You could have four separate beds or one round bed divided into the quarters of the compass, with the herbs planted in the relevant quadrant (air in the east, fire in the south, water in the west, and earth in the north).

PLANTS FOR AIR: Agrimony, alecost, bergamot, chervil, chicory, clary sage, comfrey, dandelion, dill, dock, elecampane, fenugreek, fern, horehound, houseleek, lavender, lemon verbena, lily of the valley, marjoram, mint, parsley, sage, sweet cicely, sweet pea, wormwood.

PLANTS FOR FIRE: Angelica, avens, basil, bay, betony, centaury, cinquefoil, cuckoo pint, coriander, dill, fennel, garlic, hyssop, lily of the valley, madder, mandrake, mustard, nasturtium, nettle, peony, rosemary, rue, St. John's wort, sunflower, tarragon, woodruff.

PLANTS FOR WATER: Aconite, belladonna, burdock, catnip, cereus, chamomile, chervil, cleavers, clover, coltsfoot, columbine, cornflower, daisy, feverfew, forget me not, foxglove, freesia, gardenia, geranium, hellebore, hemlock, hyacinth, jasmine, lady's mantle, lily, mallow, marshmallow, meadowsweet, mugwort, mullein, narcissus, orris (iris), ox-eye daisy, periwinkle, plumeria, poppy (red), purslane, rose, skullcap, snowdrop, stephanotis, thyme, valerian, vanilla, violet, yarrow.

PLANTS FOR EARTH: Fumitory, hollyhock, honeysuckle, lilac, mimosa, primrose, rhubarb, sage, soapwort, sorrel, strawberry, tansy, tulip, vervain, vetiver.

KITCHEN HERB GARDEN

Angelica, basil, bay, chives, coriander, dill, fennel, lemon balm, lemongrass, marjoram, mint, oregano, parsley, rosemary, sage, sweet cicely, tarragon, thyme.

COUNTRY WINE MAKER'S GARDEN

Alecost, angelica, apples, blackberry, borage, calendula, clove pinks, cowslips, grape, hawthorn, hyssop, juniper, lemon balm, meadowsweet, nettle, peppermint, primrose, raspberry, rosemary, sweet cicely, sweet woodruff, thyme, violets.

DYER'S GARDEN

Alkanet, bracken, comfrey, coreopsis, dyer's chamomile, dyer's woodruff, dyer's greenweed, hollyhock, lady's bedstraw, madder, meadowsweet, purple loosestrife, rhubarb, safflower, saint john's wort, sneezewort, sunflowers, onion, tansy, St. John's wort, weld, woad, yarrow.

HEALING GARDEN

Aloe vera, arnica, calendula, chamomile, chickweed, dandelion, fennel, feverfew, garlic, ginger, heartsease pansy, lavender, lemon balm, marshmallow, nettle, peppermint, rosemary, skullcap, St. John's wort, yarrow.

COSMETICS GARDEN

Aloe vera, angelica, calendula, chamomile, cucumber, daisy, elderflower, fennel, honeysuckle, lady's mantle, lavender, lemon, lily, lovage, marshmallow, mint, nettles, pine, rose, rosemary, sage, soapwort, strawberry, violet, yarrow.

MAGICAL GARDEN

Angelica, anise, basil, betony, bluebell, borage, calendula, chamomile, cinquefoil, elder, foxglove, hawthorn, hazel, holly, ivy, lavender, lemon balm, mint, mugwort, mullein, periwinkle, rose, rosemary, sage, St. John's wort, thyme, vervain, wormwood, yarrow, rowan.

NIGHT-BLOOMING GARDEN

Brugmansia, datura, evening primrose, four o'clock, honeysuckle, moonflower, nicotiana, night gladiolus, night phlox, night-scented jasmine, night-scented orchid, night-scented stock, petunia, regal lily, star jasmine, sweet rocket, tuberose.

Fairy Flowers and Trees

Certain trees and flowers are particularly associated with fairies and said to attract them.

ALDER (*ALNUS* SPP.): The alder grows near water and is under the protection of water fairies. It yields three dyes: red from the bark, green from the flowers, and brown from the twigs, taken to represent fire, water, and earth. The green dye is associated with fairy clothing.

APPLE (*MALUS* SPP.): The apple tree is sacred to fairies. The Apple Tree Man dwells in the oldest tree in any orchard. He can grant a good harvest for the whole orchard, and it is always his tree that is wassailed after Yule, and the last of the crop should be left on the ground for him. In the west of England, the small apples left on the trees are called the pixies' harvest. Grafted apple trees were called *ymp trees* (imp trees) in Old English and fall under the dominion of the fairies, and anyone sleeping under one is liable to encounter them. In parts of England, a Green Lady is said to dwell in every apple tree, and permission must be sought from her before chopping down the tree, and primroses are planted beneath it to appease her.

ASH (*FRAXINUS* SPP.): In Ireland some solitary ashes are sacred to fairies and cannot be cut down, even now. In Somerset ash gads were used to protect cattle against fairy mischief, while ash buds were placed in the cradle to prevent fairies substituting a changeling for a human child. In Greek myth the god Zeus was nursed in childhood by an ash nymph.

BIRCH (*BETULA* SPP.): Birches are often fairy haunted. In Russia forest spirits called leshiye live in the tops of birch trees. If you hear the murmur and rustle of leaves, this is the leshiye talking about you. In Somerset, a female spirit called the One with the White Hand flickers from birch copses, pale and gaunt as the trees. However, the birch is also a protective tree, and in England and Scotland a birch was hung with red and white rags and leant against stable doors on May Day to prevent horses from being hag-ridden, i.e., being taken out by fairies or witches and ridden to the point of exhaustion. Traditionally, the maypole is made of birch, and the besom is composed of purifying and protective birch twigs.

BLACKBERRY (*RUBUS FRUCTICOSUS*): Blackberries belong to the fairy folk. On Old Michaelmas Day (October 11) it is said that the devil enters blackberry thickets and spits on them, hence they should not be picked after that date. The Anglo-Saxons believed blackberry had the power to undo witchcraft and fairy magic: "against any evil rune and for one full of elvish tricks."[17]

BLACKTHORN (*PRUNUS SPINOSA*): In Ireland November 11 is recognised as the day of the blackthorn sprites, the Lunantishees, fairies who guard the sacred blackthorn from any human foolhardy enough to profane it by cutting the wood at this time. Like other fairy flowers, it is unlucky to bring the blossom indoors.

BLUEBELL (*HYACINTHOIDES NON-SCRIPTA*): A bluebell wood is a place of fairy spells and enchantments. The presence of bluebells in oak copses is a sure sign that mischievous fairies called Oakmen are present, and mortals should be wary. In Somerset it is believed that you should never go into the woods to pick bluebells, as it will anger the fairies. If you are a child, you will never be seen again as the fairies will take you away, but if you are an adult, you will be pixy-led and will not be able to find your way out of the woods until someone rescues you. Witches grow bluebells to attract fairies, and the ringing of the bluebell summons fairies to their moonlit revels. If you hear a bluebell ringing, this indicates the presence of a fairy. Bluebells are one of the most potent plants for fairy magic.

COWSLIPS (*PRIMULA VERIS*): These lovely spring flowers are cherished and protected by the fairies; in Dorset, England, they are called Fairycup. Elsewhere they are called Lady's Bunch of Keys or Culver's Keys and unlock the doors to the otherworld.

ELDER (*SAMBUCUS NIGRA*): The elder is inhabited by a spirit, and for this reason when it is cut, it bleeds real blood (red sap). In Lincolnshire permission must be sought of the Old Lady or Old Girl (the spirit within the elder): "Owd Gal, give me some of thy wood and Oi will give thee some of moine, when I graws inter a tree."[18] If you cut the elder without permission, you risk losing your eyesight, your health, your cattle, and your children. If you wound the tree, you must give it charms and offerings in recompense. In Denmark the elder tree was known to be

---

17 Wilfrid Bonser, "Magical Practices Against Elves," *Folklore* 37, no. 4 (1926): 350–63, http://www.jstor.org/stable/1256144.

18 Vickery, *Oxford Dictionary of Plant Lore.*

under the protection of the goddess Hulda. She lives at its roots and is the mother of the elves. According to Danish lore, if you stand under an elder on Midsummer Eve you will see the king of the elves pass by. It is safe to take a branch from the elder on January 6 without permission if you spit on the ground three times. This branch can then be used to draw a magic circle in a lonely place for the purpose of demanding magic fern seed, which will give you the strength of thirty men. Hulda will ensure that an unseen hand delivers a chalice containing the seed.

ELM (*ULMUS* SPP.): A Green Lady lives within the elm tree. Elms are called "elven" in England because they are considered to be the dwelling place of elves, who open the way to the underworld.

FAIRY RING MUSHROOMS (*MARASMIUS OREADES*): Fairy ring mushrooms appear on lawns and in meadows, leaving a bare patch, and some are as many as 600 years old. According to folklore, they are a favourite dancing place of fairies. Be warned, though: the stories tell us that if you join the fairies in their revels, you may become invisible to your companions outside the ring and find that it is impossible to leave; you will be forced to dance until you collapse and die of exhaustion. Others have found that an evening spent in a fairy ring turns out to be many years in the human realm.

FLY AGARIC (*AMANITA MUSCARIA*): These red and white spotted mushrooms are closely associated with fairies, who are often depicted sitting on them or wearing red caps reminiscent of the fly agaric itself. Some cultures, including the Celts, had a taboo on eating red food, which was said to belong to the spirit world. The mushroom causes hallucinations and was used by witches and shamans to produce visions and to travel to the spirit worlds. (Please note that it is deadly poisonous.)

FOUR-LEAFED CLOVER (*TRIFOLIUM* SPP.): The four-leafed clover enables the possessor to see fairies and spirits, heal illness, and gain good fortune. Four-leafed clovers will dispel unwanted fairy magic.

FOXGLOVE (*DIGITALIS PURPUREA*): The common name "foxglove" may be a corruption of "folks" glove, i.e., gloves of the fairies; Welsh fairies are said to wear mittens made from foxglove flowers. Foxgloves, like fairies, inhabit woody dells. This has given rise to many of the plant's folk names—Fairy's Glove, Fairy's Cap, Fairy's Thimbles, Fairy Petticoats, Fairy Weed, Little Folk's Gloves, Goblin's

Thimbles, or Thimble of the Old Fairy Woman. Growing foxgloves in your garden will attract fairies. Like other fairy flowers, it is unlucky to pick them or take them indoors.

HAWTHORN (*CRATAEGUS MONOGYNA*): The hawthorn is a tree very much associated with fairies; their trysting places are beneath its shade. When the oak, ash, and thorn grow close together, it marks a favourite haunt of the fairy folk, and solitary hawthorns growing on hills or near wells are markers to the world of the fairies. Fairies are very protective of hawthorns, and a blooming tree should never be trimmed as it angers them, and the tree should always be trimmed east to west. It is so potently magical that it is forbidden to bring it indoors except at Beltane. Falling asleep beneath a hawthorn on May Eve may result in you being spirited away to the otherworld.

HAZEL (*CORYLUS AVELLANA*): The hazel tree has many connections with fairies. To summon fairies, you should bury hazel wands under a fairy hill. Boiling jam was stirred with a hazel or rowan stick to prevent the fairies from stealing it. Hazel is the commonest wood used to make a forked divining rod, connected with elves and pixies who have all the treasures of the earth in their keeping. It was traditionally cut on Midsummer's Eve, the great fairy festival. The fairies of English hazel thickets, who had names like Churn-Milk Peg and Melch Dick, inflict painful bloat and cramps on anyone who tears off unripe nuts.

HEATHER (*CALLUNA VULGARIS*): Growing heather in the garden attracts fairies, especially white heather, which denotes their presence. Heather protects against negativity and evil spirits.

HOLLY (*ILEX* SPP.): The holly is a protective tree that wards off evil spirits. The prickly holly is lucky for men, and the smooth holly is lucky for women.

OAK (*QUERCUS* SPP.): Fairies like to dance around old oak trees. Elves live in them, and the holes found in the trunks are their means of entrance and exit. A New Forest rhyme advises "Turn your cloaks for fairy folks are in old oaks" (turning your cloak inside out protects you from being taken from your path by fairies). In England, dwarfish creatures called Oakmen live in the saplings that grow from felled oaks. If bluebells are present in the grove, this is a sure sign of their presence.

PRIMROSE (*PRIMULA VULGARIS*): The primrose is a fairy flower; according to folklore, it can make the invisible visible, and to eat primroses is a sure way to see fairies. If you touch a fairy rock with the right number of primroses in a posy, it will open to fairyland and fairy gifts, but beware—the wrong number opens the door to doom. In Somerset thirteen primroses were laid under a baby's cradle to stop it being taken by fairies. In Buckinghamshire on May Eve primrose balls were hung over the house and cowshed door as protection from malicious fairies.

RAGWORT (*SENECIO JACOBAEA*): Fairies sometimes bury their treasures beneath ragwort stalks. They are used as horses by fairies when they want to fly; they climb astride them and call out the magic words "Horse and Hattock!"

ROWAN (*SORBUS AUCUPARIA*): Rowan, or mountain ash, draws its name from the old Norse word *runa*, meaning "a charm." Its folk names include the Witch Tree or the Wicken Tree, and it is a plant very much associated with magic. It is a plant of protection, particularly from witchcraft, fairies, and lightning. When it grows in a garden, especially if it is self-seeded, it shows that the place is under the protection of the fairies. Rowan Tree Day is May 13, a fortuitous time for rowan spells of protection.

SILVERWEED (*POTENTILLA ANSERINE*): This weed is turned up by the plough in spring. One of its old names was Seventh Bread as it is said that fairies like to eat it, and it is probably assigned to them because it grows underground.

TOADSTOOLS: Mushrooms and fungi, with their strange shapes and rapid growth, are often associated with fairies, as evidenced by some of their names, which include Yellow Fairy Club, Slender Elf Cap, Dune Pixie-Hood, and Dryad's Saddle.

WILD THYME (*THYMUS VULGARIS*): At midnight on Midsummer's Night, the king of the fairies dances with his followers on thyme beds. In Shakespeare's *A Midsummer Night's Dream*, Oberon tells Puck, "I know a bank where the wild thyme blows / Where oxlips and the nodding violet grows." A charm to see fairies is to make a brew of wild thyme tops gathered near the side of a fairy hill and grass from a fairy throne. Like other fairy flowers, wild thyme is unlucky to bring into the home.

The Language of Flowers

There is a language, little known,
Lovers claim it as their own.
Its symbols smile upon the land,
Wrought by nature's wondrous hand;
And in their silent beauty speak,
Of life and joy, to those who seek
For Love Divine and sunny hours
In the language of the flowers.

. . . .

The Language of Flowers, London, 1875

Flowers have always held a wealth of lore and symbolism for us humans. Throughout history they have been associated with various gods, qualities, and symbolic relationships. This can be seen from the earliest myths of indigenous cultures, throughout the classical world and the Bible, right into the plays of Shakespeare.

The so-called language of flowers, or floriography, was largely invented in the Victorian era, though it is at least partly based on snippets of mythology, folklore, and sometimes the growing habits of plants—the clinging ivy signified faithfulness, for example, and the white violet, modesty. It became extremely popular, and most Victorian homes owned a copy of one of the many books available on the subject.

The main purpose of floriography was to send covert messages, usually to a would-be lover, via the sending of flowers. A red rose might be sent to express love, or bachelor's buttons to convey that the sender is happy being single, thank you very much. The colours of flowers were important too; while a red carnation declared love, a yellow carnation signified rejection. However, there were several different systems, and various books give conflicting meanings, which must have caused some confusion and the occasional disappointment.

By 1935, when the reaction against all things Victorian was at its height, a writer in the *Gardeners' Chronicle* remarked of the old language of flowers books "how antique in spirit they seem—how remote from the thought of the present age."[19] But fashions go in cycles, and the 1960s and 1970s saw a revival of interest in Victorian culture and the republication of early books on the subject, such Mrs Burke's *The Illustrated Language of Flowers*, and Kate

---

19   Brent Elliot, *Occasional Papers from the RHS Lindley Library: Volume Ten, April 2013, The Victorian Language of Flowers* (RHS Lindley Library, 2013).

Greenaway's *Language of Flowers*. When Prince William married Kate Middleton in 2011, the flowers in her bouquet were chosen for their meanings: lily of the valley to symbolise the return of happiness, sweet William flowers for gallantry, hyacinths for constancy of love, ivy for fidelity, and myrtle as the symbol of love and marriage.

Tussie-Mussies

A tussie-mussie is a small posy or nosegay of herbs and flowers. The name was already in use by the fifteenth century, when arrangements of aromatic herbs and protective plants were carried to freshen the air and keep sickness away while walking through unsanitary streets. Judges carried them into court to protect them from any infectious diseases that might be transmitted by prisoners.[20] The recent Queen of England was presented with a tussie-mussie at the annual Maundy Service. Long after their functional use declined, they were revived in the Victorian age with notions of romantic charm and secret messaging utilising the language of flowers.

They are a lovely way to send gifts and messages to friends and lovers. You can create a tussie-mussie, as simple or as complex as you wish, from garden flowers and herbs. Employing the list of meanings of the language of flowers or using the magical correspondences of plants, you can create a posy for protection, one to celebrate a wedding, one to let a friend know that you are thinking of them, or one to comfort the bereaved, and so on.

You will need:

- Flowers, herbs, and leaves

- Florist's wire or twine

- Scissors

- Tissue paper

- Wide ribbon

A tussie-mussie has a central flower, perhaps a rosebud stripped of its leaves, perhaps several lavender flower heads tied together, or whatever you like. Other flowers, with their stems and leaves stripped, are placed around it, in full circles of one type, as many circles as you like. Finally, a complete circle of large leaves goes around the outside edge to enclose everything else.

---

20   Stapley, *Herbcraft Naturally.*

Once you have all your circles of flowers arranged, holding the tussie-mussie tightly, cut the stems to a uniform length, then bind the posy with florist's wire or strong twine (if the posy becomes unruly, you can do this as you go along too). Wrap the stems in tissue paper or a paper doily and tie a length of wide ribbon around them.

Tussie Mussie for the Bereaved

Dark crimson rose (mourning)

Borage (courage)

Pink carnation (I'll never forget)

Lily of the valley (return of happiness)

Pansy (thoughts)

Pine (hope)

White poppy (consolation)

Rosemary (remembrance)

Tussie Mussie for a Wedding

Red rose (love and passion)

Heliotrope (eternal love and devotion)

Blue hyacinth (constancy)

Jasmine (sweet love)

Myrtle (love and marriage)

Stephanotis (happiness in marriage)

Dried Flowers

Drying flowers was a popular pastime for Victorian ladies. You can use them to make gift pictures, cards, or labels with a secret message, utilising the language of flowers.

You can buy purpose-made flower presses or press your flowers between the pages of a heavy book (the Bible was a favourite tome for this). Don't forget to sandwich the flowers between blotting paper or juice expressed from the flowers might ruin your book.

A large leaf may be used as a bookmark in your Book of Shadows or make a bookmark from pressed flowers pasted onto card stock and varnished.

You can also press dried flowers into candles. Melt the wax on the outside of the candle with a hot knife and press in your chosen flowers. These make pretty gifts or can be used in your magical work.

THE LANGUAGE OF FLOWERS	
ACACIA	CHASTE LOVE
AGNUS CASTUS	COLDNESS
AFRICAN MARIGOLD	VULGAR MINDS
AGRIMONY	THANKS
ALMOND FLOWERS	HOPE
AMBROSIA	YOUR LOVE IS RECIPROCATED
AMARYLLIS	PRIDE
ALOE	GRIEF
AMARANTH	UNDYING LOVE
ANEMONE	FORSAKEN
ANGELICA	INSPIRATION
APPLE BLOSSOM	PREFERENCE
ARBUTUS	I LOVE YOU ALONE
ASTER	DAINTINESS
AZALEA	TAKE CARE OF YOURSELF FOR ME
BACHELOR'S BUTTONS	BLESSED TO BE SINGLE
BASIL	GOOD WISHES
BAY	GLORY
BEGONIA	BEWARE
BELLADONNA	SILENCE
BELLS OF IRELAND	GOOD LUCK
BITTERSWEET	TRUTH

THE LANGUAGE OF FLOWERS

BLACK-EYED SUSAN	JUSTICE
BLUEBELL	HUMILITY
BORAGE	COURAGE
BOUQUET OF WITHERED FLOWERS	REJECTED LOVE
CACTUS	ENDURANCE
CAMELLIA	I LONG FOR YOU
CANDYTUFT	INDIFFERENCE
CARNATION (PINK)	I'LL NEVER FORGET YOU
CARNATION (RED)	MY HEART ACHES FOR YOU
CARNATION (PURPLE)	CAPRICIOUSNESS
CARNATION (STRIPED)	REFUSAL
CARNATION (WHITE)	FOR THE SWEET AND LOVELY
CARNATION (YELLOW)	REJECTION, DISDAIN
CATTAIL	PEACE, PROSPERITY
CHAMOMILE	PATIENCE/STRENGTH IN ADVERSITY
CHRYSANTHEMUM (RED)	I LOVE YOU
CHRYSANTHEMUM (WHITE)	TRUTH
CHRYSANTHEMUM (YELLOW)	SLIGHTED LOVE
CLEMATIS	A BEAUTIFUL MIND
CLOVER (WHITE)	THINK OF ME
COLUMBINE	FOLLY
COREOPSIS	ALWAYS CHEERFUL

THE LANGUAGE OF FLOWERS

Coriander	Hidden worth
Crocus	Cheerfulness
Cyclamen	Resignation and farewell
Daffodil	High regard
Daisy	Loyal love, innocence
Dahlia	Good taste
Dandelion	Faithfulness, happiness
Dead Leaves	Sadness
Edelweiss	Courage, devotion
Fern (Maidenhair)	Secret bond of love
Fir	Time
Flax	Domesticity
Forget-Me-Not	Do not forget me
Forsythia	Anticipation
Foxglove	Insincerity
Gardenia	Secret love
Garlic	Courage, strength
Geranium	Stupidity, folly
Gladioli	Sincerity, integrity
Gloxinia	Love at first sight
Goldenrod	Encouragement
Grass	Submission
Heather (Purple)	Solitude
Heather (White)	Protection, wishes will come true

THE LANGUAGE OF FLOWERS

HELIOTROPE	ETERNAL LOVE AND DEVOTION
HIBISCUS	DELICATE BEAUTY
HOLLY	DEFENCE
HOLLYHOCK	AMBITION
HONEYSUCKLE	BONDS OF LOVE
HYACINTH (BLUE)	CONSTANCY OF LOVE
HYACINTH (PURPLE)	FORGIVE ME
HYACINTH (RED OR PINK)	PLAYFULNESS
HYACINTH (WHITE)	LOVELINESS
HYACINTH (YELLOW)	JEALOUSY
HYDRANGEA	THANK YOU FOR UNDERSTANDING
IRIS	YOUR FRIENDSHIP IS IMPORTANT TO ME
IVY	FIDELITY
JASMINE	SWEET LOVE, AMIABILITY
JONQUIL	AFFECTION RETURNED
LADY'S SLIPPER	CAPRICIOUS BEAUTY
LARKSPUR	FICKLENESS
LAVENDER	LUCK
LEMON BALM	SYMPATHY
LILAC	JOY OF YOUTH
LILY (ORANGE)	HATRED
LILY (WHITE)	PURITY
LILY (YELLOW)	FALSE
LILY (CALLA)	BEAUTY

THE LANGUAGE OF FLOWERS

LILY (DAY)	COQUETRY
LILY (TIGER)	WEALTH, PRIDE
LILY OF THE VALLEY	SWEETNESS, RETURN OF HAPPINESS
MAGNOLIA	NOBILITY
MARIGOLD	CRUELTY, GRIEF, JEALOUSY
MISTLETOE	KISS ME
MINT	VIRTUE
MONKHOOD	BEWARE
MORNING GLORY	AFFECTION
MOSS	MATERNAL LOVE, CHARITY
MYRTLE	MARRIAGE AND LOVE
NARCISSUS	EGOTISM
NASTURTIUM	CONQUEST, VICTORY
NUTS	STUPIDITY
OLEANDER	CAUTION
ORANGE BLOSSOM	MARRIAGE AND ETERNAL LOVE
ORANGE MILKWEED	LET ME GO
ORANGE, MOCK	DECEIT
ORCHID	LOVE, BEAUTY
PALM LEAVES	VICTORY AND SUCCESS
PANSY	THOUGHTS
PEONY	BASHFULNESS
PETUNIA	RESENTMENT, ANGER
PINE	HOPE

THE LANGUAGE OF FLOWERS

POPPY (RED)	PLEASURE
POPPY (WHITE)	CONSOLATION
PRIMROSE	I CAN'T LIVE WITHOUT YOU
PRIMROSE (EVENING)	INCONSTANCY
RHODODENDRON	DANGER, BEWARE
ROSE (DARK CRIMSON)	MOURNING
ROSE (LEAF)	YOU MAY HOPE
ROSE (PINK)	HAPPINESS
ROSE (RED)	I LOVE YOU
ROSE (WHITE)	VIRTUE, CHASTITY
ROSE (WHITE, DRIED)	DEATH IS PREFERABLE TO LOSS OF VIRTUE
ROSE (WHITE, WITHERED)	YOU MADE NO IMPRESSION
ROSE (YELLOW)	DECREASE OF LOVE
ROSEMARY	REMEMBRANCE
SALVIA	I THINK OF YOU
SMILAX	LOVELINESS
SNAPDRAGON	DECEPTION
SORREL	AFFECTION
SPEEDWELL	FIDELITY
SPIDER FLOWER	ELOPE WITH ME
STEPHANOTIS	HAPPINESS IN MARRIAGE
STOCK	BONDS OF AFFECTION
SUNFLOWER	HAUGHTINESS
SWEET PEA	GOODBYE AND THANK YOU

THE LANGUAGE OF FLOWERS

SWEET WILLIAM	GALLANTRY
SWEET WOODRUFF	HUMILITY
TANSY	HOSTILITY
TULIP	PASSION
VALERIAN	READINESS
VIOLET (WHITE)	MODESTY
VIOLET (PURPLE)	MY THOUGHTS ARE OF LOVE
WILLOW	SADNESS
YARROW	EVERLASTING LOVE
ZINNIA	MISSED IN ABSENCE

Garden Familiars

Visitors come and go from the garden in the form of birds, insects, reptiles, and mammals. Not only are they part of the interconnected life of the garden, but they are vital in the ecosystem of the wider landscape. The garden is not your private space but is part of an intricate web of life that extends from the microbes in the soil to the birds in the trees and the frogs in the pond. In some cases, your garden can be the extent of an animal's range and the only home it knows.

All of these creatures help maintain the ecological balance of the garden. Many insects and some birds pollinate the plants, while other insects, birds, and small reptiles feed on insect pests. Managing the garden for the wildlife can range from leaving some weeds that are foods for insects, like dandelion and clover for the bees and hoverflies, to keeping an old tree that can be home to hundreds of creatures; an old oak tree, for example, can support 2,300 species.[21]

Moreover, for the witch, the animals of the garden also have a spiritual resonance—they form part of its spiritual matrix, part of its soul. They should be honoured, respected, and

---

21   https://www.woodlandtrust.org.uk/trees-woods-and-wildlife/british-trees/oak-tree-wildlife.

worked with. Moving along the Web of Wyrd, they may come to teach you lessons, aid you in your magical work, or protect you. As with most things, they will come to you when the time is right. You may become aware of synchronicities—things that seem coincidental but are not. You might become aware that the same bird greets you each morning and reappears throughout the day for several weeks or that you see a fox the same time every evening. Their messages usually mean "look at what I'm showing you" or "listen to what I am telling you," but I've included some of the common lore below:

ANTS

You might think of an ant's nest as a nuisance in the garden (though they actually do very little damage), but all the old lore tells us that ants must be treated with respect. In fact, they are said to be lucky, especially if they build a nest by your door, as they bring security and prosperity. In Cornwall it was thought they are final forms of tiny fairies, and if you place a piece of tin in a bank of ants at the waxing of the moon, it will be turned to silver. There is a common superstition that stepping on ants brings rain. An old saying declares that "swift moves the ant as the mercury rises," meaning that when temperatures rise, ants move more rapidly.

BADGERS

The seventh-century *Life of St. Columba* refers to Pictish druids as *brokan*, meaning "badgers." This is probably because the badger lives deep within the earth, the dwelling place of chthonic gods and ancestral spirits, and is therefore privy to their secrets, including the mysterious germination of life that takes place in the underworld. The badger is one of the sacred animals of the goddess Brigantia. At her festival of Imbolc, when Celtic women gathered together to celebrate the rebirth of the spring, the badger's emergence from the ground after its winter hibernation symbolized life returning to the earth. The strong and sturdy badger symbolises courage and strength.

BATS

Bats are liminal creatures, creatures of the between, seemingly part bird, part mammal. As day turns to night, they emerge from their hiding places, flying at twilight between light and darkness. No wonder they have a strange and magical reputation, associated with witches and gods and goddesses of the underworld and acting as messengers and guides between the realms. They are also a keystone species maintaining balance in the environment, some controlling insect populations and some pollinating particular flowers or spreading seeds.

BEES

Bees pollinate many of our plants—without them, humans might cease to exist. In mythology they are sacred to the summer goddess, and all the later folklore of bees suggests that our more recent ancestors realised their importance too. Tradition has it they originated in paradise and were known as "little servants of God," so it was very unlucky to kill one. If you keep bees, you should always tell them your news, such as when a family member gets married, or they might be offended and fly away. After the death of a beekeeper, a relative must go to the hive and repeat three times "Little brownies, little brownies, your master (or mistress) is dead." A bee flying into your house means a visitor will arrive.

BLACKBIRDS

Blackbirds sing at dawn and twilight, the liminal moments of the day, the times between times. They are the messengers of the goddess Rhiannon, who holds the key that opens the doors between the worlds. Their singing puts the listener into a trance, which enables him or her to travel to the otherworld. Blackbirds are a message from the higher powers. Note the direction of the bird's flight—from the left, you are being warned to behave better; from the right, you will receive a blessing.

BUTTERFLIES

If you are touched by a butterfly, it may have a message for you. Butterflies have a five-stage life cycle: first an egg, then a caterpillar, followed by a pupa that matures into a chrysalis, which, after a dormant period, breaks to reveal the butterfly. Perhaps it isn't surprising that the life cycle of the butterfly, with its many transformations, became an allegory for the existence of a human, who at first crawls on the earth, dies, and emerges from the mortal shell as a transfigured soul. Depicting a creature with butterfly wings marked it as a creature of spirit, which is why angels and fairies are often depicted with them. Butterfly can be a wonderful spirit helper that shows the way to personal growth. It is important to accept that life has cycles and stages, some active and expanding, some passive and contracting.

CATS

A visiting black cat crossing your path is good luck and an omen of good fortune to come. The cat is a creature long associated with magic, from the sacred cats of ancient Egypt to the archetypal storybook witch with her cat familiar. Aloof, knowing, and mysterious, her eyes seem to promise secrets—no wonder the Irish thought you could see fairyland by gazing into a cat's eyes.

CRANES

In symbolism, cranes are solar birds—when they return in springtime, they herald the return of the sun. Standing by the waters, cranes and herons are among the first birds to greet the dawn. The Celts associated marsh birds with the supernatural, dwelling as they do in a misty "place between places" that is neither land nor water, one of the entrances to the otherworld. As such, they are messengers between the human world and the realm of the gods, so oracles were taken from the shapes of the birds in flight. Ogma, the Celtic god of wisdom, was said to have invented the ogham alphabet after watching the flight of cranes, with the silhouettes of the birds against the sky giving him the idea for the angular letters.

Flocks of cranes always fly in a V-shaped formation, and in folklore their passing denotes the flight of a newly departed soul—an ending and a new beginning. Seeing a single crane before setting out on a journey is a very good omen. Cranes are also emblematic of vigilance and the need for watchfulness, standing watch on one leg during the night; Aristotle said that they carried stones in their mouths so that if they fell asleep, the stone would fall and the bird would wake.[22]

CRICKETS AND GRASSHOPPERS

When a cricket/grasshopper appears, it brings good luck, as long as you don't hurt it. They chirp at night if rain is on the way.

CROWS

With its night-black feathers, harsh cry, and carrion-eating habits, the crow has a somewhat dubious reputation, associating it with death, ill fortune, ghosts, and malevolent witches. This is undeserved. The truth is, crows have highly developed digestive systems, are omnivorous, and can eat anything from fruit to meat. Their eating of carrion plays an important role in the cleanup of the environment and the ongoing cycle of life. Crows are clever and cooperative birds, and though they mate for life, they cooperate with other crows in large flocks to protect their territory from predators and share information about food sources. They have exceptional problem-solving skills and even the ability to use tools. It is not surprising that crows symbolise wisdom in many different mythologies around the world as messengers that travel between the realms. As birds of prophecy, omens were taken from their flight and calls. Activities of crows at dawn and evening are weather portents: flying towards the sun in the morning indicates good weather; stalking around water in the

---

22   Aristotle, *The History of Animals*, Book VIII (trans. D'Arcy Wentworth Thompson), https://penelope.uchicago.edu/aristotle/histanimals8.html.

evening indicates a storm coming. Like magpies, the number of crows seen is important: one crow = sorrow, two crows = mirth, three crows = a wedding, and four crows = a birth.

Cuckoos

In Celtic mythology, the cuckoo is a fairy bird, spending the winter in the land of the dead. The return of the cuckoo in spring gives it much of its symbolism, standing for regeneration, rebirth, and a personal opportunity for the same. Omens were taken from the first-heard cuckoo call of the year bringing good luck or bad luck, depending on what you are doing when you hear it. It is lucky if you are standing on grass but bad luck if on barren ground. If the call comes from the right, it means good fortune, so make a wish and it will be granted; if the call comes from the left, it heralds misfortune. Cuckoos are known to lay their eggs in other birds' nests and not to care for their own young, so they also have a reputation for laziness and parasitism.

Doves

We all know the gentle dove as a symbol of peace. Doves are devoted creatures that mate for life, showing each other affection and sharing the raising of chicks. As such, they are sacred to several goddesses of love, including Inanna, Aphrodite, and Venus. The appearance of a dove is a lucky omen for lovers. If a dove appears from the right, this indicates luck in love and perhaps a marriage. A dove can also bring a friendly warning; coal miners would not go down a pit if a dove was seen near it.

Eagles

The eagle is often called the King of the Birds because it flies higher than almost any other, which the ancients believed was closer to the sphere of the gods. When the usually silent eagle cried out, it was a message from the gods themselves, one heralding great change. For the Celts, the salmon and the eagle were the oldest animals on earth, repositories of all history and knowledge and seers of all that occurred anywhere. Eagles stand for connection with greater spiritual knowledge, wisdom, and truth. When an eagle flies into sight, it brings a message from the highest powers.

Foxes

The best-known attribute of the fox is its wily nature, and we even have the phrase "cunning as a fox." Throughout the world the fox is known as a clever trickster. Foxes are stealthy and adaptable, supposed to hunt well away from their own dens to lay the blame on other foxes and be able to blend in with the background or follow twisting and turning tracks to divert hunters. The word "cunning" comes from the old Scottish word *kenning*, meaning "to know," and the appearance of a fox is a message to use your intelligence and problem-solving abilities.

FROGS

Frogs are excellent garden allies, helping keep it pest free by devouring pests such as slugs, snails, and other invertebrates; it is well worth having a pond to invite them into your plot. Moreover, frogs are important creatures in mythology and spiritual symbolism. The Celts identified them with the spirits that they believed inhabited every spring, pool, or well, particularly those at healing shrines. In several cultures the croaking of frogs during mating season was thought to call down the spring rains that cleanse and renew the face of the earth after winter, watering the sleeping seeds so that they can burst into life. Frogs are associated with creation all over the world for this reason.

In Egypt, when the Nile underwent its annual flood, it brought irrigating water and fertilising silt to the land, all heralded by the appearance of many frogs; the fertility goddess Heket was depicted as a woman with a frog's head. As well as being associated with the regeneration of the earth, frogs undergo amazing metamorphoses of their own, starting in the water as tadpoles hatching from an egg, growing limbs and evolving until the adult frog can take to the land. It is not hard to see that the message of the frog is fertility and profound transformation. It is very unlucky to kill or harm a frog.

HARES

The symbolism of the hare is very different to the symbolism of the rabbit. While rabbits live underground in communal warrens, hares are solitary creatures who spend their entire lives aboveground. They are tricksters who run fast in zigzag patterns to escape predators. Hares are usually nocturnal creatures that remain hidden during the hours of daylight, and it is only during the mating season they are abroad in daylight. The expression "mad as a March hare" refers to their wild behaviour in spring when they may be observed boxing or leaping into the air as they prepare to mate. Hares are prolific breeders, producing two to four litters a year in a shallow depression in the ground known as a "form." A female hare can even conceive while she is still pregnant. Young hares are born so well-developed that they can fend for themselves within a few hours of their birth. It is not surprising that hares are associated both with the season of spring and fertility. Apart from the breeding season, the hare is only seen at night, by the light of the moon, and the patterns visible on the full moon are sometimes thought to resemble a hare. The hare stands for swiftness, wildness, independence, fertility, and rebirth.

HAWKS

Hawks are one of the most intelligent birds, adaptable enough to live in a variety of environments. Fast and powerful in flight, they have eyesight so sharp that they can spot prey from miles away, waiting for the right moment to seize it, diving down on silent wings. Flying so high and seeing so well, in many cultures hawks were thought to be messengers from the spirit world and harbingers of change. Hawk's message may be to rise above things, view them in perspective, and wait for the right moment to act. Remember that hawks use their abilities wisely and efficiently.

HEDGEHOGS

Hedgehogs are garden heroes, eating slugs and garden pests. I leave part of the garden wild to encourage them and make sure that there are holes in the boundary fences so that they can get through, as they travel many miles in a single night. Though the hedgehog is a small, unassuming little animal, it can't be underestimated as it wears a suit of armour. When threatened by a predator, it rolls itself into a ball and the hunter is left trying to chew a mouthful of sharp spines. This clever defence has given the hedgehog a rich mythology; it often appears in fairy tales as an animal guide or bestower of wisdom. The lesson of hedgehog may be one of safety and protection, of knowing that sometimes you need to retreat from the world, roll up into a ball, and shield yourself, but also to recognise that you cannot stay that way forever and eventually will have to relax your defences and re-engage.

LADYBIRDS (LADYBUGS)

Ladybirds are wonderful garden allies. Not only do they eat aphids and other pests, some also sip nectar from flowers and carry pollen from one blossom to another, helping pollinate your plants. It is very unlucky to kill a ladybird, as they are associated with the Virgin Mary and the Goddess. It is a good omen if one lands on you, and you must not brush it off. Instead, to encourage it to fly away, you should say to it: "Ladybird, ladybird, fly away home. Your house is on fire and your children are gone."

LIZARDS

Lizards love to bask in the sun, absorbing its heat and light, moving only when necessary or when the time is right. The ancient Greeks watched the movements of lizards on a wall as a form of divination. All lizards have a residual third eye, and in some species this can detect changes in light conditions. This mystical third eye has given the lizard connections with inner or psychic sight and the power of dreams, so you may need to pay attention to these.

Some lizards can shed their tails when threatened and will eventually grow new ones, an amazing symbol of regeneration and renewal, as well as of the need to make sacrifices in order to move forward.

MAGPIES

The magpie is a bird of omen, and the number that appear are important. There are several rhymes on the subject, such as:

> One for sorrow, two for joy
> Three for a girl and four for a boy
> Five for silver, six for gold
> Seven for a secret never to be told
> Eight's a wish and nine's a kiss
> Ten a surprise you should not miss,
> Eleven for health, twelve for wealth,
> Thirteen beware it's the devil himself.

To see one alone is always unlucky, according to the rhymes, and you should avert the bad fortune by greeting it with the words "Hello, lord magpie!" It is a bad omen to see a magpie when setting off on a journey.

MOLES

Moles are almost blind and can only detect changes of light with their poor eyesight. However, do they have powerful noses and an amazing sense of smell. Mole reminds us that we cannot always only rely on what we see but must use our others senses too, including intuition. Moles have powerful front legs and paws, enabling them to efficiently dig their underground tunnels and chambers so that they can live snugly down in the belly of Mother Earth with the roots and seeds. They were often associated with witches and herb cunning. You might mutter at molehills on your lawn, but you can use the finely tilled soil from molehills to transplant your seeds.

MICE

In Greek mythology mice were sacred to the sun god Apollo and a symbol of abundance, fertility, and the harvest. They were regarded as underworld animals because of their habit of living underground and in dark places, travelling between the world of men and the underworld along secret paths, getting through the tiniest crack to escape danger.

OWLS

Owls are thought of as ghostly creatures. In most of Europe owls were associated with witches, who were thought to be able to turn themselves into the birds. Owls had such a fearful reputation that people would not even touch a dead one. As well as its association with ill omen, the owl is a symbol of wisdom, linked with goddesses of wisdom, such as the Celtic Sulis, the Greek Athene, and the Roman Minerva. The Celts believed that it was one of the five oldest beasts on earth (with the blackbird, stag, eagle, and salmon) and thus possessed much ancient knowledge.

RABBITS

Like the hare, the rabbit is associated with moon deities, and in many cultures, from Asia to North America, the rabbit is a clever trickster. Rabbits are common witch familiars and spirit forms; tales often recount how witches were discovered after being wounded while in rabbit guise and then found to be carrying the same wounds on their human form. Rabbits are gentle, sensitive creatures, symbols of fertility, new beginnings, renewal, and good luck. An old superstition is to say "white rabbits" on the first day of every new month for luck.

RATS

Rats are sacred to gods and goddesses of the underworld, depicted with Cernunnos in his underworld aspect and embroidered on the veil of the Roman underworld goddess Proserpine. In Egypt the rat symbolized utter destruction but also wise judgment because rats always choose the best bread to steal. The rat has had a very bad press, and it is certainly true that rats can carry disease and cause widespread famine, yet the rat is honoured in Buddhism because it is a clever animal and an able forager. Rats can overcome great obstacles.

RAVENS

The raven shares much of the mythology of the crow, and indeed, the ancients don't seem to have made a distinction between different members of the corvid family. Crows and ravens are both known to feed on carrion, hence their association with death and death deities such as the Celtic battle goddess the Morrigan. However, crows congregate in flocks while ravens tend to live alone with their life-long mates. The raven is perhaps the most intelligent of birds, able to communicate, use tools, solve puzzles, and even play cunning tricks. The Norse god Odin had two ravens called Munnin and Huginn, or "memory" and "thought." They flew up and down the world tree, bringing him news of everything that happened on earth.

In lore the raven is the most prophetic of birds, hence the phrase "the foresight of a raven." The raven's croak is distinctive, and the bird has been known to mimic human speech, giving it an association with prophecy and oracular utterance. The Irish phrase "raven's knowledge" implies the discovery of secrets. Ravens are considered omens of change. If ravens are seen flying towards each other, it is an omen of quarrels. If a raven perches on the roof, it means prosperity for the family. If you hear a raven before setting out on a journey, you will achieve all you want from the trip. If they are seen preening themselves, rain is on the way.

ROBINS

In Pagan lore the robin rules six months of the year, the wren the other six months, the robin beginning his rule after the winter solstice. In mediaeval times the wassailing ceremony to welcome the New Year involved hanging up gifts of food for the robins who brought luck for the coming year. When you see the first robin of the year, it is still the custom to make a wish, for if the bird flies away before you have decided what you want, you will have no luck in the coming year. In Norse myth the robin was sacred to Thor, god of lightning, and was under his protection; its presence averting lightning. Harming a robin is very bad luck and will result in your house being struck by lightning, ills of the hands and legs, or even death:

> *The robin and the lintil, the laverock and the wren,*
> *Them that harries their nests will never thrive again.*

If you see one sheltering in a tree or hedge, rain is on the way. If it sits on an open branch, chirping, good weather is coming.

ROOKS

It means good luck if rooks settle on your land. They are said to be able to predict the future; they know when the tree in which they are nesting is about to fall and will move. If rooks leave an area where they have been settled, it is a bad omen for the landowners. If they build high, the summer will be fine; if low, the weather will be wet and cold. If they perch together, facing the wind, a storm is on the way. As the old rhyme says, *When rooks and gulls twirl high in the sky, it's a certain sign that a gale is nigh.*

SNAKES

A snake in the garden might be a message from the Goddess. Snakes were companions of goddesses of healing, fecundity, and abundance as the snake usually lives within the body of Mother Earth and is aware of all her secrets. In Greek and Roman temples, the snake was a powerful guardian spirit and was encouraged in homes to keep down vermin. Because the snake sheds its skin each year and appears renewed, it represents healing and revitalization.

SPARROWS

If two sparrows appear from the right, this is good luck for lovers. It is unlucky to kill or cage a sparrow. They sing when rain is on the way. The sparrow is a symbol of the gods of the household and important to the well-being of home and family.

SPIDERS

The spider is the archetypal spinner and weaver, with its web representing the pattern of life itself. It was associated with all spinning and weaving goddesses, those twisters of fate who spin the thread of human destiny, as well as the world, the stars, the cosmos, and the web of energies that joins it all together. Because the spider is associated with powerful goddesses, it is unlucky to kill one. It preys on flies, symbols of corruption, evil, and disease: *If you wish to live and thrive, let the spider run alive.* The tiny money spider confers riches to anyone it runs over. It is considered very lucky if a spider drops from a ceiling onto your face. They are weather predictors too. When a spider spins long, radial strands in their webs or builds a flimsy web high, a spell of dry weather is coming. When rain is coming, they spin short strands.

SWALLOWS

The swallow is a harbinger of spring. In ancient Greece, returning swallows were thought to predict the safe return of Dionysus, the vegetation god, but, as Aristotle cautioned, "One swallow does not make a summer,"[23] meaning that the appearance of one bird doesn't indicate a trend, though the appearance of flocks of them does. From early times swallows have made their nests in the eaves of buildings, and for the Romans they were sacred to the Penates, the household gods, so it is lucky if they nest on your house, offering protection from lightning, fire, and storms. Destroying a nest or killing a bird meant disaster for the house and its inhabitants. It is bad luck if the swallow deserts its nest. If a swallow is disturbed, it means a bad harvest. To see swallows fighting is a bad portent.

---

23   Aristotle, *Nicomachean Ethics.*

Squirrels

Because the squirrel is fleet of foot and can travel though trees without ever touching the ground, it has been associated with messenger gods like Hermes and Mercury. In Norse mythology the squirrel Ratatoskr scrambles up and down the world tree Yggdrasil, carrying messages from the top to the bottom. Squirrels bury nuts to eat in the winter and are a emblem of being prepared. They are also seasonal omens: *When squirrels early start to hoard, winter will pierce us like a sword.* They are quick and always busy, and often playful. Anyone who shoots a squirrel is destined to have bad luck.

Toads

Toads were common witch familiars and shape-changing forms. A toad was supposed to cry out to warn its witch master of danger. The toad reflects the fertility and abundance of the earth and is a symbol of healing. It is sacred to Hecate. Toad is a wonderful garden familiar. He will eat slugs, snails, and other invertebrates, so you can count on him to keep your garden pest-free. Finding one is a lucky omen.

Wrens

The wren is the ruler of the dark half of the year. Wren ceremonies at the winter solstice were enacted up to the nineteenth century and have been revived in several places. It is extremely unlucky to kill a wren. In France anyone who killed a wren could expect his house to be destroyed by fire or his fingers to shrivel and drop off. In England anyone who harms a wren will suffer a broken bone shortly afterwards.

Seasonal Garden Rituals

The gardening year is a cycle—the balmy days of spring, when life returns; the full days of summer, when the earth blossoms; and the abundant bounty of autumn followed by the frozen days of winter, when the garden sleeps and readies itself for the cycle to begin anew. This reflects the great tide of energy that flows in and out of the world with the seasons. Our ancestors sought to honour the seasonal current and work with it, with a myriad of feasts and rituals throughout the year.

Here are a few of my personal garden rituals, by which I seek to honour the seasons, the gods, and the spirits of the garden.

SPRING

In spring we can feel energy building in the natural world as it responds to the increasing light and warmth. Vigorous life is returning to the land; everywhere shoots push up through the earth, trees bud, flowers blossom, and animals and birds begin to mate; the earth is waking up. It is a time of renewal, promise, and hope, when the sun god gains strength, the vegetation god emerges from the earth, and the maiden goddess is wreathed in flowers.

Tool Blessing

In very early spring, my thoughts turn to getting to work in the garden. The garden tools are taken out of their storage in the shed, brushed off, cleaned, and sharpened, and I like to bless them before the real gardening begins with these words:

> Lord and Lady,
> Bless these tools that I have prepared in your honour
> Bless my endeavours this year
> May there be plenty; may there be abundance
> Lord and Lady,
> Blessed be.

Blessing the Seeds

Before the seeds are planted, they are blessed in the name of the Lord and Lady. We often do this as part of the coven Ostara ritual, but when that is not possible, I lay them on the God and Goddess shrine in the garden, weather permitting (otherwise on my altar in the house), and say:

> Come, our fairest Lady, grant blessing unto the seeds which become
> the flowers of tomorrow. Come, O gracious Lady, and protect that
> which is newly born, that children and animals grow strong beneath
> thy hands. Let the seeds be blessed in thy name, O Goddess.
>
> Come, our gentle Lord, grant blessing unto the seeds which become
> the flowers of tomorrow. Come, O gracious Lord, and protect that
> which is newly born, that children and animals grow strong beneath
> thy hands. Let the seeds be blessed in thy name, O Lord.

Seed Planting Blessing

As I plant my seeds, I like to bless them and imbue them with my intention. A good time to plant seeds is the new moon, a time of new beginnings. Hold the seeds in your hands. Say:

> *Spirits of the garden, I honour you.*
>
> *I call upon you to nurture these seeds,*
>
> *Bring them to growth, bring them to increase.*
>
> *I give you thanks and blessings.*

Put the seeds in their pot, cover them with soil, and water them.

Seedling Protection Spell

When the seedlings are starting to come up in the greenhouse, I ask for some protection for them. I light a green votive candle in the greenhouse and say:

> *Lord and Lady, garden spirits, protect my seedlings; let them grow freely,*
>
> *nursed by the earth and the sun, until they are ripe. Blessed be.*

SUMMER

In the summer, basking in the light of Father Sun, Mother Earth is in the full flush of her maturity, soft and ample; foliage is lush, and the perfume of flowers fills the air. The crops have been planted and are growing nicely, and young animals have been born. The herbs reach their greatest potency, and I pick and prepare them for later use. Winter seems far away, and I want to spend all my time outdoors.

Early Summer Flower Ritual

Decorate your garden altar with seasonal flowers. Light two green candles in garden lanterns and say:

> *Come, Lady of Flowers, so that I may honour you and sing your praises.*
>
> *In your season every tree is clothed with leaves; the grass grows high in the pastures.*
>
> *You wear a thousand colours, a thousand different forms.*
>
> *You are also the goddess of the fields, for if the crops have blossomed well,*
>
> *The harvest will be good; if the vines have blossomed well, there will be wine.*
>
> *Honey is your gift; you call the bees to the violet and the clover and the wild thyme.*
>
> *Let me use life's flower while it still blooms. I pray you, Goddess, bless me.*

Allow the candles to burn out.

High Summer Fertility Ritual

Consider the Goddess at this time of year, by whatever name you know her. She is the earth beginning to bear, responding to the light of the Sun God, at this time of longer hours of daylight and greater warmth. In this short ritual she is addressed as the vital life force that flows throughout the world and throughout us. Light a red candle in a garden lantern on your garden altar and say:

Goddess,
Your vital force flows throughout the world,
Pushing up with every shoot
Each fledgling bird
Each opening flower.
You are the life giver
The woman of power
Who rejuvenates the earth.
Flow through me too
And let me know your touch.

Reflect on this for a while, and let the candle burn itself out.

Autumn

With autumn we enter into the time of harvest, when all the work in the vegetable garden comes to fruition, of ripeness when the juicy red apples are ready for picking, branches bending under the weight of their fruit. The grapes are ripening on the vine. Mushrooms sprout under the harvest moon. It's a busy time of picking and nutting, preserving and storing. Even if you do not grow food, consider the harvest of seeds that grows on your plants to feed the wildlife.

Ritual for the Harvest

This is a celebration of the Goddess as Queen of the Harvest. Fresh herbs or flowers are gathered and made into bouquets or wreaths to be blessed in the ritual and later hung up as a blessing and protection in the house. A loaf of bread is baked. Go out into the garden. Put the bouquets or wreaths on the ground. Say:

Goddess, Queen of the Harvest, I come to honour you,
You have given of yourself, You have sprouted the seed and nurtured the shoots,
You have opened the flowers and set the fruit; I come to give you thanks.

Take up the bread. Proceed sunwise (clockwise) around the plot, laying pieces of bread on the ground around its borders, saying:

> *I walk sunways around my dwelling,*
> *In the name of the Queen*
> *Who did protect me,*
> *Who will preserve me,*
> *In peace, in plenty, in righteousness of heart.*

Take up the bouquets or garlands and say:

> *Queen of the Harvest, bless these herbs which I have prepared in your honour.*
> *They are the wind and the rain, the soil and the sun made manifest, grown from*
> *your womb. Bless them, I pray you, as I honour you and give you thanks.*
> *Let this ritual end with love and blessings. Blessed be.*

WINTER

In winter, the hours of daylight dwindle, cold comes, and the powers of growth wind down. Most of my plants die off, and frost lines their tattered remains. The bone structure of the garden becomes visible with the empty beds and the naked arms of the trees. But just because the garden seems to be sleeping, it doesn't mean that nothing is happening; magic is busy stirring in the earth. Microorganisms in the soil are converting leaves and fallen plant matter into soil nutrients, and the earthworms are turning the soil. Seeds fall onto the ground, ready to sprout when days lengthen once more and warmth returns. I am happy knowing that in the abandoned fallen leaves and plant stems, insects and small mammals dream away their time in hibernation, grateful that I left them shelter.

Wassailing the Tree Spirits Ritual

On Twelfth Night, January 6, the apple trees are wassailed to honour the Apple Tree Man, the spirit of the orchard. His tree is always the oldest in the orchard or the one that bears the heaviest crop. He can grant a good harvest for the whole orchard as well as other benefits. The last of the crop should be left on the ground for him.

It is best to use some cider made from his apples, with pieces of toast floating in it. Everyone present drinks to the health of the tree and takes a piece of toast. The rest of the toast is put into the branches of the tree for the birds, and the remaining cider is poured on the roots of the tree. Everyone should bow to the tree, and drums are played to scare away evil spirits. This song is sung to it:

Old apple tree, we wassail thee, and hoping thou wilt bear

For the Lord doth know where we shall be till apples come another year

To bear well and bloom well so merry let us be.

Let every man take off his hat and shout to the old apple tree

Old apple tree, we wassail thee, and hoping thou wilt bear

Hat-fulls, cap-fulls, three-bushel-bagfuls

And a little heap under the stairs.

Hip! Hip! Hooray!

Garden Spells

Acorn Charm

Carry an acorn in your pocket to protect you from storms, getting lost, or evil intent. Carry three acorns for beauty, youthfulness, and achievement in life.

Ivy Protection

Grow ivy on your walls to protect you from malice.

Birch Cross Protection

Tie two twigs of birch with red thread and hang over your front door or garden gate for protection.

Thunderstorm Water

Collect water during a thunderstorm and use it for breaking bad luck and deadlocked situations. Drink the water and ask the storm spirits to bring you new insights in your meditations or in your dreams.

Fairy Dew

Dew is the first exhaled breath of the earth at dawn. Collect it from your garden. Bottle it, keep it refrigerated, and use it in spells, cast under the light of the moon, to get the Sight and for astral travel.

Garden Gnomes

Ceramic gnomes may be considered rather twee, but they represent the protective powers of earth fairies in the garden.

Message on the Wind

Take a feather, hold it in your hand, and think hard about the message you wish to send, visualising the person you wish to send it to. Tie this onto a tree so that the wind can blow it, saying:

> *Spirits of the air, carry this message for me*
> *Blown on the wind*
> *Carried on your breath*
> *Carry this message for me, spirits of air*
> *And I will pour you a libation of sweet white wine.*

Dispelling Bells

The sound of bells dispels negativity. Hang a windchime or line of small bells in your garden to put it under the protection of the air spirits. As the bells sound, any trouble will be driven away.

Bonfire Spell

If you wish to be rid of something—a bad habit or a painful situation, for example—write it on a piece of paper and throw it onto the garden bonfire and watch it burn away.

Spell to Encourage Rats and Mice to Leave

This traditional spell is worth a try! Chant:

> *Rats and mice*
> *Leave this poor person's house*
> *Go away over to the mill*
> *And there you'll get your fill.*

Sweethearts' Blossom Spell

Take a lily bulb and plant it in a clean pot that has never been used before. While you plant, say:

> *As this root grows*
> *And as this blossom blows*
> *May my future lover's heart be*
> *Turned unto me.*

The Osiris Healing Spell

The ancient Egyptians would bury an Osiris doll (god of vegetation, death, and rebirth) covered in seeds, and when it sprouted in the growing season they would know that the god had been reborn. You can use this ancient power of regeneration in a healing spell.

Take an oblong of cloth and cover it with quick-germinating seeds, perhaps edible ones such as aduki beans or mustard cress. Tie off the "head" and the "body" to make a vaguely human shape, saying:

> *As Osiris shoots and grows, so all things are reborn.*
> *As these seeds grow, let me grow in strength and health.*

Water and keep damp but not wet. In a few days the Osiris doll will be covered in fresh leaves and shoots. Eat these and visualize taking the strength and healing of Osiris within.

Ash Leaf Charm

A Cornish tradition is that a leaf from an even ash (one that has the same number of branches each side) is a particularly lucky charm. Pick the leaf, saying:

> *Even ash, I do thee pluck*
> *Hoping thus to meet good luck.*
> *If no good luck I get from thee*
> *I shall wish thee on the tree.*

Keep the leaf in your purse or wallet.

Pin Healing Spell

The ash is a tree of healing, a tradition preserved in folklore, whereby the ash tree reputedly had the ability to cure disease by taking it from the sufferer. The following is a very old healing spell: wear a pin for three days, then go to an ash tree and say:

> *Ashen tree, ashen tree, pray buy this sickness of me.*

Insert the pin into the tree. The disease then appears as knobs on the tree, and you will be free of it.

Making a Wand

Woody plants can provide powerful magical tools such as wands and staffs. However, you will need to get to know the tree over time and form a relationship with it and ask for its permission. There will be a moment when the energies are right for taking the wood, and you must not miss it or there may not be another chance. You should leave something in return—something that is meaningful or valuable to you, or preferably something of yourself such as some hair or a drop of blood. When you have your wood, it must be left for a few months to season, then you can carve it if you wish. Do not varnish it and do not add crystals until you have worked with the tool for a while and intuit what would enhance its powers. Your wand will always be connected to the spirits of place and the tree you took it from.

Making a Besom

The broom or besom is a magical tool in its own right, used for ritually sweeping and cleansing the sacred space; birch is a tree of new beginnings, purification, and dispelling negativity. It is a symbol of fertility; in the old times women would ride broomsticks around the field, leaping as high as they could; the higher they leapt, the higher the crops would grow. Today it is used as a fertility tool during the handfasting rite, when the newlywed couple leap over it to bless their marriage (or sometimes once for each child they would like to have)!

The ash pole, birch twigs, and willow binding should be collected in a conscientious fashion, though the actual construction of the besom is a fairly simple matter. The twigs are bound to the pole with willow shoots, which should first be soaked in water to make them soft and flexible. As they dry, they will shrink and make the binding tighter. The birch twigs can then all be cut off to the same length. As you work on your besom, think of the functions of its various components and bind them in. The besom should be consecrated with the following words:

> God and Goddess, deign to bless this besom that I would consecrate and set aside.
> Let it obtain the necessary virtues for acts of magic in the names of the Lord and
> Lady. Let it be an instrument of cleansing whose influence is felt in all the realms.
> God and Goddess, I call upon you to bless this instrument that I have prepared in
> your honour.

Make a few symbolic sweepings with the broom and say:

> Let blessing be.

Weather Lore

Ash before oak
Expect a soak.
Oak before ash
Expect a splash.

If ash leaves come out before oak leaves, it will be a rainy summer. If oak leaves come out before ash leaves, there will only be occasional showers.

Onion skin very thin
Mild winter coming in.
Onion skin thick and tough
Coming winter cold and rough.

A bumper crop of nuts presages a hard winter.

When a halo rings the moon or sun
Rain is approaching on the run.

If leaves stay late on the trees, the approaching winter will be hard.

Rainbow at morn
Good weather has gone.
Rainbow after noon
Good weather comes soon.

If the winter sunset is pale yellow, it indicates wind or rain on the way. If it is pale green, there will be frosts or snow.

Mackerel sky
Not long wet, not long dry.

A sky full of cirro-cumulus clouds indicates changeable weather.

Red sky at night
Shepherd's delight.
Red sky in the morning
Shepherd's warning.

Evening red and morning glory
Sets the traveller on his way.
Evening grey and morning red
Brings down showers upon his head.

Trace the sky in the painter's brush
And the winds around you soon will rush.

Wispy cirrus clouds, the highest in the sky, foretell approaching winds.

The Garden Pharmacy
Making Your Own Herbal Remedies

Your garden contains plants with valuable healing properties that can be used to treat and prevent common health problems. Using them can be as simple as making a cup of herbal tea. However, there are some important safety considerations to be taken into account.

- Make sure you have identified your plant correctly.

- Remember that anyone can be allergic to anything.

- Larger amounts of some herbs are not compatible with prescription medicines; always check with your healthcare professional before using herbal remedies on a regular basis.

- Always consult a medical practitioner if you have any acute or persistent health concerns.

- Make sure that you have looked up the method of preparation and the safe dosages.

- Do not take medicinal amounts of any herb for an extended period.

Tools Needed
- Saucepan (not copper or aluminium)
- Double boiler (or a bowl over a pan of boiling water)
- Kettle
- Muslin
- Kitchen scales
- Measuring jug
- Bottles and jars
- Pestle and mortar

Internal Remedies
Infusions and Decoctions

Herbs may be prepared in a variety of ways for internal and external use, so let's look at some basic methods.

Many of a herb's components, such as its minerals, vitamins, sugars, starches, hormones, tannins, volatile oils, and some alkaloids, dissolve well in water, and for this reason, herbs are often taken as infusions or teas (tisanes). Infusions can be made from the soft green and flowering parts of a herb.

Usually, an infusion is made with boiling water, as when you make tea, but some herbs have constituents such as mucilage and bitter principles that are destroyed by heat, so in that case a cold infusion is made.

Some of the harder, woodier parts of a plant, such as seeds, roots, buds, and barks, need to be boiled in water for a while to extract their properties. This is called a decoction. If the herbs are dried, they should first be pounded into a powder. Never use an aluminium or copper pan as it can react with the brew and taint it.

Herb Tea Basic Recipe

2 TEASPOONS FRESH OR 1 TEASPOON DRIED HERBS

250 ML OR 1 CUP WATER

Put the herbs in a teapot or a pot with a lid, pour on boiling water, and infuse for 10–20 minutes. Strain and drink, sweetened with honey or sugar if desired. Take one to three times daily.

Strong Infusion

An infusion indicates a greater measure of herbs to water: 4 teaspoons fresh or 2 teaspoons dried herbs to 250 ml of water, or double the quantity of herbs in the recipes. You can use a double strength infusion to make a gargle for a sore throat, for example. Take one to three times daily.

Cold Infusion Basic Recipe

2 TEASPOONS FRESH OR 1 TEASPOON DRIED HERBS

250 ML OR 1 CUP WATER

Use a non-metal container and put in the herbs and water. Close the lid or cover with cling film (plastic wrap) and leave overnight. Strain before use. Take one to three times daily.

Decoction

2 TEASPOONS FRESH OR 1 TEASPOON DRIED HERBS

250 ML OR 1 CUP WATER

Put the herbs in a pan and pour on the water. Cover and let the herbs macerate in the cold water for a few hours. Bring to a boil and simmer gently 15–20 minutes. Strain. Take one to three times daily.

Tinctures and Glycerites

These are fluid extracts of herbs using either alcohol or glycerine to extract plant chemicals and preserve them in an easily usable form that can be stored. Plant constituents are generally more soluble in alcohol than water, and alcohol will dissolve and extract resins, oils, alkaloids, sugars, starches, and hormones, though it does not extract nutrients such as vitamins or minerals. A remedy made this way is called a tincture. Brandy or vodka is usually used. Never use alcohols designed for external use, such as rubbing alcohol.

If you don't want to use alcohol for any reason or are formulating remedies for children, you can make a glycerite instead. You can use glycerine to extract phytochemicals from herbs in a similar manner to how alcohol is used to make a tincture, so you can convert any tincture recipes to a glycerite. Vegetable glycerine can be purchased from pharmacies or online and is a syrup made from vegetable oil; it is very sweet but doesn't raise blood sugar, so it is safe for diabetics. Glycerine is a weaker solvent than alcohol, so glycerites won't be as potent as an alcohol-based tincture and you will need a larger dose for a therapeutic effect. They won't keep as long as a tincture and are not good at making extractions from hard barks and dried roots. Make sure you use a food-grade vegetable glycerine.

TINCTURE (FOLK METHOD)

You can just pack your herbs into a glass jar and pour your chosen spirit over it, but if you want to be more precise, put 100 grams dried or 200 grams fresh herbs into a clean jar and pour on 500 ml of vodka or brandy. Make sure the herbs are completely covered. Seal and keep in a warm place for two to four weeks, shaking daily. Strain through muslin and store in a dark bottle in a cool place for two to six years. Because a tincture is much stronger than an infusion or decoction, you only need a few drops in a glass of water as a medicinal dose. Alternatively, a few drops may be added to a salve or bath for external use.

GLYCERITE (FOLK METHOD)

You can just pack your herbs into a glass jar and pour your glycerine over it, but if you want to be more precise, put 100 grams dried or 200 grams fresh herbs into a clean jar and pour on 500 ml of slightly warmed glycerine. Seal and keep in a warm, dark place for two to four weeks, shaking daily. Strain through muslin and store in a dark bottle in a cool place for about a year. If you add water to your glycerite or use fresh herbs with a lot of water content, it will spoil much faster. Take a teaspoon three times daily. Glycerine is soothing for a sore throat in itself. Glycerine is used in cosmetic products to soften, moisturise, and plump the skin, so you can use your herbal glycerites externally—dilute with rosewater to use as a skin toner or add them to salves, creams, and homemade soaps.

Syrups

Some herbs are bitter tasting and are more palatable when taken in the form of syrup, particularly for children. The sugar preserves the herbs. Thick syrup sticks to tissues, bringing the herbal benefits to sore throats and coughs.

SYRUP (FOLK METHOD)

To make syrup, first make your herbal infusion or decoction (see above), then for every 250 ml of infusion or decoction add 250 grams of sugar and heat gently until the sugar is dissolved. Simmer gently until thickened. Pour into sterilised bottles and label. This will keep six to twelve months unopened in a cool, dark place. Once opened, keep in the fridge for one to two months. If you wish, you can use honey instead of sugar, though the heating process destroys most of the honey's own properties.

Acetas: Herbal Vinegars

By just placing a few springs of herbs in vinegar, you can make herbal vinegar, which is not only pleasant tasting when sprinkled on salads but also therapeutic.

However, you can make a stronger version in the same way that you make a tincture, and this is an alternative to using alcohol. Though vinegar won't draw out as many phytochemicals from the herbs as alcohol, it does extract the vitamins and minerals from the plants.

Acetas—or vinegar extractions—are not as strong as tinctures, so the dose needed is higher. Take two teaspoons three times a day. You can dilute your herbal vinegar with water to take internally or use it externally in baths and compresses. Acetas generally have a cooling, anti-inflammatory effect, so are useful for conditions such as sore throats and inflamed skin. They will store for one to two years in a cool, dark place.

ACETA FOLK METHOD

To make an aceta, put 100 grams dried or 200 grams fresh herbs into a clean jar and pour on 500 ml of cider vinegar. Seal and keep in a warm place for 2 weeks, shaking daily. Strain through muslin and store in a dark bottle in a cool place for two to six years.

If you can, use raw cider vinegar.[24] Raw cider vinegar (the kind with the mother in it, rather than the barren pasteurised kind) contains antioxidants, vitamins, and minerals such as magnesium and potassium and helpful probiotic enzymes and bacteria. It stimulates digestion and has been shown to help lower blood pressure and increase HDL ("good") cholesterol. Though vinegar is acidic, cider vinegar has an alkaline effect on the body when consumed, which many people believe helps treat arthritis.

Electuaries (Herbal Honey)

An electuary is simply a herb or spice mixed with honey, so they are incredibly simple to make and will store for one to two years if dried herbs are used or up to 6 months if fresh herbs are used (the water content from the fresh plant matter shortens the shelf life). Honey extracts both the water and oil-based components from the herbs and is soothing and calming when added to a remedy. Take a teaspoonful one to four times a day.

ELECTUARY (FOLK METHOD)

Make your electuary with fresh plant material if you can. Simply chop your plant, put it in a glass jar, and cover it with slightly warmed honey. (You will need about two parts honey to one part fresh plant material or two parts honey to a half part dried herb/spice.) Seal the jar and leave in a dark place for three weeks. Warm the jar slightly, then strain off the honey into a clean, sterilised jar.

Oxymels

Oxymels are a sweet and sour blend of honey and vinegar, combining the benefits of both. If you've ever taken apple cider vinegar and honey, you've had an oxymel. The easiest way to make a herbal oxymel is to mix an already prepared herbal electuary with a prepared herbal vinegar, generally a 50:50 mix. You can come up with your own recipes by simply combining different herb vinegars and electuaries, mixing sage electuary with rosemary vinegar, for example.

Another way to make an oxymel is to quarter fill a sterilised jar with dried herbs or half fill with fresh herbs and top up with a 50:50 mix of honey and slightly warmed vinegar. Put on a lid and keep in a cool, dark place, shaking daily. (Avoid using a metal lid, as this may

---

24   For an easy recipe to make your own, please see my *Hearth Witch's Compendium* (Llewellyn, 2017).

be corroded by the vinegar and taint your product.) After two to four weeks, strain through muslin into a sterilised storage bottle.

For a quick way to make an oxymel, you can use the hot method. Simmer your herbs and vinegar together very gently without boiling for 10–20 minutes. Strain out and stir in the honey while the vinegar is still warm.

The usual dosage of an oxymel is one to two teaspoons three or four times a day as needed (when you have a cold, for example). You can put a spoonful of oxymel in warm water and drink that or even put a spoonful in a glass and top up with sparkling water or tonic water to create a herbal mocktail.

An oxymel should keep at least six to nine months in the fridge. Discard if you notice any mould.

External Remedies

BATHS

Adding herbs to a bath is a great way of getting the relaxing qualities of herbs (absorbed through the skin and inhaled) and for treating some skin conditions and aching muscles. You can put some herbs in a sock or muslin bag and drop this into the bath, but the bath water isn't really hot enough to extract the herbs' qualities. The best way is to add 500 ml of herbal infusion or decoction to the bath water and soak.

STEAM INHALATIONS

Steam inhalations of herbs may be used to relieve cold symptoms (try using peppermint, thyme, or ginger).

STEAM INHALATION (BASIC METHOD)

1 LITRE BOILING WATER

2 TEASPOONS HERB (FRESH IF POSSIBLE)

Pour boiling water over the herb and inhale. Place a towel over your head to trap the vapour.

SALVES

Herbs can be made into salves or ointments, which can then be applied to the affected area.

SALVES (FOLK METHOD)

250 ML OR 1 CUP VEGETABLE OIL SUCH AS SUNFLOWER, OLIVE, OR GRAPESEED

2 TABLESPOONS HERB

150 GRAMS OR 5 OUNCES BEESWAX OR SOY WAX, GRATED

In a double boiler, simmer the herb in the oil for 20–40 minutes. Strain and return the oil to the pan and add the wax and melt. Pour into warm glass jars. This is my preferred method.

You can also set a macerated oil (see page 74) into a salve using this method. Slightly warm your prepared oil and add the beeswax, allowing 2 tablespoons of grated beeswax to 500 ml (2 cups) of infused oil after the herbal material has been strained off. Pour into shallow jars to set.

COCONUT BALMS

Coconut oil, solid at room temperature, is a perfect consistency for a simple balm. You can simply gently simmer your herbs at a low temperature in a double boiler or slow cooker in the coconut oil for one to two hours, then strain into shallow jars to set. Coconut adds its own benefits to a balm: it is anti-inflammatory and can reduce pain and swelling. It is intensely moisturising and contains antimicrobial lipids, lauric acid, capric acid, and caprylic acid, which have antifungal, antibacterial, and antiviral properties.

CREAMS

Creams are less greasy and more quickly absorbed into the skin than salves and balms, but they are trickier to make. It involves blending oil and water in an emulsion, and they don't naturally want to blend. A cream will not keep as long as a salve, and if using fresh herbs for the purpose, it should be stored in the fridge.

A cream or lotion is basically a mixture of water and oil. As we all know from school, oil and water don't mix, so they will need another agent to bind them together, and this is called an emulsifier. You can use beeswax or soy wax; special emulsifying waxes are available online. You can make a basic cream just from vegetable oil, water, and emulsifying wax. Of course, this is a book about using plants, and you'll want to add other ingredients for their properties and natural perfumes. You can substitute herb and flower infusions or purchased floral waters (hydrosols) for the plain water, vary the oils and emulsifiers used, and add essential oils, aloe vera gel, honey, glycerine, and so on. You can add a preservative to make your product store longer, though most of the natural creams in this book have a very short shelf life or will need to be kept in the fridge. I suggest you make small quantities and use them up quickly. Because the cost is so much less than a shop-bought cream, you can afford to use them on your body as well as your face.

The basic method is to prepare the oil part and the liquid part separately before bringing them together.

Combine the emulsifying wax and oil(s) in a double boiler. Most creams use a combination of pouring oils, such as grapeseed or almond, and more solid oils, such as coconut or shea butter.

Your water needs to be warmed in a separate pan but must reach the same temperature as the oils, as this will help the two elements combine when they come together. Then the water part is dripped into the oil part very slowly, whisking constantly with a wooden spoon, hand whisk, or electric whisk until they are fully combined and emulsified.

The cream is then allowed to cool down a little. Now you can add other ingredients such as essential oils, glycerine, preservatives, etc.

Stir and quickly transfer to your storage jars before it thickens too much.

TROUBLESHOOTING

MY CREAM WON'T EMULSIFY: The two parts of your cream, the oil mix and the water mix, need to be at the same temperature. If it doesn't work the first time, allow the mixture to separate out, pour them off, and try again.

MY CREAM HAS GONE MOULDY: Using fresh or dried plant-based material in your creams is great for your skin and has many benefits, but it usually means that the cream will not last more than a few days or a couple of weeks in the fridge. In addition, it is vital that all your equipment, including the final jars and their lids, are sterilised to prevent mould. If the recipe calls for water, distilled water is best as tap water can contain bacteria. If using tap water, boil and cool it first.

HYDROSOLS

To make a homemade distilled flower hydrosol, take a large pan and put a metal trivet on the bottom of it. Pack your flowers around it (but not on it) and add just enough distilled water to cover them. Put a small heatproof bowl on top of the trivet. Bring water to a boil.

Now place a large heatproof bowl on top of the big saucepan and fill it with icy cold water and ice cubes. This will cause the rising steam to condense back into water droplets and drop back down onto the bowl. (Add more ice if it starts to warm up.) Simmer for a while before carefully removing the pan from the heat and taking out the small bowl—there will be some condensed liquid in it. Allow it to cool. The condensed water is hydrosol (flower water).

Compresses and Poultices

Compresses and poultices are a way of applying the benefits of herbs externally to the skin.

COMPRESS

For a compress, prepare a clean cotton cloth and soak it in a strong hot herbal infusion or decoction. Use this as hot as possible on the affected area, taking care to not burn yourself. Cover with a warm towel and leave for 30 minutes and change the compress as it cools down. Use one to two times a day.

POULTICE

Whereas a compress uses a cloth soaked in a liquid herbal infusion, a poultice employs herbs directly applied to the skin and then covered with a warm cloth. Bruise fresh herbs and apply directly to the skin and cover with a warm cloth. Use one to two times a day.

Macerated (Infused) Oils

Fats and oils extract the oily and resinous properties of a herb, and these are often the anti-bacterial, antifungal, and wound-healing components. Infused oils are used for external applications. Unlike essential oils, they do not need to be diluted for use.

COLD MACERATED OIL (FOLK METHOD)

The beauty of this method is that it is very simple and you don't have to weigh or measure anything. Cut up your fresh herb and put it in a sterilised glass jar. Pour in vegetable oil (olive, sunflower, almond, etc.), enough to make sure the herbs are covered. Leave on a sunny windowsill for 2 weeks, shaking daily. Strain into a clean jar. This will keep in a cool, dark place for up to 1 year.

Heat-Macerated Oil (Folk Method)

Using a hot maceration is quicker to make than a cold oil infusion. In a double boiler, put in your chopped herbs (again, you don't need to weigh or measure) and pour in enough vegetable oil to cover them. Simmer very gently, covered, for two hours. Turn off the heat and allow the oil to cool before straining. You can add fresh herbs to the oil if you wish and repeat the process for a stronger oil.

Gargles and Mouthwashes

To make your own herbal gargle or mouthwash, simply make a herbal infusion (or decoction) of your chosen herb. Allow it to infuse for 15 minutes. Strain, then gargle with it.

Your Magical Workshop

You can use your garden plants in your magical and spiritual work, and they will be more powerful because you have grown and collected them yourself.

Equipment Needed

- Pestle and mortar

- Bottles and jars

- Kitchen scales

- Measuring jug

- Ribbons, string, wire

- Cloth or bags

- Candles

- Charcoal blocks

The Magical Virtues of Plants

Each ingredient possesses its own virtues and energies. It has its own vibration, depending on its characteristics, makeup, and the environment it grew in, taking in nutrients from its surroundings and energy from the sun, becoming a unique being. Always remember that you are working with the virtues inherent in the plant to achieve the result you want, whether that is to evoke the energy of a particular deity or season, for protection, for cleansing, love, purification, or abundance, and so on. These are known as a plant's correspondences, and at the heading of each herb in the A–Z herbal are the correspondences for the planetary ruler, element, and associated deities, followed by the plant's magical virtues.

Let's look briefly at what some of those things mean:

PLANETS

SUN: The sun is dynamic and expansive. Herbs ruled by the sun turn towards the sun or have yellow flowers. The sun rules over prosperity and general protection.

MARS: Mars is the planet of war, so Mars plants symbolise a warlike spirit and generally have thorns or stings. Mars energy is assertive, spontaneous, and daring.

SATURN: Saturn is the planet of aging, limitation, and death, so Saturn plants are slow-growing or long-living and woody, thrive in the shade, have deep roots, or are poisonous, foul smelling, or considered evil. Saturn's energy is to do with limitation, change, the crystallisation of efforts, and endings. Because this is a kitchen herbal, very few of the plants in this book fall under Saturn.

MERCURY: Mercury is the planet of communication, so Mercury plants include fast-growing weeds, creepers and winding plants, or plants with hairy, fuzzy, or finely divided leaves. They may be aromatic. Mercury energy rules the mind and intellect.

VENUS: Venus is the planet of love and beauty, so Venus plants overwhelm the senses with sweet scents and lovely flowers, red fruits, or soft, furry leaves. Venus energy is feminine, creative, harmonious, and loving.

MOON: The moon governs the tides, and moon plants often grow near water or have a high water content or juicy leaves. They may have white flowers or moon-shaped leaves or seed pods. Moon energy is subtle, feminine, and inward looking. The moon rules the instinct, emotions, and psychic abilities.

JUPITER: Jupiter is the bringer of abundance, so Jupiter plants are usually big and bold and often edible. Jupiter is benign, expansive, and optimistic.

ELEMENTS

EARTH: The powers of earth are concerned with what is manifest, the material, the fixed, the solid, the practical, with what is rooted. Earth magic is concerned with manifestation, business, health, practicality, wealth, stability, grounding and centring, fertility and agriculture. Earth plants tend to be nourishing or earthy smelling.

AIR: The powers of air are concerned with the intellect, the powers of the mind, knowledge (as opposed to wisdom), logic, inspiration, information, teaching, memory, thought, and communication. Air magic is usually concerned with the intellectual or the spiritual, and in ritual air is symbolised through the use of perfume or incense. Air plants are often freshly fragrant, such as mint.

WATER: Water is associated with the emotions, feelings, and the subconscious, and water magic is usually concerned with divination and scrying. Water plants are juicy and fleshy or grow near water.

FIRE: Fire magic is concerned with creativity, life energy, and zeal. Fire gives us vitality, igniting action, animation, and movement. It sparks courage and acts of bravery. It heats passion and enthusiasm. Fire is the power of inner sight and creative vision, directing it and controlling it to make it manifest in the world. Fire plants tend to have fiery sap or a hot taste like ginger or warm perfumes like clove and cinnamon.

DEITY CORRESPONDENCES

Various religions have assigned specific plants to different gods and used them in the worship of those deities or associated them in mythology. Where I have assigned gods and goddesses to herbs it is because those plants were connected with those particular deities either in their mythology or worship. They are not arbitrarily assigned, as they are in many books.

Incorporating Herbs in Magic

There are numerous ways you can incorporate the energy of a herb into your spiritual and magical practice, and here are just a few:

LIVING ENERGY PRESENCE

Simply having a particular plant growing in your garden will bring the living energy of that plant into your environment. Some plants, such as basil, are believed to be protective spirits in their own right.

DISPLAYED FOR MAGICAL PURPOSES

The energy of a plant can be brought into your environment by creating a herbal talisman or herbal charm bag, always concentrating on your purpose and intent and then hanging it in the place it is most needed, such as the kitchen or bedroom.

WREATHS

A wreath is simply an arrangement of flowers or leaves woven into a ring. Hang a wreath on your front door to protect the magical threshold between inside and outside and prevent negativity from entering.

CARRY ABOUT THE PERSON

Throughout the ages, people have put leaves of particular herbs in their pockets or purses when they wanted to carry the energy of that herb with them.

PLACED UNDER THE PILLOW

Placing a herb beneath the pillow to absorb its energy is an ancient practice.

CHARM BAGS

This is one of the simplest forms of magic using herbs. Herbal charm bags are fabric pouches filled with dried plant matter. Put the ingredients into the pouch one by one, stating your desire each time. You can blend several different dried herbs to suit your purpose. Sew it shut, and then either carry it with you, put it in the appropriate room of your house, or sleep with it under your pillow, according to its purpose.

ASPERGERS (SPRINKLERS)

Aspergers are sprinklers made from woody herb stems such as sage, rosemary, or mint used for scattering consecrated water or herbal infusions in order to purify a place or person of negative vibrations and energies. To make one, take some fresh sprigs of herbs about 15 cm (6 inches) long and bind them together at one end using white thread. To use the asperger, dip it into the liquid and sprinkle it around the area (a circle, temple, house, or shop, for example) or person to be purified.

POTIONS

Potion is a generic term for herbal preparations made in a ritual way. They are made according to the same methods as infusions and decoctions made for healing but are brewed with magical intent, preferably at the correct moon phase and season, and perhaps with appropriate words and symbolic actions. The purpose of a potion depends on the plants chosen.

EATEN OR DRUNK

When you ingest a plant, you make an intimate connection with it, absorbing its vibrational energy into your body and your own energy field, changing its frequency; it becomes part of you forever. When you do this with intent, consciously, as part of spiritual practice or ritual, it becomes a communion of spirits. Plants can be consumed in teas, potions, food, or infused in wine.

THE RITUAL CUP

Herbs and flowers infused in wine or wine made with herbs, fruit, or flowers can be used as a ritual drink. You will need to tailor the plants used to your purpose for different sabbats and events such as handfastings.

POWDERS

Herbs, barks, and roots can be powdered together for use in magic. You can scatter a powder around your house or possessions to protect them, put a pinch of money-drawing powder in your purse, put them in charm bags, sprinkle them on candles, or use to consecrate tools and amulets.

OFFERINGS

When performing spells and rituals, it is customary to make offerings to the gods and spirits. Such offerings can take the form of bread and cakes baked with suitable herbs left in the ritual venue, incense, libations of herbal wines, or simply bunches of herbs left in the places you work to thank the spirits for their help. Please never leave wire, ribbons, or plastic tied to these, as this is just littering, and the spirits will be angry.

IN CONJUNCTION WITH CANDLES

Infused oils can be used to anoint the candles used in candle magic or you can stud a candle with seeds (do be careful because as they burn, they can explode) or warm the outside of the candle and then roll it in dried herbs. This adds the energy of the herbs to a ritual or spell, or you can perform a candle magic spell.

INCENSE

You can use your kitchen herbs and spices in your ritual incenses. Loose incense is probably the easiest type of incense to make and the most useful kind for magical ritual. All the measurements in this book are by volume, not weight, and I use a spoon to measure out small quantities when I am making a single jar of incense or a cup for large quantities and big batches. Therefore, if the recipe says 3 parts rosemary, ½ part thyme, and 1 part oregano, this means three spoons of rosemary, half a spoon of thyme, and 1 spoon of oregano.

CLEANSING

If you feel that your home has accumulated negative energy or if there is a bad atmosphere lingering after an argument, you can take several measures to cleanse it. (It is a good idea to do this on a regular basis in any case.) Doing this with burning dried plants is known all over the world. Native Americans call it smudging, while in Scotland it is known as saining, for example. This method can also be used to cleanse the aura and any magical tools or ritual objects.

RITUAL OILS

Infused oils made from herbs, flowers, and spices can be used in spells and rituals to anoint people and candles or consecrate tools, talismans, and amulets and so on.

FLOWER ESSENCES

A flower essence is the bio-energetic imprint of a flower transmitted, by a process of solarisation, to water, which then holds the memory of the vibrational essence of the plant. Flower essences work on energy pathways to heal on an emotional, mental, and spiritual level, and the spiritual aspect of the remedies is why I have included flower essences in this section.

IN CONJUNCTION WITH MEDITATION

The vibrational energy of herbs can be helpful in your meditation practice and chakra work. Try holding a sprig or leaf of a particular herb within your aura as you meditate.

Harvesting and Storing

Your garden plants can provide you with a supply of useful material for use.

HARVESTING

- Use an open basket or cardboard box for harvesting to prevent crushing the material.

- Collect from healthy plants; don't pick damaged leaves or flowers.

- Double check what you are harvesting to make sure you have identified the right plant. Don't mix different plants in your collecting basket.

- Gather on a dry, sunny day.

- Leaves are best collected in spring or early summer, flowers as they bloom, berries as they become ripe, and roots in the autumn.

DRYING

You will need to attend to any plants you have collected quickly, before they start to deteriorate.

You can dry plants either by hanging or spreading them flat on absorbent paper in a warm place or using a dehydrator or drying in a very low oven.

If you are harvesting the whole aerial parts of a plant (such as a bunch of nettles), you can make small bunches of stems and hang them up out of direct sunlight. When dry, crumble them into paper bags or dark glass jars.

Large flowers can be separated out on trays to dry. Leave enough air circulation between them. When dry, separate the petals.

Berries can be dried in a warmed oven, which is then turned off before the trays of fruits are put in. Leave the door of the oven open and leave for 3–4 hours.

Roots should be washed and chopped into small pieces. Spread on a tray and put in a warmed oven, turned off, for 2–3 hours.

Seeds can be collected by hanging the seeding heads of flowers upside down in a paper bag. They will fall off into the bottom of the bag as the plant dries.

STORING

Badly stored plant material will soon deteriorate and lose its potency. Store in sterilised dark glass containers with airtight lids. If you don't have dark glass jars, you can wrap thick paper around the outside of clear jars. Do not use metal or plastic containers.

Part 2

The A–Z Herbal

Aloe Vera

Aloe barbadensis syn. *Aloe vera*

· · · · · · · · · · ·

PLANETARY RULER: Moon

ELEMENT: Water

ASSOCIATED DEITIES: Moon goddesses,
Artemis, Aeacus, Amun Ra, Chandra, Indra,
Rhadamanthus, Vulcan, Yama, Venus

MAGICAL VIRTUES: Healing, protection,
divination, spiritual development

Although it resembles a cactus, aloe vera is actually a member of the lily family and is a stemless succulent plant growing up to 100 cm (40 inches) tall. Aloe vera has thick succulent pale green leaves with lighter spots. The edges of the leaves are barbed but not sharp enough for injury. When broken, they contain a viscous, clear gel. If you want to use your plant, make sure it *is* an aloe vera, as there are around 350 species of aloe.

The botanical name *Aloe* derives from the Arabic *alloeh*, meaning "bitter and shiny substance" and *vera* from the Latin word for truth. Despite the nomenclature *barbadensis* ("of Barbados") it is native to North Africa and the Arabian Peninsula and thrives in warm, dry climates. I can only put mine outside in the summer months; for most of the year they become house plants. In the summer, the older plants each produce a flowering stem that bears spikes of narrow yellow or orange flowers. As long as you can keep your plants fairly warm, they are easy to grow. They prefer a sandy soil or well-drained compost and like to dry out between watering; nothing looks sadder than an overwatered aloe vera. The plants soon produce offshoots that you can pot on and give away to friends.

Various types of aloes have been used medicinally for thousands of years. The ancient Egyptian Ebers Papyrus, from about 1550 BCE, gives twelve formulas for mixing aloe vera with other herbs for pain and inflammation. The first-century CE herbalist Dioscorides gave a detailed description of it in his *De Materia Medica* ("On Medical Material"), which is our prime historical source of information about the medicines used by the Greeks, Romans, and other cultures of antiquity. In it, he recommended aloe for the treatment of wounds, skin irritation, sunburn, acne, and hair loss.[25] The Roman writer Pliny prescribed aloe vera juice as a laxative. Alexander the Great transported wagons of fresh aloe vera plants to the sites of his battles to treat the wounds of his soldiers. It is even reputed that Aristotle convinced him to annex the island Socotra to ensure a steady supply of plants from the aloe groves there.[26]

In ancient Egypt aloe was known as the "plant of immortality" for its healing properties, its benefits in keeping the skin looking young and fresh (both Cleopatra and Nefertiti were reputed to have used aloe vera in their beauty care), and because its antibacterial and anti-fungal qualities were employed in the embalming of the dead. The Mayans christened it the "Fountain of Youth."

In myth and lore, aloe is a protective plant. For the people of ancient Mesopotamia, aloe was used to ward off and expel evil spirits, a practice mentioned on the clay boards from Nippur, which date back to 2,200 BCE. In Africa it is hung over house doors to drive away evil spirits and kept in kitchens to prevent (and treat) burns and kitchen mishaps. In the Middle East, after completing a pilgrimage to Mecca, aloe is hung over doorways to ensure protection. In Mexico a red ribbon tied around an aloe vera leaf wards off evil, bad luck, and malevolent spirits.[27]

MAGICAL USES

Hang a leaf of aloe vera above your front door for protection and keep a plant in your kitchen. Dry the leaves and use them in incenses of protection or add aloe vera gel to protective salves and talismans.

In modern Pagan practice, aloe vera is associated with the feminine, the moon, intuition, divination, and spiritual development. The leaves may be dried and used in incenses dedi-

25   https://archive.org/details/Dioscorides_Materia_Medica.
26   https://www.aloe-medical-group.com/en/aloe-vera/history.html?l=2.
27   https://journeys.dartmouth.edu/folklorearchive/2018/11/13/red-ribbon-on-aloe-vera.

cated to the moon goddess to bring understanding and insight and invoke her help during divination. The third eye position on the forehead may be anointed with aloe vera gel. Add aloe vera gel to salves or dry and add to incenses and talismans of the moon goddess, the moon, or water.

The sap squeezed from the fleshy leaves may be added to a shampoo used to cleanse the hair and body in the ritual bath for cleansing and protection.

CULINARY USES

None.

COSMETIC USES

Aloe vera gel is one of the best herbs you can use on your skin. Its anti-inflammatory effect soothes irritation, while its emollient nature softens, moisturises, and reduces wrinkles. It has the added benefit of tightening the skin, and its antibacterial quality means it has an anti-acne effect. You can apply fresh aloe gel directly to your skin or add it to your home-made facial cleansers and moisturizers, such as the **Aloe Vera Cream** below. Use it in a homemade after-sun cream or apply the gel directly to the skin.

Aloe vera gel is also useful for frizzy hair—smooth a little gel on dry and split ends before styling. Add to shampoo to treat an itchy scalp.

Using fresh aloe is better as commercial products lose some of the vital properties during processing and may be adulterated with alcohol.

MEDICINAL USES

The plants provide two separate liquids—the thick, clear aloe gel that is found in the centre of broken leaves, which is used topically (i.e., on the skin), and aloe vera latex (also called aloe juice or aloe resin), which oozes from the base of the leaf when it is cut and is bitter tasting, yellow, and watery, which should not be used. Use the clear gel only, and only for external use.

Aloe gel is well-known and widely used as a topical remedy for skin irritation. I like to keep a plant in the kitchen as it is a handy first-aid remedy for minor burns, fungal infections, ringworm, nappy rash, eczema, dermatitis, psoriasis, insect bites, sunburn, cuts, and skin abrasions—just take a fresh leaf and open it to extract the clear gel within and apply this directly to the affected area. It reduces pain, speeds healing, and encourages cell repair, due in part to the presence of aloectin B, which stimulates the immune system.

Caution: *Applying aloe gel to the skin is considered to be generally safe and rarely produces side effects, though in some sensitive people it can cause contact dermatitis. Aloe vera belongs to the lily family of plants, so individuals who are allergic to other members of the lily family (which includes garlic, onions, crocus, hyacinth, lilies, and tulips) may also be sensitive to aloe. If a rash, redness, or swelling develops at the site of application, the aloe gel should be washed off with cool water. It should not be used during breastfeeding as it can act as a purgative on the baby.*

Oral ingestion of the bitter yellow aloe vera latex is potentially toxic and may cause abdominal cramps and diarrhoea, which in turn can decrease the absorption of prescription drugs. Aloe gel should not be taken by mouth because aloe latex may be mixed with it.

The "aloe vera juice" you can buy in health food shops to drink is generally made from the whole leaf, crushed and ground to produce a liquid, which is then filtered and stabilised, followed by various steps of filtration and stabilization. Taking aloe juice regularly may lead to reduced potassium levels in the body, resulting in muscle weakness and potentially dangerous changes in heart rhythm. Drinking it over prolonged periods of time has been associated with kidney damage; some deaths have been attributed to kidney failure caused by long-term or high-dose oral use of aloe vera juice.

Recipes

ALOE & CUCUMBER UNDER-EYE GEL

1 TEASPOON ALOE VERA GEL

3 TEASPOONS CUCUMBER, PEELED

Put the cucumber into a blender (or mash up with a pestle and mortar), then stir in the aloe vera gel. Pop into a clean jar and store in the fridge for up to 3 days. Apply to the under-eye area morning and evening.

ALOE VERA CREAM

70 ML OR 4 TABLESPOONS ALOE VERA GEL

30 ML OR 2½ TABLESPOONS MACERATED
CALENDULA OR LAVENDER OIL

5 ML OR 1 TEASPOON HERBAL TINCTURE
(CALENDULA, LAVENDER, OR LILAC)

20 DROPS ESSENTIAL OIL OF YOUR CHOICE
(LAVENDER, ROSE, JASMINE, AND CALENDULA
ARE ALL GOOD FOR THE SKIN)

Put the aloe gel in a bowl and gradually whisk in the herbal infused oil a teaspoon at a time. Whisk in the tincture and essential oil until combined. Spoon into sterilised jars, label, and date.

It is that easy! Most homemade creams can be very greasy and take a long time to be absorbed into the skin, but this makes a light, fluffy, non-greasy cream that is easily absorbed into the skin. You can use your homemade herbal oils and tinctures in it, but it comes without all the heating and fuss of an emulsified cream. Depending on what oils and tinctures you choose, you can make this as a healing cream or a beauty cream.

Aloe Vera Aftershave Gel

110 ML OR 20 TEASPOONS ALOE VERA GEL

5 TEASPOONS DISTILLED WATER

3 TEASPOONS WITCH HAZEL

10 DROPS ESSENTIAL OIL OF YOUR CHOICE (CEDAR IS NICE)

Combine all the ingredients. Keep in a cool, dark place for up to 2 weeks.

Aloe Vera Lotion

250 ML OR 1 CUP ALOE VERA GEL

1 TEASPOON VITAMIN E OIL

10 DROPS ESSENTIAL OIL OF YOUR CHOICE

25 GRAMS OR 1 OUNCE EMULSIFYING WAX

120 ML OR ½ CUP VEGETABLE OIL

Mix the gel, vitamin E, and essential oil. In a double boiler, melt the wax and vegetable oil over a gentle heat. Add to the aloe mix a little at a time, using an electric whisk. This will keep in the fridge for 6 weeks. It makes a soothing skin lotion and eases the pain of sunburn.

Begonia

Begonia spp.

PLANETARY RULER: Mars

ELEMENT: Fire

ASSOCIATED DEITIES: Gods and
goddesses of justice and harmony

MAGICAL VIRTUES: Balance, harmony, peace, justice

With over 2,000 species, begonias originate in the subtropical and tropical moist climates of South and Central America, Africa, and southern Asia. The first person to document them was a Franciscan monk called Charles Plumier, who found fibrous-rooted begonias in Brazil in 1690. He named the plant after the governor of the French Antilles, Michel Bégon. The pretty flowers first reached Europe from Central and South America and the Caribbean islands. Initially, in Europe, begonias were a rich man's indulgence as, like orchids, they needed heat and specialised care. It was only after they were selectively bred to withstand more demanding conditions that they became affordable for most gardeners.

Begonias are categorized according to root types into fibrous-rooted, tuberous, and rhizomatous. Fibrous-rooted begonias have only fibrous roots, prefer bright light, and are more sun tolerant. Tuberous begonias grow from tubers, have single or double flowers, and are shade-loving bedding plants. Rhizomatous begonias grow from a modified stem called a rhizome.

In modern lore, the different-coloured flowers contain their own symbolism. White begonias mean innocence, red begonias are romance and passion, and pink is friendship.

MAGICAL USES

Keep a begonia plant in your home or plant in the garden by the door to promote harmony.

Use dried begonia flowers in herbal talismans and sachets, which you can carry or hang in your house for balance and accord.

A **Begonia Flower Essence** helps with releasing negativity and hurt stemming from past events. It helps to integrate the experience, heal the heart, and release the pain.

The dried flowers can be used in spells and incenses that call for and promote justice.

CULINARY USES

Begonias are a source of vitamin C and are eaten from Japan, India, Indonesia, China, Brazil, Mexico, and Paraguay to the Philippines. In China, the leaves of *Begonia fimbristipula* are dried to make a tea. The tart sap has even been used to curdle milk for cheese making.[28]

Generally, it is the tuberous begonias that are eaten. A few websites say wax begonias are cancer-causing but there is no supporting evidence. Tuberous begonias have edible leaves and flowers with a sour, citrus-like taste that can be used raw or cooked, for flower garnishes, and in spreads, dips, and salads.

COSMETIC USES

You can dry begonia petals to use in begonia crafts and natural beauty recipes. They make a nice addition to soothing bath salts and give them a delicate floral scent.

> *Caution:* Begonias contain oxalic acid, so they should be consumed in moderation and avoided by people with kidney disease, rheumatism, or gout. In some sensitive people, the sap of begonias can cause irritation and contact dermatitis.

---

28 Sangeeta Rajbhandary, "Traditional Uses of Begonia Species (Begoniacae) in Nepal," https://www.academia.edu/32450803/TRADITIONAL_USES_OF_BEGONIA_SPECIES_BEGONIACAE_IN_NEPAL.

Recipes

Begonia Flower Essence

Gather a few mature flowers. Float them on the surface of 150 ml spring water in a bowl and leave in the sun for 3–4 hours. Make sure that they are not shadowed in any way. Remove the flowers. Pour the water into a bottle; to preserve it, top up with 150 ml brandy or vodka. This is your mother essence. To make up your flower essences for use, put seven drops from this into a 10 ml dropper bottle and top that up with brandy or vodka. This is your dosage bottle. The usual dose is four drops of this in a glass of water four times a day. When making flower essences, it is important not to handle the flowers—it is the vibrational imprint of the flowers you want to be held by the water, not your own imprint. Begonia flower essence helps to heal the hurts of the past.

Begonia Justice Talisman

RED CLOTH OR A PURCHASED RED POUCH

2 TEASPOONS DRIED BEGONIA FLOWERS

1 HORSE CHESTNUT

7 JUNIPER BERRIES

SMALL RED JASPER STONE

Assemble at the waxing moon. You will need an oblong piece of cloth big enough to take all the ingredients when folded in half and sewn up. Choose a sturdy fabric. Take the cloth and fold it in half, right sides together. Sew up three sides, reinforcing your intent with each stitch (you can chant it as you sew), and then turn it right-side out. Put the ingredients into the pouch one by one, stating your desire each time. Sew it shut, then carry it with you when you need justice.

. . . .

BEGONIA BATH SALTS

HANDFUL OF COARSE SALT

HANDFUL OF DRIED BEGONIA FLOWERS

Gently blend the flowers into the salt. Store in a pretty glass jar with a tightly fitting lid. Add a handful to your bath, stir in, lie back, and relax!

. . . .

BEGONIA SYRUP

1 LITRE OR 4 CUPS WATER

25 TO 30 BEGONIA FLOWERS, PREFERABLY RED

50 GRAMS OR ¼ CUP SUGAR

1 TEASPOON CITRIC ACID

Pour the water over the flowers and stand overnight. Strain, discarding the flowers. Add the sugar to the retained liquid. Heat gently for 20 minutes (do not boil), add the citric acid, and strain again. Keep refrigerated and pour over fruit salads, puddings, and ice cream.

Borage

Borago officinalis

- - - - - - - - - - - - - - - -

PLANETARY RULER: Jupiter

ELEMENT: Air

ASSOCIATED DEITIES: Warrior gods, Euphrosyne

MAGICAL VIRTUES: Courage, strength,
warrior magic, joy, gladness, expansion

Borage's numerous folk names give us a clue to its many attributes—Bee Plant, Starflower, Cool Tankard, and Herb of Gladness, to name just a few. Already this tells us that it is a plant beloved by bees, it has star-shaped flowers (which give their name to its commercially available starflower oil), it relates to brewing, and it was used to treat depression; in fact, the Welsh name for the plant, *llawenlys*, translates as "herb of gladness."

Borage is a hardy annual plant originating in the Mediterranean that has now spread throughout Africa, Europe, and the Middle East. It was taken to America by colonists. The star-shaped blossoms begin as pink before turning a beautiful blue, flower most of the summer, and are irresistible to bees. The stem and dark green leaves are covered with prickly hairs. The plant readily self-seeds, so if you start off with one borage plant, it will quickly spread and pop up all over the garden year after year.

The origin of the name *borage* is unclear. It may relate to the Italian *borra* or the French *bourra*, meaning "hair" or "wool," from the low Latin *burra*, referring to the thick covering of short white hairs on the plant. Another possibility is from the Latin *corago* (*cor* meaning "heart" and *ago* meaning "I bring"), and the lore of borage is certainly associated with courage. Its Celtic name is *borrach*, or courage, as Celtic warriors prepared for battle by drinking wine in which borage had been steeped. This quality was recognised throughout the Classical world. The Roman writer Pliny (23–79 CE) recorded the motto "I borage bring courage."[29] During the Crusades, before their departure and to ensure their valour, knights would be given a stirrup cup of wine in which borage flowers had been steeped. Medieval knights even had the flower embroidered on scarves, which they carried to bring them bravery in battle. In folklore, carrying borage will bring you courage, and there is an old saying that "a garden without borage is like a heart without courage." It was even claimed that if a girl put borage in her lover's wine, it would give him the courage to propose. We now know that borage stimulates adrenaline production, which might indeed give courage a boost.

Borage has been a valuable medicinal herb since ancient times, and as a remedy for depression it has been extolled by herbalists through the centuries. Pliny the Elder (23–79 CE) believed it gave to life the spirits, courage and comfort to the heart, driving away sorrow.[30] He called it Euphrosynum after Euphrosyne, the goddess of joy, one of the Three Graces. The Greek physician Dioscorides (40–90 CE), in his *De Materia Medica*, suggested borage to "cheer the heart and to lift the depressed spirits."[31] The sixteenth-century English herbalist Gerard extolled the virtues of borage "for the comfort of heart, to drive away sorrow, and increase the joy of the minde."[32] Francis Bacon (1561–1626) wrote that borage had "an excellent spirit to repress the fuliginous vapour of dusky melancholie."[33] The famous Nicholas Culpeper wrote of it as one of the "herbs of Jupiter and under Leo, all great cordials and strengtheners of nature," adding that the "flowers…put into wine make men and women glad…and drive away all sadness."[34] John Evelyn (1620–1706) recommended it "to revive the hypochondriac and cheer the hard student."[35] Research has shown that people who suffer from depression experience a dramatic drop in adrenaline, and as borage can increase adrenaline production, it may act as a natural antidepressant. So powerful was it believed to be that Pliny believed borage was the Nepenthe mentioned in book IV of Hom-

---

29   Pliny the Elder, *Natural History*.
30   Ibid.
31   https://archive.org/stream/de-materia-medica/scribd-download.com_dioscorides-de-materia-medica_djvu.txt.
32   Gerard, *Gerard's Herbal*.
33   Quoted in Staub, *75 Exceptional Herbs*.
34   Culpeper, *Culpeper's Herbal*.
35   Evelyn, *Acetaria*.

er's *Odyssey*: a substance that, dropped into wine, "eased men's pains and irritations, making them forget their troubles—a drink of this, once dipped in wine, would guarantee no man would let a tear fall on his cheek, not even if his father and his mother died."[36]

Borage is a favourite plant of bees, not just the honeybee, but also bumble bees and other smaller bees, which is why it is called Bee Plant and Bee Bread. At one time borage was grown by beekeepers near their hives to boost honey production. Borage is a wonderful addition to a wildlife garden and provides an abundance of nectar for bees to enjoy.

The usefulness of borage in the garden does not end there. It can help nearby plants resist pests and disease. Borage adds trace minerals to the soil it is planted in and is great added to the compost heap or can be employed for mulching. As a companion plant, it deters cabbage and tomato caterpillars while attracting beneficial pollinators. Planting borage close to tomatoes, squashes, spinach, cabbages, cucumbers, fruit trees, and strawberries will improve their growth and fruit production.

MAGICAL USES

Borage is used in charms, spells, rituals, and potions to stimulate courage and strength. Carry some flowers in a small pouch close to your heart when you need these. Drink **Borage Tea** to give you a lift when facing a difficult situation.

Borage is particularly useful when exploring the warrior path and trying to cultivate inner strength and determination. Take **Borage Tea** or **Borage Wine** or use the dried flowers and leaves in an incense to explore the warrior aspects of your own personality.

Borage Tea or **Borage Wine** may also be taken at Lughnasa if the traditional chases and battles are to be undertaken. Use the dried leaves and flowers in an incense to invoke warrior gods or their qualities of strength, courage, and endurance.

Borage has expansive Jupiter energies. A **Borage Flower Essence** may be of benefit to those who fear failure or who are anxious and depressed, and can help feelings of joy and enthusiasm. Use dried borage flowers in incenses of Jupiter when evoking these qualities.

Borage is sacred to the goddess of joy. Use it in the form of incense, tea, or wine. Carry a herbal talisman containing borage when you need to bring joy into your life.

Borage Wine or **Borage Infused Wine** can be taken at the sabbat feast to make merry and bring gladness to the hearts of the participants.

---

36   https://www.theoi.com/Text/HomerOdyssey4.html and Pliny the Elder, *Natural History*.

Borage Tea can be drunk to aid psychic awareness or added to the ritual bath in preparation for inner journeying, vision quests, and shamanic practices of an arduous nature. Add dried borage flowers to psychic incenses or anoint yourself with **Macerated Borage Oil**.

CULINARY USES

Borage was a popular culinary herb in the Middle Ages, and right into the early part of the nineteenth century the young tops of borage were boiled as a potherb, and the young leaves added to salads. In Poland and Russia, it is still used to flavour pickled gherkins, is eaten as a vegetable in Germany, while in northern Spain and northwestern Italy, it is added to ravioli and pansotti fillings.[37] All parts of the plant have a delicate flavour reminiscent of cucumber.

The bright blue flowers may be picked and eaten fresh in salads or candied for cake decoration. Add fresh flowers to a glass of Pimms or freeze them in ice cubes to be added to cocktails, lemonade and summer drinks.

Gather the leaves when the plant is coming into flower. Pick the young leaves only and reject any that are damaged. They are best used fresh as they do not retain their flavour when dried of frozen. They may be added to poultry, fish and cheese dishes, most vegetables, used fresh in salads, or added to pickles and salad dressings. Add the young leaves to summer drinks.

Parts of the plant are sometimes used as a flavouring agent in wine, gin and non-alcoholic beverages. It was formerly a common addition to cool tankards of wine, cider and claret cup. Try the **Borage Infused Wine** below.

When steeped in water, borage leaves and flowers add a cool cucumber flavour—just add lemon to make a refreshing summer drink.

COSMETIC USES

A commercially available oil is produced from the seeds and is generally marketed as starflower oil. This has moisturising and softening effects so may be included in face creams.

Borage is a cooling, cleansing herb with skin softening and anti-inflammatory properties. Add **Macerated Borage Oil** to your homemade skin care products, rub it into your skin, or pour a little into your bath.

Use steam-wilted borage leaves as a face mask for dry skin.

---

37   https://www.countrylife.co.uk/nature/borage-the-pimms-ingredient-that-powered-the-crusaders-and
-lifted-dusky-melancholie-229439.

Medicinal Uses

All parts of the borage plant contain medicinal properties. It is used by herbalists to treat eczema, rheumatoid arthritis, stress, PMS, coughs, and depression.

Borage is useful at times of stress, as it is a restorative for the adrenal cortex. An infusion of the flowers and leaves in wine (**Borage Infused Wine**) or **Borage Tea** can be used to stimulate the adrenals and increase the ability to cope during times of stress. It is particularly useful for someone who has been on steroids for any length of time, restoring the adrenal glands. It can be used for fevers and during convalescence,

A poultice of the fresh leaves can be used to soothe bruises and inflammations.

The plant has a high mucilage content. Externally, the pulped fresh leaves are employed as a soothing and cooling poultice for inflammatory swellings, bruises, insect bites, rashes, and inflamed skin.

Borage has been used for many years as an antidepressant, mainly in the form of **Borage Tea**, which also may be useful for fevers, diarrhoea, and bronchitis.

Borage seeds are used to make a commercially available oil.[38] It has a higher percentage of the polyunsaturated omega-6 fatty acid gamma-linolenic acid (GLA) than any other natural source.

> *Caution:* *While eating small portions of borage occasionally as food is not believed to present a risk for most individuals, taking the aerial parts of borage for extended periods of time or ingesting a very large amount (several servings) at one time should be avoided. Very large doses of borage aerial parts may contain enough pyrrolizidine alkaloids to cause liver damage. Borage herb should not be taken by people with liver conditions. Pregnant women and epileptics should not take borage seed oil (starflower oil). Do not use internally if you are on blood thinning medication (including aspirin) or blood thinning herbs such as danshen, devil's claw, eleuthero, garlic, ginkgo, horse chestnut, panax ginseng, papain, red clover, or saw palmetto.*

38　James E. Simon, Nancy Beaubaire, Stephen C. Weller, and Jules Janick, "Borage: A Source of Gamma Linolenic Acid," in J. Janick and J. E. Simon (eds.), *Advances in New Crops* (Portland, OR: Timber Press, 1990), 528.

Recipes

BORAGE TEA

250 ML OR 1 CUP BOILING WATER

2 TEASPOONS FRESH BORAGE LEAVES

Pour the water onto the herb and infuse for 10–15 minutes. Strain and drink to boost adrenal production and as a mild antidepressant.

BORAGE WINE

3 LITRES OR 12 CUPS PLUS 1 LITRE OR 4½ CUPS WATER

1 LITRE OR 4½ CUPS BORAGE FLOWERS AND LEAVES

450 GRAMS OR 2¾ CUPS RAISINS

900 GRAMS OR 4½ CUPS GRANULATED SUGAR

JUICE AND GRATED PEEL OF ONE LEMON

1 CUP BLACK TEA

WHITE WINE YEAST (AVAILABLE ONLINE)

WHITE WINE YEAST NUTRIENT (AVAILABLE ONLINE)

Wash and chop the flowers and leaves. Put into a large pan with 3 litres or 12 cups water and bring to boil. Simmer for 5 minutes, remove from the heat, and leave to infuse for 24 hours. Strain and set aside the liquid. In a clean pan, bring 1 litre or 4½ cups water to boil and add the sugar, stirring until dissolved. Remove from the heat. Combine the infused borage liquid and the sugar water in a fermentation bin. When the liquid has cooled to lukewarm, add the yeast and nutrient according to manufacturer's instructions, plus the raisins, tea, and juice and grated peel of lemon. Fit the lid and leave for a week, stirring daily. Strain into a demijohn and top up with cold boiled water if necessary. Fit an airlock and leave to ferment out in a warm place. When fermentation is completed (when the airlock stops bubbling completely), siphon into a clean demijohn, fit a bung, and leave to clear for a few weeks, allowing any sediment to sink to the bottom. Siphon into clean, sterilised bottles and fit a cork or lid. Store as you would any other wine. *Note:* Some of the water may be substituted by 2 litres or 8½ cups pure apple juice.

BORAGE INFUSED WINE

Take a bottle of white wine and remove a glassful. Add 2–3 borage leaves or a handful of flowers to the wine in the bottle. Seal the bottle. Allow to infuse overnight and then strain out the wine into a clean bottle.

BORAGE AND POTATO SOUP

1 LARGE ONION

OIL

4 LARGE POTATOES

1 LITRE OR 4¼ CUPS VEGETABLE STOCK

4 FRESH BORAGE LEAVES

Chop the onion. Heat the oil and add the onion. Cook gently for 5 minutes. Peel the potatoes, add to pan, and gently fry for a few seconds. Add the vegetable stock. Simmer with the lid on for 40 minutes. Add the borage leaves for last 5 minutes. Liquidise and serve hot or cold.

MACERATED BORAGE OIL

Pick the flowers and young leaves of borage. Put them on a tray and leave them overnight to wilt and lose some of their water content. Pack them into a glass jar and cover with vegetable oil. Fit a lid and leave this on a sunny windowsill for 3 weeks, shaking daily. Strain the oil into a clean jar. Use directly on your skin for rashes and irritations or add it to your homemade cosmetics. Store in a cool, dark place for 6–12 months.

. . . .

Borage Flower Essence

To help heal anxiety and depression, gather a few mature borage flowers. Float them on the surface of 150 ml or ½ cup spring water in a bowl and leave in the sun for three to four hours. Make sure that they are not shadowed in any way. Remove the flowers. Pour the water into a bottle; to preserve it, top up with 150 ml or ½ cup brandy or vodka. This is your mother essence. To make up your flower essences for use, put seven drops from this into a 10 ml dropper bottle and top that up with brandy or vodka. This is your dosage bottle. The usual dose is four drops of this in a glass of water four times a day. When making flower essences, it is important not to handle the flowers—it is the vibrational imprint of the flowers you want to be held by the water, not your own imprint.

Calendula

Calendula officinalis

. . . .

PLANETARY RULER: Sun

ELEMENT: Fire

ASSOCIATED DEITIES: Aphrodite, Apollo,
Ganesh, Lakshmi, Rama, Virgin Mary, Vishnu

MAGICAL VIRTUES: Solar rituals, protection, love,
marriage, mourning, remembrance, divination

First, know your marigold. Make sure you correctly identify your plant as *Calendula officinalis,* the pot marigold, as other types of plants that are also called marigold can be toxic; it should not be confused with *Tagetes,* for example, which is also called marigold. The calendula or pot marigold is a hardy annual herb native to central and southern Europe and Asia. It has bright orange or yellow single or double many-petalled flowers that blossom from summer right through to the autumn. The seeds are curved and rough.

The name of this plant comes from the Latin *calends* or *kalendae,* the word for the first day of each month and the origin of our word *calendar.* In ancient Rome the calendula was said to be in bloom on each calend throughout the year.

It is certainly associated with the passage of time. The Italians called it Peasant's Clock because its flowers tell the hour, closing when the sky gets darker. Because it is so light sensitive, in England it was called Husbandman's Dial and Summer's Bride. The petals even close when rain is due. In Wales it was said that if the flowers had not opened by 7 am, it would rain and thunder all day.[39] In Devon and Wiltshire there was a superstition that picking marigolds or looking at them too long would make thunder come too soon.

Its sensitive petal opening and closing habits made it a herb very much associated with the sun. In Greek myth, when the sun god Apollo fell out of love with Clytia and she became jealous, he turned her into a calendula flower. In another myth, a girl called Caltha fell in love with Apollo but because she constantly gazed at the sun, she pined away and changed into a calendula flower. A similar tale is often told of flowers that seem to turn to the sun or have a corolla that looks rayed and sunlike.

Marigolds are part of every Hindu celebration, from the welcoming of an important person and weddings to rituals for the gods, with marigold garlands hung above doorways. They represent the sun, brightness, and positive, auspicious energy.

In another myth, marigolds were created from the tears Aphrodite shed at the death of her lover Adonis. Perhaps this is why marigolds were a symbol of mourning and fond memories in Greece; as such, they are often represented on monuments. In Germany calendula was only planted in cemeteries and not thought to belong in gardens. Marigolds were strewn at graves. According to folklorist James Frazer, in Bavaria it was the tradition to decorate graves with them on All Soul's Day.[40]

In the Middle Ages, the name of the Virgin Mary was often added to beautiful things, hence the names Marygold and Marybud for the calendula, one of her symbols because it bloomed at all the festivals celebrating the Virgin Mary and because people believed that by her association with the flowers, they could ward off evil (a property previously associated with sun deities). Garlands of marigold flowers were hung on doors to prevent evil from entering, and marigold petals were also scattered on the floor under the bed to offer protection to sleepers.

Marigolds were associated with love and utilised in love charms. If a girl planted marigold in the footsteps of her beloved, it would tie him to her forever. In German lore, if a man wanted to be popular with girls, he should always carry a calendula root and a violet-coloured silk handkerchief. To dream of marigolds is said to mean a happy and wealthy marriage. On St. Luke's Day (October 18), a girl anxious to know who her husband would be could pulverise marigold flowers, marjoram, thyme, and wormwood to a powder and simmer this powder with honey and vinegar, rubbing the mixture over herself before going to bed and saying three times, "Saint Luke, Saint Luke, be kind to me. In dreams let

39   de Cleene and Lejeune, *Compendium of Symbolic and Ritual Plants in Europe.*
40   Frazer, *The Golden Bough.*

me my true love see." Marigold was also commonly used as an aphrodisiac. French husbands even thought that if their wives spent too long looking at marigolds, they would become unfaithful!

Marigolds were considered plants of divination and prophecy. Petals placed under the pillow could induce visionary dreams and enable the identification of a thief or robber. Walking barefoot through marigold flowers enabled girls to understand the language of birds.

The specific name *officinalis* shows that calendula was included on the official list of herbal medicines. It has been grown in physic gardens since the Middle Ages, when it was also commonly sold in European markets, and used medicinally in the treatment of intestinal problems, fevers, smallpox, insect bites, and snake bites. At one time the flower was thought to strengthen the eyesight and comfort those in distress. According to the archaic Doctrine of Signatures (by which the appearance of a plant indicated its use), the yellow colour of the flower marked it out as a cure for jaundice. In Wiltshire it was called the Measles Flower as it was believed to cure measles. Sixteenth-century herbalist John Gerard recommended it for smallpox as well as measles, for swellings, and for comforting the spirit.[41] During the American Civil War, the leaves of the marigold were used by doctors on the battlefield to treat open wounds.

MAGICAL USES

Marigold flowers represent the sun and its passage through the wheel of the year, particularly the solstices and equinoxes. The dried petals may be used in incense, as a bathing herb, or be thrown onto the bonfire at these sabbats. It is one of the sacred herbs of Midsummer.

Marigold petals can be added to water, infused in oil, or dried and added to incense used in rituals of divination or in the consecration of divinatory tools.

Place a pouch of dried marigold flowers beneath your pillow at night to induce clairvoyant dreams.

With the strength of the sun, marigold is also a powerful herb of protection and may be added to incenses, charm bags, oils and powders, used in spells and rituals, or grown in pots around the home.

Calendula Tea or calendula flower essence may be taken when you need to connect to your higher self, release pain, and heal the past with empathy rather than anger.

Calendula petals may be used in love spells or added to love sachets and incenses.

---

41   Gerard, *Gerard's Herbal.*

CULINARY USES

The pot marigold is so called because it was added to pottage (a kind of stew), not because it is grown in a pot. Calendula petals have been used for culinary purposes since ancient times. Their use was certainly documented in ancient Rome, while Culpeper (1616–1654) explained that it was common to dry and store the petals for winter use when they were added to soups, stews, and porridge.[42]

The petals have long been used as a cheap substitution for the very expensive saffron. Certainly, all the bags of "saffron" I saw in the souks of Egypt were marigold petals.

Marigold petals add colour and flavour to rice, chowder, custard, soups, cream cheese or yogurt dips, and potato salad. Add them to baked goods and egg dishes or use as a garnish for salads and vegetables. They can be candied, made into wine, vinegar, marigold buns, or added to cordials. Historically, marigold petals were used for colouring butter and cheese—try the **Marigold Butter** or **Marigold Curd Cheese** below. To give up their colour, they must first be bruised, then finely chopped.

COSMETIC USES

The active compounds of calendula combat inflammation and promote the formation of new tissue. Calendula is restorative and soothing for the skin and helps protect it. It is especially useful for dry and aging skin, though it can be used on all skin types. Add **Macerated Calendula Oil** or **Calendula Infusion** to your homemade creams (such as the **Calendula Cream** below) and lotions or pour some into your bath. Try the **Calendula Milk Bath** for a full body treatment.

The petals have healing properties, and a **Calendula Infusion** may be used as a skin wash or toner for oily and acne-prone skin.

Calendula Infusion makes a colour-enhancing hair rinse for red hair. To use, wash your hair as usual and rinse well with warm water. Have your infusion ready in a jug or (better still) spray bottle. Spritz it on your hair and massage it gently through your hair and into your scalp. Leave it on for at least five minutes. Rinse and style as usual.

MEDICINAL USES

Calendula promotes the tissue healing of burns. Used as a wash, a **Calendula Infusion** takes the sting out of burns, scalds, insect bites and stings, and also acts as a styptic to stop the bleeding of deep cuts. Use **Calendula Electuary** as a wound dressing.

---

42   Culpeper, *Culpeper's Herbal.*

Calendula Infusion may be used to bathe sore eyes or pour the infusion into a foot bath to bathe sore and tired feet. Soak a pad in the infusion to make a compress for slow-healing wounds or varicose ulcers.

Calendula is antifungal. Use **Calendula Infusion** externally as a body wash for vaginal thrush. Use as a mouthwash for oral thrush. It also makes an effective douche for yeast infections. **Calendula Tea** is gentle enough to be applied to thrush in children's mouths.

The bitter taste of the flower petals activates the liver and aids in the digestion of fats. It can help heal an irritated gastric system. Take **Calendula Tea** or a teaspoon of **Calendula Electuary** for inflammatory problems of the digestive system such as gastritis, peptic ulcers, regional ileitis, and colitis.

Calendula Salve decreases the inflammation of sprains, stings, varicose veins, and other swellings and soothes burns, sunburn, rashes, dry skin, wounds, dry eczema, sore nipples in breastfeeding, scalds, and skin irritations.

Use **Calendula Infusion** as a healing mouthwash for mouth ulcers and gum disease, and after tooth extraction.

Calendula Macerated Oil may be used on chilblains, haemorrhoids, and broken capillaries.

> Caution: *Make sure you correctly identify your plant as* Calendula officinalis, *the pot marigold, as other types of plants that are called marigold can be toxic. Preparations of calendula flower are considered safe for most people, but to be on the safe side, do not take internally if you are pregnant or breastfeeding, for two weeks before surgery, or if you are using prescription sedatives.*

Recipes

Calendula Milk Bath

1 TABLESPOON ROLLED OATS

1 TABLESPOON MILK POWDER

1 TABLESPOON DRIED CALENDULA PETALS

1 TABLESPOON DRIED CHAMOMILE FLOWERS

Combine the ingredients in a muslin bag (or an old stocking, cut off). Tie it under the tap while you are filling the bath. Soak in the bath. This is good for rashes and irritated skin. If you are vegan, this still works well if you leave out the milk powder.

Calendula Electuary

20 FRESH CALENDULA FLOWERS (PETALS ONLY)

450 GRAMS OR 1 POUND HONEY

Remove the petals from the flowers and put them in a clean jar. Slightly warm the honey in the microwave and pour over the petals. Seal the jar. Leave for one month. Slightly warm the honey again and strain out the petals (discard the petals). This makes a good dressing for wounds and burns, as well as being good on toast!

Calendula Tea

1 TEASPOON CALENDULA (PETALS ONLY)

250 ML OR 1 CUP BOILING WATER

Pour the water over the petals. Cover and infuse for 10 minutes. Strain and drink for digestive problems.

· · · · · · · · · · · · · · ·

Calendula Salve

250 ML OR 1 CUP VEGETABLE OIL (SUNFLOWER, OLIVE, ALMOND, ETC.)

40 GRAMS OR 1½ OUNCES BEESWAX OR SOY WAX (OR HALF WAX, HALF COCOA BUTTER)

25 GRAMS OR 1 OUNCE CALENDULA (PETALS ONLY)

In a double boiler (or in a slow cooker), simmer the petals in the oil for 30 minutes. Strain. Return the liquid to the double boiler, add the wax (and cocoa butter if using) until melted. Pour into sterilised wide-necked jars. Label. Will keep one year. Use for skin irritations.

· · · · · · · · · · · · · · ·

Calendula Infusion

20 FRESH CALENDULA FLOWERS (PETALS ONLY)

280 ML OR 1 CUP WATER.

Simmer gently together for 20 minutes, strain, and use while slightly warm. Use as a wash for burns and cuts, as an antifungal wash, or gargle.

· · · · · · · · · · · · · · ·

Macerated Calendula Oil

Pack a clean glass jar with fresh calendula (petals only). Pour on enough vegetable oil to cover. Leave on a sunny windowsill for 2 weeks, shaking daily. Strain the oil into a clean, sterilised jar and label. Store in a dark place for 6–12 months. This is soothing and healing for your skin.

· · · · · · · · · · · · ·

Marigold Butter

70 GRAMS OR 2½ OUNCES FRESH PETALS

100 GRAMS OR ¼ CUP PLUS 3 TABLESPOONS BUTTER OR MARGARINE

Combine the ingredients and spread on scones, bread, etc. Will keep in the fridge for 2–3 days.

· · · · ·

. . . .

Calendula Cream

8 TABLESPOONS MACERATED CALENDULA OIL (SEE ABOVE)

50 GRAMS OR 2 OUNCES EMULSIFYING WAX

5 TABLESPOONS MARIGOLD INFUSION

2 TABLESPOONS MARIGOLD TINCTURE

Prepare the oil part and the liquid part separately before bringing them together. Combine the infusion and tincture and warm them gently. Separately, combine the emulsifying wax and calendula oil in a double boiler until the wax has melted. It is important that the water part (the infusion and tincture) reaches the same temperature as the oil and wax part, as this will help the two elements combine when they come together. To combine, the water part is dripped into the oil part very slowly, whisking constantly with a wooden spoon, hand whisk, or electric whisk until they are fully combined and emulsified. Stir and quickly transfer to your storage jars. Will keep about 2 months in the fridge. This is good for dry and aging skin but can be used on all skin types.

. . . .

Calendula Soap

250 GRAMS OR 9 OUNCES MELT-AND-POUR SOAP

2 TABLESPOONS DRIED CALENDULA PETALS

1 TABLESPOON RUNNY HONEY (OPTIONAL)

10 DROPS ESSENTIAL OIL OF YOUR CHOICE

Cut up the soap base and put into a microwavable jug with the honey. Melt on a low heat in the microwave—this will take a couple of minutes. (If you don't have a microwave, you can do this in a heatproof bowl set over a pan of boiling water.) Remove from the microwave and stir in the petals, honey, and essential oil. Pour into moulds to set.

CALENDULA LIP BALM

130 ML OR 9 TABLESPOONS ALMOND OIL

20 GRAMS OR ¾ OUNCE CALENDULA PETALS

70 GRAMS OR 2½ OUNCES BEESWAX OR SOY WAX

1 TEASPOON HONEY (OPTIONAL)

1 TEASPOON VITAMIN E OIL

Put the almond oil in a pan with the flowers. Warm very gently for 5 minutes. Remove from the heat and leave overnight. Strain the oil into a double boiler. Add the wax and honey (if using) until the wax has melted. Remove from the heat and add the vitamin E oil. Pour into sterilised small wide-mouthed jars. Label. Keeps 2–4 months. You can use grapeseed oil or sunflower oil in place of almond oil if you have a nut allergy.

MARIGOLD CURD CHEESE

1 LITRE OR 4¼ CUPS WHOLE MILK

1 TABLESPOONS MARIGOLD PETALS

PINCH SALT

1 TEASPOON VINEGAR OR VEGETABLE RENNET

Pour the milk into a pan with the petals and salt. Bring to boil, take off the heat, and stir in the vinegar. Leave it for 10 minutes. The mixture will curdle, with the curds rising to the top and the whey (the watery part of the milk) sinking to the bottom. Set a muslin cloth over a bowl and use a slotted spoon to scoop the curds into it. Tie up the corners, suspend it over the bowl, and leave to drip for at least 4 hours. Unwrap and put the curds into a covered dish in the fridge. Will keep for 3 days refrigerated.

Marigold Wine

1 LITRE OR 4¼ CUPS MARIGOLD PETALS

1 ORANGE

4 LITRES OR 17 CUPS WATER

1.1 KILO OR 5½ CUPS SUGAR

1 TEASPOON WHITE WINE YEAST (AVAILABLE ONLINE)

1 TEASPOON WINE YEAST NUTRIENT (AVAILABLE ONLINE)

225 GRAMS OR 1½ CUPS RAISINS

Put the petals and the juice and zest of an orange into a fermenting bin. Meanwhile, in a large pan, heat the water and stir in the sugar until it has dissolved. Pour it over the petals. When the liquid has cooled to lukewarm, add the yeast and nutrient according to manufacturer's instructions. Put on the lid and leave for 5 days, stirring daily. Strain the liquid into a demijohn and add the raisins. Fit an airlock and leave to ferment out. When you are sure the fermentation has finished, siphon into a clean demijohn, fit a bung, and leave to clear for 6 months. Siphon into clean sterilised bottles and store as you would any other wine.

Carnation

Dianthus spp.

PLANETARY RULER: Sun

ELEMENT: Fire

ASSOCIATED DEITIES: Jupiter, Zeus, Virgin Mary

MAGICAL VIRTUES: Protection, energy,
love, marriage, mourning

Carnations are native to the Mediterranean. The Greek philosopher Theophrastus (371–287 BCE) called them dianthus from the Greek words *dios* (divine) and *anthos* (flower).[43] The common name *carnation* comes either from the Latin *corona* (crown) since it was one of the flowers used in Roman chaplets[44] or from the Latin *caro*, meaning "flesh," a reference to the colour of the flower.[45] They are also called pinks, a name that doesn't come from the colour but from the Old English word *pynken*, meaning notched or cut, referring to the edges of the petals; we still use this word for pinking shears, the serrated scissors used in dressmaking. In the past, they were sometimes called gillyflowers, meaning "July flowers," since this is when they usually bloom. Along with the original pink (*Dianthus caryophyllus*), the name carnation is also applied to the other 300 varieties of dianthus grown as annuals,

---

43 Gledhill, *The Names of Plants.*
44 Watts, *Elsevier's Dictionary of Plant Lore.*
45 Carl Linnaeus, *Species Plantarum* (Stockholm: Laurentius Salvius, 1753).

biennials, or perennials. Growers in the sixteenth century developed the deep red and white varieties that are still popular today.

Pinks were used to impart a slight clove flavour to wine and ale (the *caryophyllus* part of the name refers to cloves), especially the sweet wine presented to brides at the wedding ceremony, hence the folk name Sops in Wine. In the Middle Ages, clove pinks were used as a substitute for the prohibitively expensive cloves (*Eugenia caryophyllata*) in spiced wine and beer. Chaucer wrote of "clove-gilofre...to putte in ale, whether it be moyste or stale."[46] It is said that the Spaniards and Romans used carnation flowers as a spicy flavouring in wine.[47]

Carnations are associated with love in many parts of the world, a symbol of fascination, marriage, and conjugal harmony. In China the carnation is the flower most frequently used in weddings, while in the West, carnations are a traditional first wedding anniversary flower. Naturally, this meant that they were employed in love potions. In the late seventeenth century, the countess of Dorset was said to have used carnations in a love potion along with bay leaves, marjoram, and lavender. In the Victorian language of flowers, the various colours of carnation had different meanings—deep red carnations indicated love, paler red carnations meant admiration, white carnations represented pure love, striped ones indicated regret that love could not be returned, and purple carnations indicated capriciousness.

In France purple carnations are a symbol of mourning and condolence used as funeral flowers. Red carnations symbolise workers' movements in Europe.

According to a Christian legend, carnations first appeared at the crucifixion when the Virgin Mary shed tears for her son, and carnations sprang up from where they fell. Thus, the carnation became the symbol of a mother's undying love.[48] This is perhaps one of the reasons it is a traditional Mother's Day symbol in the USA. The meaning has evolved over time, and now a red carnation is to be worn if one's mother is alive and a white one if she has died. Similarly, in Korea, carnations are worn on Parents' Day.

At the University of Oxford (UK), carnations are traditionally worn to all examinations; white for the first exam, pink for interim exams, and red for the final exam. An apocryphal tale relates that a white carnation was kept in a red inkpot between exams so by the last exam it was fully red. It is true that a white carnation placed in a coloured liquid (such as

---

46   Chaucer, *The Canterbury Tales.*

47   "The Biology of *Dianthus caryophyllus* L. (Carnation)," Australian Government Dept. of Health, Version 2.1, February 2020, www.health.gov.au.

48   http://www.teleflora.com/carnation/flowers-plant-info/carnation-detail.asp and Watts, *Elsevier's Dictionary of Plant Lore.*

food colouring) will absorb colour into the flower. The green carnations worn in the USA on St. Patrick's Day are made this way, as was the green carnation popularised by the gay writer Oscar Wilde as a symbol of homosexuality and referenced by gay composer Noël Coward's song "We All Wear a Green Carnation."

In Italy carnations were considered a protection from witchcraft on the dangerous night of St. John's Eve (Midsummer's Eve)—according to folklore, if you give a witch a flower, she will have to stop and count the petals before she can move.

MAGICAL USES

Use carnation petals in protection incense, sachets, and talismans. Use a **Macerated Carnation Oil** to protect possessions (wipe a little on and ask for protection). Plant carnations in the garden or keep in pots by your door as a magical safeguard against harm.

Add carnation petals to incenses of love, use in love spells, or drink **Sops in Wine** with a lover. Use in handfasting bouquets, chaplets, and decorations, have **Sops in Wine** as the handfast cup, or just float carnation petals in the ritual cup. If you wish, you can place stems of white carnations in green food colouring and use for gay love spells; though it is not really necessary to dye them, you might like the symbolism and associations.

Carnations vibrate with the energy of the sun, strength, and health. Use them in incense, spells, potions, and rituals of healing and calling for power, vitality, and wellness.

Carnation is one of the sacred herbs of Midsummer and can be used in wreaths, decorations, in the wine, food, and incense, or simply thrown onto the bonfire for protection.

Purple carnations may be employed in rituals for the dead and mourning.

The flower heads can be dried for potpourri and scented sachets.

CULINARY USES

Carnation petals are edible. If you are lucky enough to have some clove-scented pinks (*Dianthus caryophyllus*), you can use the sweet petals in a variety of ways (other varieties of carnation are edible but disappointing). Remove the petals from the calyx and the white base before use as this is bitter tasting, and use the petals sprinkled over salads and fruit, candied for cake decoration, to flavour liqueurs and drinks, to flavour vinegar or conserves, or make a syrup from them that can be poured over desserts and used in summer drinks and cocktails.

COSMETIC USES

Carnation essential oil is used in commercial perfumery and soap making. It takes 500 kilograms of carnation flowers to make 100 grams of the essential oil. You can't make your own essential oils effectively at home, but you can make a **Macerated Carnation Oil**, which you can use to soothe your face and body or in massage to treat skin problems. Add it to your homemade skin care creams. Carnations promote the healing, conditioning, and softening of the skin, making them useful for wrinkles, irritated skin, acne, rashes, rosacea, and eczema.

In mediaeval times carnations were steeped in rosewater to make a perfume for the hair. Try the **Mediaeval Hair Tonic** below.

Carnations are naturally quite high in saponins (soap). If you make your own soap, carnation petals are a lovely addition, but you can simply simmer the leaves in water, strain, and use the liquid to cleanse your skin. If your skin is irritated, you may find this gentler and more soothing than conventional soap.

MEDICINAL USES

Carnations have some painkilling properties. Externally, carnations can aid aching muscles, skin inflammations, and swellings. Soak in a warm bath to which **Carnation Vinegar** or a carnation infusion has been added. This may also help alleviate menstrual cramps.

The herbalist Culpeper (1616–1654) wrote that carnations "strengthened the brain and heart,"[49] while Gerard (1545–1612) stated that "the conserve of the floures of the clove gillofloure and sugar, is exceeding cordiall, and wonderfully above measure doth comfort the heart, being eaten now and then."[50] The petals would be steeped in white wine until the petals went pale and then strained, but you can try **Carnation Tea** instead, which can be taken for nervousness, stress, and minor depression, and may be of use in cases of seasickness.

Carnation Tea may be used as a tonic for the digestive and urinary system.

Use a carnation steam for chest congestion. In a large basin, pour 1 litre or 4¼ cups boiling water over 2 teaspoons carnation petals (fresh if possible). Lean over the basin with a towel over your head and inhale the steam.

> *Caution: Carnations may cause allergic symptoms in sensitive people or contact dermatitis in pets. Avoid use during pregnancy as it may cause uterine contractions in sufficient doses. Excess use may cause toxicity. Internal use of carnations should be avoided in cases of spleen/kidney deficiency.*

---

49   Culpeper, *Culpeper's Herbal.*
50   Gerard, *Gerard's Herbal.*

Recipes

Carnation Tea

1 TEASPOON FRESH CARNATION PETALS

250 ML OR 1 CUP BOILING WATER

Pour the water over the petals. Cover. Infuse 10 minutes, strain, and drink as a tonic for the digestive and urinary system.

Macerated Carnation Oil

To make a cold macerated oil, cut up carnation petals and put them in a glass jar. Pour in enough vegetable oil (olive, sunflower, almond, etc.) to cover them. Leave on a sunny windowsill for 2 weeks, shaking daily. Strain into a clean jar. This will keep in a cool, dark place for 6–12 months. Use to soften and condition your skin.

Sops In Wine

HANDFUL OF CARNATION PETALS

BOTTLE OF WHITE WINE

Put the petals in a jug and pour on the wine. Cover and leave for 4 hours. Strain the wine into a clean jug.

Carnation Vinegar

Pack a jar with carnation petals. Cover with white vinegar. Fit a lid. Leave on a sunny windowsill for 2 weeks, shaking daily. Strain into a clean jar and label. This can be used in salad dressings or added to the bath for aching muscles and menstrual cramps.

Mediaeval Hair Tonic

Fill a jar with strongly scented chopped carnation petals and cover with rosewater. Fit the lid. Infuse 3 days, shaking daily. Strain the liquid into a clean jar and keep in the fridge for up to one month. Rub this through your hair and into your scalp.

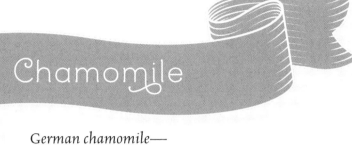

Chamomile

German chamomile—
Matricaria recutita (syn. Matricaria
chamomilla or Chamomilla recutita)
Roman chamomile—Chamaemelum nobile

PLANETARY RULER: Sun

ELEMENT: Water

ASSOCIATED DEITIES: Cernunnos, Ra,
Baldur, sun gods, St. Anne, Hecate

MAGICAL VIRTUES: Protection, healing,
sun, motherhood, peace, harmony

The term chamomile (or camomile) actually refers to a range of different daisy-like plants, all of which are members of the *Asteraceae* family, the two most commonly used being German chamomile (*Matricaria recutita*) and Roman chamomile (*Chamaemelum nobile*). Chamomiles are native to Europe, North Africa, and temperate Asia. Roman chamomile is a low-growing perennial plant. The root is fibrous, the stems hairy and branching, the leaves feathery. The flowers appear in late summer with yellow centres and white florets. The whole plant is aromatic. German chamomile is an annual with feathery leaves and flowers with yellow centres and rayed white petals.

The name *chamomile* comes from the Greek *kamai*, meaning "on the ground," and *melon*, meaning "apple" because the scent was thought to resemble apples. The genus name

Matricaria is derived from the Latin *matrix* (womb) or *mater* (mother), and both refer to the herb's reputation for treating women's complaints in the ancient world.

Chamomile has been used as a healing herb for thousands of years. In 90 BCE its regular use was recommended by the physician Asclepiades, who was so skilled in his use of herbs that he said he would renounce his profession if he ever became ill; he died at a ripe old age as the result of an accident.[51] Culpeper (1616–1654) wrote extensively about it as a treatment for many ailments.[52] Gerard (1545–1612) said "it eases and mitigates pain, it mollifies and smooths, and all these operations are in our vulgar 'Cammomill.'" The Egyptians, Gerard tells us, thought so highly of it that they consecrated it to their deities.[53] In Germany it was said that a good cup of chamomile tea did more good than three doctors.

Chamomile's reputation extends to healing other plants as well as people. It is known as "the plant physician" and is said to be able to cure any plant it grows next to and keep it free of insects. For some reason even bees hate the scent and will not venture near it.

In the language of flowers, it is "strength through adversity," probably from its ability to withstand being walked all over when used as a lawn plant; as Shakespeare notes in *King Henry* IV, "the chamomile, the more it is trodden on, the faster it grows."[54] When walked on, its strong, fragrant scent will often reveal its presence before it is seen. For this reason, it was employed as one of the aromatic strewing herbs in the Middle Ages, spread over floors to freshen rooms and keep insects away.

Chamomile was widely used as a herb of protection. Chamomile stems were put in the first sheaf of corn as a magical safeguard against vermin, along with St. John's wort. In Germany it was believed that carrying it protected against bewitchment, and branches were hung in the house to prevent witches entering. At Candlemas it was hung above the door to protect from witchcraft. Chamomile flowers were gathered on St. John's Day (Midsummer's Day), when they are at their most powerful—after Midsummer, it was said, witches flew over them and took all their medicinal power.

The Norse called chamomile Baldur's Brow because the flower was as pure as his forehead. In Egypt chamomile was dedicated to the god Ra. Wild chamomile was a plant in Hecate's garden.

Chamomile makes a good compost activator dried, powdered, and added to the heap.

---

51 Pliny the Elder, *Natural History*.
52 Culpeper, *Culpeper's Herbal*.
53 Gerard, *Gerard's Herbal*.
54 Part 1, Act II, Scene 4.

MAGICAL USES

Chamomile is a herb of the sun with its solar yellow centre surrounded by an aura of white rays. As a power plant, it connects with the sun's power of regeneration, healing, and protection. For this reason, it was planted on graves as a symbol that the soul would be reborn, just as the sun is reborn each morning. **Chamomile Tea** may be taken to connect with sun energies, to heal and regenerate the spirit within. **Chamomile Infusion** may be used in the ritual bath. Dried chamomile flowers are used in incenses to connect with the sun or invoke sun gods. Include in herbal amulets to boost their power.

Plant on graves and use in funeral wreaths and memorial flowers as a symbol of rebirth.

Chamomile is one of the sacred herbs of Midsummer and may be thrown onto the festival fire, used in the incenses and garlands or added to the ritual cup. **Chamomile Mead** makes a suitable drink.

Chamomile is also a protection plant: **Macerated Chamomile Oil** may be used to form a magical barrier around doors and windows to prevent negativity entering—smear it around the door and window frames with a prayer for protection. Hang chamomile over the doorway to prevent negativity entering. Plant in the garden as a guardian herb.

The dried flowers may be used in an incense or tea to induce a calm and relaxed state prior to meditation.

CULINARY USES

The best-known use of chamomile is its use as an herbal tea, and these are available commercially or you can make your own with dried or fresh chamomile flowers. If you've already made a cup of chamomile tea, don't throw the tea bag away. Use it to infuse the water you cook rice in for an unusual, subtle flavour.

Freeze the flowers in ice cubes and drop them into drinks and cocktails.

Chamomile can be infused into jam, wine, and mead. The Spanish wine flavoured with camomile, manzanilla, means "little apples."

The fresh young leaves of chamomile can be eaten in salads or used as garnishes.

COSMETIC USES

Chamomile is good for all skin types but especially sensitive skin prone to inflammation. Use **Chamomile Tea** as a facial wash. Put a cold chamomile tea bag on each eye to soothe tired, puffy, and sore eyes, as well as reduce dark circles.

Use powdered, dry chamomile flowers mixed with ground almonds and honey (or just a little water) as a facial exfoliant scrub.

Chamomile is a natural skin lightener that also fades spots and acne scarring. Use **Chamomile Tea** as a wash or apply **Macerated Chamomile Oil**. On the hair, a **Chamomile Tea** rinse can be used to lighten fair hair and bring out blond highlights. It will also soothe dandruff.

Use a **Chamomile Steam Treatment** to unblock your pores and leave your skin glowing.

MEDICINAL USES

German chamomile is the flower of an annual plant *Matricaria recutita* (syn. *Matricaria chamomilla* or *Chamomilla recutita*). The perennial English or Roman Chamomile (*Chamaemelum nobile*) is sometimes listed in old herbals by the old name *Anthemis nobilis*, and this was the chamomile used by the famous English herbalists Gerard and Culpeper. If you are in England, the chamomile you would use is likely *Chamaemelum nobile*; in the rest of the world, German chamomile is more common, but both have very similar properties.

Chamomile has a relaxing and sedative effect and has been used as a sleep aid and for stress and anxiety. Take a cup of **Chamomile Tea** or tie some chamomile flowers in muslin, drop into your bath, and have a relaxing soak before bedtime or try the **Sleepy-Time Chamomile Bath** recipe below. You can sew chamomile flowers into a small sleep pillow to place on top of your usual pillow to give you a good night's sleep.

Chamomile is a gentle remedy for digestive problems, indigestion, acid, IBS, bloating, gastritis, spastic colon, acute diarrheal episodes and colic, [55] irritations and inflammations of the stomach and intestines. Drink one cup of **Chamomile Tea** between meals three to four times a day.

Chamomile relaxes tense, aching muscles and menstrual pain. It is considered safe for children. You can add **Chamomile Infusion** to your bath or rub on **Macerated Chamomile Oil**.

A **Chamomile Steam** is anti-allergenic useful for hayfever and asthma and can be inhaled to relieve a stuffy nose or congested chest.

Chamomile's anti-inflammatory and antibacterial properties make it a wonderful topical remedy for many skin conditions such as eczema, insect bites, rashes, and sore, itchy skin. Use **Chamomile Infusion** as a wash or in a cream or apply **Macerated Chamomile Oil** to the affected areas

---

55   Chevallier, *The Encyclopedia of Medicinal Plants.*

Chamomile has a soothing effect on the tissues inside the mouth, nose, and throat. It can alleviate canker sores and other mouth irritations, while its antibacterial qualities may treat and prevent gum diseases such as gingivitis. Use **Chamomile Infusion** as a mouthwash for inflammations of the mouth or gargle with it for a sore throat.

A chamomile cream is useful for breastfeeding mothers in the treatment of cracked nipples.

A chamomile poultice will soothe external swelling, inflammatory pain, or congested neuralgia. Fill a muslin bag with chamomile flowers and steep in hot water before applying to the affected area.

To treat haemorrhoids, apply a chamomile poultice or use **Chamomile Infusion** as a skin wash.

> **Caution:** *Chamomile is generally considered a very safe herb, but it should not be taken by people who are allergic to it. Those who are sensitive to members of the Asteracea family (including ragweed, feverfew, and yarrow) may also want to avoid chamomile. It is advisable to avoid the oral intake of chamomile if you are on blood-thinning medication, sedatives, aspirin, and NSAIDS and pregnant or breastfeeding. It may interact with ginkgo biloba, garlic, saw palmetto, St. John's wort, and valerian.*

Recipes

CHAMOMILE TEA

1 TEASPOON DRIED HERB OR 2 TEASPOONS FRESH FLOWERS

250 ML OR 1 CUP BOILING WATER

Pour boiling water over the herb and infuse for 5–10 minutes in a covered vessel such as a teapot. Strain and drink. This is relaxing before bed and good for digestive problems.

CHAMOMILE INFUSION

3 TEASPOONS DRIED HERB OR 5 TEASPOONS FRESH FLOWERS

250 ML OR 1 CUP BOILING WATER

Pour boiling water over the herb and infuse for 10 minutes, covered. Strain. This may be used as an antiseptic skin wash or mouthwash or added to your bedtime bath to aid sleep.

MACERATED CHAMOMILE OIL

FRESH CHAMOMILE FLOWERS

VEGETABLE OIL

Pack the flowers in a glass jar, pour on the oil to cover, and fit the lid. Leave on a sunny windowsill for 2 weeks, shaking daily. Strain into a clean jar. Will keep 6–12 months in a cool, dark place. This is an anti-inflammatory and antibacterial oil for irritated skin conditions.

Chamomile Steam Treatment

1 LITRE OR 5 CUPS BOILING WATER

2 TABLESPOONS CHAMOMILE FLOWERS

Pour boiling water over the herbs in a heatproof bowl placed on a mat. Leave to infuse a few minutes, then lean over the bowl, putting a towel over your head to keep in the steam to clear a stuffy nose or unblock your pores.

Chamomile Baby Powder

2 TABLESPOONS CHAMOMILE DRIED FLOWERS,
   GROUND IN A COFFEE GRINDER

3 TABLESPOONS BICARBONATE OF SODA (BAKING SODA)

5 TEASPOONS CORNFLOUR (CORNSTARCH)

Mix the ingredients together. Put through a sieve to get any large particles out. Keep the fine powder in an airtight container for up to 6 months.

Chamomile Shampoo

25 GRAMS OR 1 OUNCE DRIED CHAMOMILE FLOWERS OR
   A LARGE HANDFUL OF FRESH

600 ML OR 2½ CUPS BOILING WATER

30 ML OR 2 TABLESPOONS LIQUID CASTILE SOAP

1 TEASPOON VEGETABLE GLYCERINE

Pour boiling water over the herbs and leave overnight. Strain and combine with the soap and vegetable glycerine. This should keep in the fridge for 2–3 weeks.

Hair Lightening Chamomile Treatment

2 TEASPOONS CHAMOMILE INFUSION

JUICE OF ONE LEMON

To lighten blond hair, mix the infusion and lemon juice. Rub it through your hair and sit in the sun for an hour or two. Rinse thoroughly.

. . . .
Sleepy-time Chamomile Bath

1 TABLESPOON CHAMOMILE FLOWERS

½ TABLESPOON LAVENDER FLOWERS

½ TABLESPOON ROSE PETALS

½ TABLESPOON MILK POWDER (OPTIONAL)

Combine the ingredients and tie in a muslin bag. Throw it in a warm bath and soak before bed.

. . . .
Chamomile Skin Wash

2 TEASPOONS DRIED CHAMOMILE FLOWERS

200 ML OR 14 TABLESPOONS WATER

2 TEASPOONS HONEY (OPTIONAL)

150 ML OR 10 TABLESPOONS ROSEWATER

120 ML OR 8 TABLESPOONS GLYCERINE

120 ML OR 8 TABLESPOONS LIQUID CASTILE SOAP

15 ML OR 1 TABLESPOON WITCH HAZEL

Put the chamomile and water in a pan. Simmer gently for 5 minutes, then stir in the honey, if using. Take off the heat and leave aside for an hour. Strain into a bottle with the other ingredients. Shake before use. You can use this as a gentle face or body wash in the shower. This should keep 2 weeks in the fridge.

. . . .
Chamomile and Lavender Sleep Pillow

Oblong of cotton fabric

Needle and thread

60 GRAMS OR 2 OUNCES DRIED CHAMOMILE

15 GRAMS OR ½ OUNCE DRIED LAVENDER FLOWERS

Sew the herbs into the cotton cloth to make a small pillow or bag. Use at the side of your regular pillow to promote restful sleep and a clear head.

Chamomile Mead

4½ LITRES OR 1 GALLON WATER

2 KILOS OR 4 POUNDS HONEY

HANDFUL CHAMOMILE FLOWERS

JUICE OF 1 LEMON

WHITE WINE YEAST (AVAILABLE ONLINE)

WINE YEAST NUTRIENT (AVAILABLE ONLINE)

Put three quarters of the water and all the honey into a pan and bring to boil. Remove from the heat. Add the chamomile flowers. Allow to cool to lukewarm. Add the juice of the lemon and the yeast and nutrient according to manufacturer's instructions. (A nutrient must be used as some modern honey is deficient in important minerals.) Pour everything into a demijohn, top up with more water, if necessary, and fit an airlock and keep in a warm place. Allow to ferment out (until the airlock stops bubbling completely), then siphon into bottles. This should be matured for at least a year before drinking. Store as you would any other wine.

Chamomile Ale

225 GRAMS OR 8 OUNCES DRIED CHAMOMILE FLOWERS

9 LITRES OR 2 GALLONS WATER

900 GRAMS OR 4½ CUPS GRANULATED SUGAR

JUICE OF 1 LEMON

BEER YEAST (AVAILABLE ONLINE)

Simmer the chamomile flowers in the water for 2 hours. Strain into a fermenting bin or covered non-metal bucket and stir in the sugar until it has dissolved. Add lemon juice and cool to lukewarm. Add the yeast according to manufacturer's instructions. This will be ready to drink in one week. Unlike beer, ale does not keep for a long period, so it will need to be drunk within 2 weeks.

Clover

Trifolium spp.

. . . .

PLANETARY RULER: Mercury

ELEMENT: Earth

ASSOCIATED DEITIES: Aphrodite, Freya, Hathor, Venus

MAGICAL VIRTUES: Luck, visionary herb, Beltane,
faithfulness, love, fairy contact, abundance

My lawn is full of clovers, and I make no attempt to weed them out because they are so beneficial. The bees adore them, and honey made by bees feeding on clover is delicious. It attracts many beneficial insects including parasitic wasps that kill aphids and other insects that can destroy the vegetable garden. It is wonderful for nitrogen fixation in the soil too, pulling in atmospheric nitrogen and storing it in its roots. When the plant dies, nitrogen is released back into the soil as food for surrounding plants. This is not a modern discovery; from the seventeenth century, farmers added red and white clover to their fields to feed them. This and the fact that clover makes good hay gave rise to the phrase "to be in clover," meaning abundance.

This little plant, often regarded as a weed that grows in many a lawn and roadside verge, has more than its fair share of folklore.

St. Patrick used the threefold shape of the clover leaf to explain the three-in-one nature of the Holy Trinity (Father, Son, and Holy Spirit). In Christian lore, Eve took some four-leaf clovers with her when she was banished from the Garden of Eden as a reminder of her happy time in paradise. However, its reputation as a plant of luck and prosperity is most prevalent in Celtic countries, and it is likely that much of its lore predates Christianity altogether.

Clovers generally have three leaves, and four leaves are rare, so just finding one might be considered extraordinary luck. Four is a number of balance—four directions, four elements, four seasons, and so on. One traditional rhyme associates it with four common aspirations:

> One leaf is for fame
> And one leaf is for wealth
> And one for a faithful lover
> And one to bring you glorious health
> Are all in the four-leaved clover.

Otherwise, the four leaves are taken to represent faith, hope, love, and luck. For Christians, the four-leafed clover represented the cross, and possession of one would protect against evil spirits, the attentions of fairies, witches, and ill luck. Maybe before the advent of Christianity it was a solar cross, a symbol that dispelled evil in ancient times.

Clovers were used in love magic. According to popular folklore, place a four leafed clover under your pillow to dream of your perfect partner. If you are seriously looking for a partner, place a clover leaf in your shoe and the first man you meet will be your destined lover. Or pin the clover to your door and the first unmarried man that passes will be yours. Scatter in front of a new bride for luck and protection.

If we are to judge by fairy tales, clovers were much loved by the fairy folk. According to one story, a milkmaid accidentally picked a four-leaf clover with the grass she used to soften the weight of the pail on her head. When next she looked at her cow, she saw dozens of fairies milking it. In many documented recipes, a salve of four-leaf clover was said to open the Sight and allow a person to see fairies and spirits.

Clover is protective, a holy herb that shielded against dark forces. There is an old rhyme that runs *Trefoil, vervain, St. John's wort, dill/Hinders witches of their will.* In Cornwall a four-leaf clover is said to bring back a real child stolen by the pixies through placing the clover on the changeling.

It is said that snakes will not go where clover grows. The similar-looking shamrock was said to have been planted in Ireland by St. Patrick, who expelled all the snakes from the island, a metaphor for overcoming the power of the Pagans. Shamrock means "small clover," though it is not a clover at all, but an oxalis.[56]

The word *clover* is possibly from the Latin *clava*, meaning "club," the three-knotted club of Hercules, the symbol of the suit of clubs in playing cards. In Anglo-Saxon it was called *cloeferwort* (a wort is a medicinal herb).

MAGICAL USES

Clover is a visionary herb and may be employed in teas, wine, incense, salves, and potions to aid access to the spirit world, especially for fairy contact at Beltane, as a doorway between the seasons, and at the great fairy festival of Midsummer.

Consecrate the ritual pentacle and copper tools, such as herb knives, with a clover infusion or **Clover Macerated Oil**. Use **Clover Macerated Oil**, incense, and infusion in rituals and spells for increase, earth, abundance, and prosperity. Carry a clover for luck.

According to an old spell, to stay young, gather dew at dawn on May Day. Steep three clover stalks in it, out of the sunlight. The next day rub some of this water on your face and every subsequent day until it is used up. (It's worth a try!)

Use in incense, spells, herbal talismans, and as an anointing oil for spells of rituals of love and to honour the goddess of love.

CULINARY USES

Both red clover and white clover are edible. Clovers are high in protein and contain trace minerals and beta-carotene plus vitamins B and C. The leaves have a grassy taste, and the flowers are sweet if picked on a sunny day.

The flowers can be made into herb teas or they are lovely added fresh to a salad, especially potato salad. You can freeze the blossoms in ice cubes to jazz up drinks and cocktails. The flowers of red clover make a lovely wine. Clover flowers (red or white) can be dusted with flour and pan fried in oil to make a crispy snack.

The leaves can be added raw to salads or cooked in soups, stews, and sauces.

The seeds can be soaked and sprouted. A protein-rich flour can be made from the dried, ground-up flowers and seed pods. Sprinkle this on cooked food.

---

56 Bruton-Seal, *Hedgerow Medicine*.

COSMETIC USES

Red clover contains isoflavonoids that help slow down signs of ageing on the skin, increase collagen production, and add moisture. Use a red **Clover Macerated Oil** directly on the skin or add it to your homemade skin creams, cosmetic preparations, and soaps. Add to lip balms to protect your lips.

Red Clover Coconut Hair Balm is smoothing and moisturising for your hair and will help combat dandruff. Massage it in, leave it for two hours, then wash out well. Alternatively, you can just brush a little through dried and split ends.

MEDICINAL USES

The flower heads and young leaves of both red and white clover may be used medicinally, though they have slightly different properties. Pick newly opened flowers in early summer. The plant should be dried quickly, as if it ferments, the coumarin it contains converts to dicoumarol, which is a blood thinner.

Red clover (*Trifolium pratense*) is used to treat PMS and menopausal symptoms. It contains chemicals called isoflavones, which are as phyto (plant-derived) oestrogens, with an oestrogenic effect to maintain normal oestrogen levels. Taking **Red Clover Tea** may help delay osteoporosis in women who have not yet reached menopause. Some menopausal women find it a relief for hot flushes.

Red Clover Tea improves the elimination of toxins, increases the flow of urine, moves mucus out of the lungs, increases bile, and is a gentle laxative. It is a soothing expectorant for coughs and bronchitis.

Red Clover Macerated Oil contains calcium and magnesium, which can help ease muscle pain and tension. Use as a massage oil. It is also good for rashes, eczema, and psoriasis.

Like red clover, white clover (*Trifolium repens*) is anti-inflammatory. In the form of a poultice, the mashed flowers of clover applied directly to the skin help insect bites and small wounds. **White Clover Tea** can be used to treat fever, coughs, and colds, and its antirheumatic and analgesic (painkilling) properties make it useful for rheumatic aches, arthritis, and gout. Use it cooled as an eye wash or to clean wounds.

> *Caution:* Do not take medicinal amounts if pregnant or breastfeeding or if you have hormone-dependent conditions such as endometriosis, uterine fibroids, or cancers of the breast, ovaries, or uterus. Men with prostate cancer should also avoid taking red clover. Do not use medicinal amounts if you are on antiplatelet or anticoagulant drugs, oestrogen replacement therapy, oral contraceptives, or tamoxifen.

· · · · ·

Recipes

Red Clover Tea

4 TO 6 RED CLOVER FLOWERS

250 ML OR 1 CUP BOILING WATER

Pour boiling water onto the flowers. Infuse 10–15 minutes and strain. Take when you are having a hot flush or PMS. You can take for menopausal symptoms, coughs, and bronchitis. Do not take for longer than 6 weeks.

White Clover Tea

4 TO 6 WHITE CLOVER FLOWERS

250 ML OR 1 CUP BOILING WATER

Pour boiling water onto the flowers. Infuse 10–15 minutes and strain. Drink hot with a little honey or try cooling, adding mint sprigs and ice cubes for an iced clover tea. This is used for its mild painkilling properties for arthritic conditions and to ease coughs and colds. Do not take for longer than 6 weeks.

Clover Macerated Oil

Fill a jar with clover flowers (you can use red or white) and cover with vegetable oil. Fit a lid and leave on a sunny windowsill for 2 weeks, shaking daily. Strain into a clean jar and label. Will keep 6–12 months in a cool, dark place. Use on the skin to boost collagen production and ease irritated skin or use with massage for muscle pain.

. . . .

Red Clover Wine

2 LITRES OR 2 QUARTS RED CLOVER FLOWERS

4½ LITRES OR 1 GALLON BOILING WATER

3 LEMONS

2 ORANGES

900 GRAMS OR 4½ CUPS SUGAR

WHITE WINE YEAST (AVAILABLE ONLINE)

WINE YEAST NUTRIENT (AVAILABLE ONLINE)

Put the flowers in a fermenting bin and pour over boiling water. Add the juice of the oranges and lemons. Cool to lukewarm and add the yeast and nutrient according to manufacturer's instructions. Fit the lid. Leave for 5 days, stirring daily. Strain into a sterilised demijohn and fit an airlock. Leave to ferment out completely, then siphon into another clean, sterilised demijohn and leave to clear. Siphon into clean bottles and store as you would any other wine.

. . . .

Clover Flour

Pick as many white clover flowers as you would like. Dry them thoroughly, preferably in a dehydrator. Grind them up in a coffee grinder or with a pestle and mortar. You will be left with a gluten free flour that tastes like peas.

. . . .

Red Clover Coconut Hair Balm

2 TABLESPOONS COCONUT OIL

1 TABLESPOON RED CLOVER FLOWERS

Coconut oil, solid at room temperature, is a perfect consistency for a balm. In a double boiler (or you can use a slow cooker), gently simmer the flowers in coconut oil for 1–2 hours. Strain into shallow jars to set.

. . . .

Red Clover Shampoo

200 ML OR ¾ CUP BOILING WATER

10 GRAMS OR 2 TEASPOONS RED CLOVER FLOWERS

2 TABLESPOONS LIQUID CASTILE SOAP

Pour boiling water over the flowers. Leave to infuse until cool. Strain the liquid into a bottle. Add the liquid soap. Shake before use. Will keep 7-10 days in the fridge.

. . . .

To Get the Sight Salve

7 FOUR-LEAF CLOVERS

2 TABLESPOONS ALMOND OIL

14 GRAMS OR ½ OUNCE BEESWAX OR SOY WAX

In a double boiler, put the clover flowers into the oil and warm for 20 minutes. Strain the oil from the flowers and return the oil to the pan. Add the wax and allow it to dissolve, then beat the mixture with a wooden spoon until it sets. Use to anoint the third eye to aid in psychic work.

. . . .

Opening the Sight Sachet

1 FOUR-LEAF CLOVER

7 GRAINS WHEAT

7 CM OR 3" SQUARE OF PURPLE CLOTH

PIECE OF WHITE THREAD

Lay the four-leaf clover and the seven grains of wheat on the cloth, and tie up the parcel with the white thread, knotting it seven times. Carry the charm with you when you wish to encounter fairies, but do not carry it continually. It will work on seven occasions.

Daisy

Bellis perennis

PLANETARY RULER: Venus

ELEMENT: Water

ASSOCIATED DEITIES: Alcestis, Aphrodite, Apollo,
Artemis, Belenos, Belidis, Flora, Freya, Jesus Christ,
Saule, St. Margaret, Thor, Venus, Virgin Mary

MAGICAL VIRTUES: Protection (especially for children),
innocence, purity, fidelity, youth, love, spring, childhood

Gardeners who like perfect bowling green lawns might curse the little lawn daises that poke their heads above the grass, but I welcome them, along with buttercups, clover, and any other wildflowers that want to brighten up my lawn. The daisy is such a cheerful little flower and is an important pollen source for bees. This hardy perennial is native to Europe and Asia and grows to a height of just 8–16 cm (3–6 inches). The stem is hairy, as are the leaves, which are toothed and finely serrated, forming a flat rosette near to the ground. The flowers, which bloom from spring to autumn (equinox to equinox), have a bright yellow centre and single or double rows of white or pale pink petals.

The common name "daisy" is a contraction of its old name, Day's Eye (Old English *daeges eage*), as it looks like a little sun that only opens in the day and closes its petals at night. It is not surprising that it is associated with sun gods and goddesses, such as the Baltic sun goddess Saule; anything round and rayed suggests the sun.

It starts to flower around Easter (or the Spring Equinox); indeed, in France, children attending the Easter mass might be given eggs painted with daisies. Custom has it that spring has not arrived until you can put your foot on twelve daisies (others say seven or nine). In southwest Ireland children celebrated the coming of spring and the first daisies of the year by picking them and exchanging them for pennies.

They are associated with maiden goddesses of spring and blossoming. The botanical name *bellis* comes from the Latin *bellus*, which means "pretty." In classical myth the daisy is said to have been created when the nymph Belidis changed herself into a daisy to avoid the amorous attentions of the orchard god Vertumnus or when Boreas, god of the north wind, tried to get the attention of Flora, goddess of flowers, and sent a gust of snowflakes into the flowering meadows. Flora just laughed and turned each snowflake into a tiny daisy.

Just as the year is young and innocent in the spring, the daisy is symbolic of innocence, purity, virtue, and sweet youth. In Christian lore it is dedicated to the Virgin Mary, hence the folk name Mary's Flower. Daisies are said to have sprung from the Virgin Mary's tears as the holy family fled to Egypt, while in medieval paintings the daisy stood for the purity and innocence of the Christ Child.

It is a flower very much associated with children, especially the newborn, specifically for their protection. The folk name of Bairnswort is thought to originate in Scotland and refers to the childhood pastime of making daisy chains, the stems split with the thumbnail and the next flower threaded through, made and worn by children for protection, a custom that continues though the original meaning has been lost. Daisy chains were placed beneath a child's pillow to shield them from disease.

The protective power of daisies was also employed by adults. On St. John's Day (Midsummer's Day) it was the custom to gather daises before dawn and put them on the roof as a protection against lightning. They were called John's Flowers in Switzerland. In Bavaria it was believed that if you are going on an important journey, you should pick daisies between 12 noon and 1 o'clock and wrap them in paper and carry them for luck and protection. To protect against plague, daisies dug up on St. John's Day were preserved and kept as a protective charm.

Daisies are also a symbol of faithful love; in the thirteenth century the daisy was called *Flos amoris* or "love flower." If a knight was promised love, he was allowed to depict a daisy on his armour. If the damsel in question was considering his proposal, she wore a garland of daisies on her head. In Chaucer's *The Legende of Goode Women*, Queen Alceste is transformed into a daisy because, according to Chaucer, her virtues outnumbered the flower's petals. This was a retelling of an ancient Greek myth in which Alcestis was the daughter of Pelias. Her betrothed, Admetus, became fatally ill. Apollo appealed to the Fates to spare him, but they would only do so on condition that another person should consent to die in his place. Alcestis agreed to do this and was restored to earth in the form of a daisy, a reward for her selfless and faithful love.

Daises were employed in love spells and love divination. Who has not played the game "He loves me, he loves me not" with a petal plucked off at each chant and the final petal deciding the issue? One American version runs:

> One I love, two I love, three I love I say,
>
> Four I love with all my heart and five I cast away,
>
> Six he loves, seven she loves, eight they both love,
>
> Nine he comes, ten he tarries,
>
> Eleven he courts and twelve he marries.[57]

A similar custom is simply to count the petals to see if your love is returned—if there is an even number, then it is not, but an odd number means it is. Actually, the petals are usually odd numbered, and if you start with "he loves me," then you usually get the required answer. Or sit in a flowering meadow, close your eyes, and pull up a handful of grass; the number of daisies in the handful is the number of unmarried years remaining to you. If you want to attract love, wear a daisy. If you want to dream of an absent lover, daisy roots should be placed under your pillow.

The common phrase "pushing up daisies" means to be dead and buried. An old superstition was that if you put your foot on a daisy in spring, it would be growing over you (or someone close) by autumn. In Germany it was said that if many daisies flower in the spring, then many infants will die in the autumn, and the hay crop will be bad.

They have long been used medicinally, mentioned by the Roman Pliny the Elder, and the English herbalist Gerard (1545–1612) said that daisies "mitigated all pains" while the crushed leaves cured bruises and swellings, hence another of its folk names, Bruisewort. The daisy was used in ancient times, sometimes in combination with yarrow, to counter the shock of battle injuries. Its Latin name *Bellis* means "beautiful," so *Bellis perennis* could translate as "perennial beauty." Bellis could also stem from *bellum*, meaning "war," maybe because daisies grew in fields of battle and military doctors of the Roman Empire would soak bandages in their juice to bind soldiers' wounds. It was a common folk cure for toothache.

---

57   Watts, *Elsevier's Dictionary of Plant Lore.*

According to the antiquated Doctrine of Signatures, the daisy opens and closes like an eye, suggesting that it can ease infection or inflammation of the eye. In Ireland an infusion of daisy was used as an eyewash.

MAGICAL USES

The daisy is a perfect symbol of spring, the strengthening sun, blossoming, and the youthful year, which can be utilised in your Ostara celebrations. We sometimes use daisies to decorate the altar and the ritual cup, floating them in the wine. The dried flowers and leaves can be added to incenses.

Daises represent innocence and purity, particularly of women. They may be used to greet the arrival of a baby or to garland a young girl celebrating the rite of passage at onset of menstruation.

They are plants of protection for children. Place a posy of daisies or a daisy chain in a child's bedroom.

In the Northern Tradition daisies are sacred to Freya and may be used in rituals to honour her, in an incense, strewn around the boundary of the circle, used to decorate the altar, or worn as a garland by the invoking priestess.

Daisies are sacred to sun gods and goddesses. They may be employed in rituals of the sun and solar deities, especially at Ostara and at Midsummer, the zenith of the sun's power.

Daisies picked between noon and one o'clock have special magical qualities. They bring success in any venture when they are dried and carried.

CULINARY USES

The young leaves contain high amounts of vitamin C and can be added raw to salads. They have a mild, slightly sour flavour. In the past they were popularly cooked as a vegetable and served with meat, and can be added to soups, stews, and sandwiches.

Daisy flowers make great decorative additions to salads and cocktails. **Daisy Tea** has a slight lemony taste and is uplifting and refreshing.

The young, closed flower buds can be pickled in vinegar and used as caper substitutes.

COSMETIC USES

Bellis perennis has been used for centuries for cosmetics dating back to ancient Egypt and is still used in commercial products like creams, gels, lotions, and makeup.

Daisy has a unique combination of polyphenols that naturally suppress melanin production, which helps reduce the appearance of dark spots on the skin and lightens and brightens the complexion naturally. Use a **Macerated Daisy Oil** or daisy cream on age spots and uneven skin tone.

The daisy carries a high concentration of exfoliating acids and is very high in malic and tartaric acids, which aid in natural cell turnover. Add dried daisy petals to exfoliating preparations or use **Daisy Tea** and a rough washcloth to remove dead cells from the surface of your skin, leaving it looking bright and glowing.

Tie the flowers in a muslin bag and add to your bath to refresh dull skin.

MEDICINAL USES

Daisies are one of our most common plants, and the fresh or dried flowers and leaves may be used both internally and externally.

Daisies are astringent and stem bleeding. They can be used for treating wounds in the form of a wash or poultice. They contain antibacterial agents and were once used on the battlefield for treating wounded soldiers. Daisy is helpful in healing sores, fresh wounds, and scratches. Use **Daisy Tea** as a wash or apply **Daisy Salve**. A traditional name for the plant is Bruisewort from its traditional use in treating bruises. Smear **Daisy Salve** on the affected area or apply a poultice of the crushed leaves.

Daisy Tea is antitussive, anti-inflammatory, and expectorant and can help catarrh and coughs, bronchitis, colds, and sinusitis.

For sore eyes, use an eyebath of **Daisy Tea**.

Chew the fresh leaves to relieve the pain of mouth ulcers. **Daisy Tea** may be used as a mouthwash or gargle to aid a sore throat and mouth inflammation.

The anti-inflammatory and analgesic properties of **Daisy Tea** may help relieve arthritis and sore muscles. For stiff necks, lumbago, and general aches and pains, make a **Daisy Decoction**, strain, and dab it on the skin or add it to a warm bath and soak. **Daisy Salve** may be rubbed onto inflamed joints and sore muscles.

As a mild diuretic, **Daisy Tea** aids the excretion of toxins via the kidneys, which may be useful in treating gout, arthritis, and skin problems, including acne and boils.

Daisy promotes sweating and contributes to lowering fevers. Use as a compress on the forehead or drink **Daisy Tea**.

> *Caution: Daisies are generally considered safe, and there are no known side effects. It is wise to avoid medicinal amounts during pregnancy and breastfeeding. However, some people are allergic to the daisy (Asteraceae) family, so use with caution if there is any risk of a reaction.*

Recipes

Daisy Salve

LARGE HANDFUL OF DAISY FLOWERS AND LEAVES

250 ML OR 1 CUP VEGETABLE OIL

14 GRAMS OR ½ OUNCE BEESWAX OR SOY WAX

In a double boiler, put the flowers and leaves into the oil and simmer for 2 hours. Strain out the flowers and return the oil to the pan. Add the wax to melt. Remove from the heat, pour into jars, and label. Will keep around a year. Use on bruises.

Daisy Tea

250 ML OR 1 CUP BOILING WATER

1 TEASPOON DRIED OR 2 TEASPOONS FRESH FLOWERS

Pour the water over the flowers and infuse for 10 minutes. Strain and allow to cool slightly before drinking for coughs and colds.

Daisy Decoction

50 GRAMS OR 2 OUNCES FLOWERS AND LEAVES

500 ML OR 2 CUPS WATER

Boil together for 2 minutes. Remove from the heat. Strain after 10 minutes. Add to the bath to soothe aching muscles.

. . . .

Macerated Daisy Oil

Cut up daisy leaves and flowers, pack into a glass jar, and cover with vegetable oil (olive, sunflower, almond, etc.). Put on the lid. Leave on a sunny windowsill for 2 weeks, shaking daily. Strain into a clean jar. This will keep in a cool, dark place for up to 1 year. Use on age spots and uneven skin tone.

Dandelion

Taraxacum officinale

. . . .

PLANETARY RULER: Jupiter

ELEMENT: Air

ASSOCIATED DEITIES: Hecate, Green
George, Theseus, Brighid, sun gods

MAGICAL VIRTUES: Solar rituals,
healing, divination, increase

If you've ever tried to eliminate dandelions from your garden or lawn, you will know it is almost impossible. Leave behind the tiniest bit of root and it will regrow, while the fluffy seeds float freely on the wind and spread the plant everywhere. But wait—every part of the dandelion is useful, a gift of free food, wine, beer, dye, cosmetics, magic, and a whole pharmacy within itself, available most of the year. Truly a gift from the gods!

The tenacious dandelion is a hardy perennial plant, probably native to China and Asia but now spread throughout the world, commonly found in gardens, pastures, lawns, meadows, waste ground, and on roadsides. It has a fleshy root and a hollow stem that contains a milky white juice. The leaves are lance shaped and form a rosette at the stem base. The bright yellow flowers bloom from late spring to early autumn and are followed by the fluffy white seed heads. Dandelion is an important food source for wildlife. The flowers contain a good supply of nectar, attracting many insects, especially bees. Small birds eat the seeds while rabbits love the leaves.

The common name comes from the French *dent de lion* or "lion's tooth," which seems a little strange and is generally said to refer to the shape of the leaves. However, the lion is an ancient symbol of the sun, and the rayed golden flowers resemble little suns, so the name is possibly a corruption of "rays of the sun."[58]

The dandelion is one of the three emblems of the goddess Brighid/Bride, who was Christianised as St. Brigit (the others being the lamb and the oyster-catcher bird). In Uist it is called *bearnan Bride* ("the little notched flower of Bride"), while other Gaelic names translate as "little flower of God" and "St. Bride's forerunner." Like the dandelion, Brighid is associated with the coming of spring at Imbolc (February 1), her festival, and the increase of the sun; she wears it at her breast, and the sun is said to follow. People would go to wells dedicated to her to watch the sun dance at the vernal equinox and, later, Easter. A further association comes from the "milk" that can be expressed with the stems. Like other "milk" yielding plants, they are associated with Brighid as patroness of flocks and herbs. A common belief was that the dandelion "milk" nourished young lambs in spring.

It has been used in medicine and folk remedies since ancient times for a variety of ailments. The name of the genus, *Taraxacum*, is derived from the Greek *taraxos* (disorder) and *akos* (remedy), an allusion to the plant's use as a remedy. Dandelion root was said to cure any disease, but you had to dig out the whole root and not leave any behind—the devil will try to nip a bit off, which makes the cure useless. In Warwickshire folk medicine it was said to be good for the blood; it was recommended in the Highlands of Scotland as a tonic and in America as a blood purifier. Dandelion was used by Arab physicians in the eleventh and twelfth centuries as a general curative.

It is best known as a diuretic (urine promotor), hence many of its folk names—Stink Davie, Wet-a-Bed, Mess-a-Bed, Pissimire, Pittle Bed, and Wet-Weed. Indeed, its English folk name of Piss-a-Bed is echoed in the French *pissenlit* and the German *pissblume*. In counter magic, children in the Fens (eastern England) would be given the flowers to smell on May Day, which was said to stop them wetting the bed for twelve months.

It is a plant with a great deal of folklore attached to it, and many of its folk names call it a clock: Clocks and Watches, Blowball, Peasant's Clock, Doon-Head-Clock, Fortune Teller, One o' Clocks, Clocks, Fairy Clocks, Farmer's Clocks, Schoolboy's Clocks, Shepherd's Clock, Tell-Time, Time Flower, Time-Teller, or Twelve o' Clock. The spherical seed heads can be blown for temporal divinations of all kinds. You can find out how long you have left to live by blowing once on a dandelion seed head; the number of seeds left correspond to

---

58   Bruton-Seal, *Hedgerow Medicine*.

the number of years you have left. Or blow on the seed head to tell you how many years will pass before you get married or how many children you will have.

In Somerset it was called the Weather Clock since when the seed head is fluffy, it means fine weather, but when it is limp, it indicates rain. The flowers themselves close before rain and dew fall. The blooms are very sensitive to weather conditions: in fine weather all the parts are outstretched, but if direct rain threatens, the whole head closes up.

In France girls put a dandelion leaf beneath their pillow to dream of their future husband. To dream of dandelions is unlucky, however, indicating tough times ahead.

Magical Uses

The dandelion is very much associated with solar energies. Its golden colour and nourishing vitamin and mineral content make it a plant of bright energy and vitality. It can be added to sun incenses to increase their power or in incense, potions, spells, and rituals for strength and healing.

Dandelion Leaf Tea may be taken to enhance psychic powers, and the dried flowers may be added to divination incenses.

Blow the dandelion seeds to send thoughts to a loved one.

Burying dandelions in the northwest corner of the garden brings favourable winds.

The white, downy seeds also associate the dandelion with lunar energies, supplying the balancing spirit. Collect these seeds under the light of the full moon and use them in incenses and talismans.

The traditional time to make **Dandelion Wine** is St. George's Day, April 23. St. George may well be the Christian incarnation of a much earlier vegetation deity who overcame the dragon of winter and ushered in the summer. This is a wonderful wine for the Beltane ritual cup.

Culinary Uses

Dandelions are rich in minerals, especially potassium, and vitamins including A, B, C, and D, but people have largely forgotten them as a food source. Up until the 1800s Americans pulled up grass from their yards to plant dandelions, while before the First World War dandelions were grown as a commercial crop in Britain. In Britain the roots were lifted from two-year-old plants to make dandelion coffee; the roasted and ground roots were sold for two shillings per pound. However, when food is scarce, people remember, and during the Second World War the British radio doctor Charles Hill recommended dandelion leaves as a food.

The leaves can be eaten fresh in salads, boiled like spinach, or made into a tea. You can pop a dandelion leaf into a sandwich. Pick the young leaves in early spring for eating (the older ones get bitter) before the plant has flowered. For a more delicate flavour, you can blanch the plant in a similar way to endives; put an upturned flowerpot over the plant during the winter.

The root can be boiled as a vegetable or added raw to salads. The root may be roasted and ground as a substitute for coffee. Gather the roots during the autumn.

The flowers taste slightly sweet and can be eaten raw or used to decorate salads. Try dipping them in batter and deep-frying them. **Macerated Dandelion Flower Oil** can be used in salad dressings, as can **Dandelion Vinegar.** For a vegan alternative to honey, try **Dandelion "Honey."**

Dandelions can be added to tonic beers and wines, which aid digestion.

COSMETIC USES

Dandelions are great for the skin as they are rich in antioxidants, minerals, and vitamins. They have anti-aging properties, are anti-inflammatory, help prevent free radical damage, reduce fine lines and the appearance of scars, as well as encourage healthy skin cell production, even out skin tone, and stimulate circulation. Furthermore, they can have a protective effect against sun damage and improve skin hydration. Do you still want to weed out your dandelions?

Macerated Dandelion Flower Oil can aid dry skin and is especially good for the delicate skin around the eyes. You can also use the oil in the preparation of your homemade skin care products.

Make a dandelion infusion and use as a face wash for the treatment of large pores, age spots, blemishes, sunburn, and chapped skin.

Dandelions are also good for the hair. Rich in vitamins and minerals, they stimulate root growth. Use dandelion infusion as a hair rinse, dilute **Dandelion Vinegar** half and half with water as a hair rinse, or massage **Dandelion Tincture** into your scalp.

MEDICINAL USES

Every part of the dandelion can be used medicinally, and it has been described as a self-contained pharmacy. Dandelion is a good all-round health tonic, rich in vitamins A, B, C, D, and minerals, including potassium and calcium.

The bitter nature of dandelion leaves aids digestion by stimulating the secretion of digestive fluids and promoting the appetite.

Dandelion root is a powerful detoxifying herb, encouraging the elimination of toxins due to infection and pollution—including hangovers—by working on the liver and gall bladder to remove waste products and stimulating the kidneys to remove toxins via urine. This is useful in many conditions including constipation, acne, eczema, psoriasis, boils, and arthritic conditions including gout. It is a safe liver herb and stimulates bile production, useful in the treatment of jaundice, hepatitis, gallstones, and urinary tract infections. Use **Dandelion Root Decoction**.

Dandelions are diuretic and can be used to treat swollen ankles and fluid retention, but without the consequent loss of potassium of orthodox drugs. Use **Dandelion Leaf Tea**.

For rheumatism and arthritis, take **Dandelion Leaf Tea** or **Dandelion Coffee** to help the joints and stimulate the removal of acid deposits. **Macerated Dandelion Flower Oil** can ease muscle tension and stiff joints when rubbed into the affected parts.

Macerated Dandelion Flower Oil applied to the skin helps reduce inflammation and irritation and may help soothe eczema, psoriasis, acne, and skin rashes.

In folk medicine the white latex sap within the flower stem has been used to treat warts and pimples simply by breaking the stem and dabbing the milk on the affected area.

A few dandelion flowers can be eaten raw and may cure a headache.

> *Caution: Dandelion is considered safe in food amounts and safe for most people in medicinal quantities. However, medicinal amounts are best avoided during pregnancy or breastfeeding to be on the safe side. If you are allergic to ragweed, daisies, chrysanthemums, or marigolds, you should avoid using dandelion or use with caution. Some people find that they have a reaction to the white latex found in dandelion stems. Dandelion may decrease the efficacy of some antibiotics, so check with your healthcare provider. Do not take if you are on lithium or taking other diuretics. Dandelion root should not be used by individuals with gallstones, gallbladder complaints, obstructed bile ducts, gastroesophageal reflux disease (GERD), gastritis, or ulcers. Dandelions slightly lower blood sugar so diabetics should carefully monitor sugar levels.*

Recipes

DANDELION WINE

2 LITRES OR 8½ CUPS DANDELION FLOWERS (WHEN LIGHTLY PRESSED DOWN)

2 LITRES OR 8½ CUPS BOILING WATER

1100 GRAMS OR 5½ CUPS GRANULATED SUGAR

1 LITRE OR 4 CUPS WARM WATER

225 GRAMS OR 1½ CUPS RAISINS

WHITE WINE YEAST (AVAILABLE ONLINE)

2 ORANGES

Collect the flowers on a sunny day and remove the green stalks. Place in a fermentation bin and pour on boiling water. Fit the lid. Leave for 3 days, stirring daily, then strain into a demijohn. Dissolve the sugar in the warm water and add to the demijohn. Add the raisins and wine yeast according to manufacturer's instructions. Add the juice and grated rind of the oranges. Fit an airlock and leave until fermentation is complete (until the airlock stops bubbling completely). Siphon off into a clean, sterilised demijohn and leave for at least 12 months. Siphon off into bottles and store as you would any other wine.

DANDELION ROOT DECOCTION

2–3 TEASPOONS DANDELION ROOT

250 ML OR 1 CUP WATER

Boil together and simmer gently for 15 minutes. Strain. Use to encourage the elimination of toxins and remove waste products from the body.

Dandelion Beer

225 GRAMS OR ½ POUND DANDELION PLANTS, INCLUDING THE ROOTS

2 TABLESPOONS ROOT GINGER, GRATED

RIND AND JUICE OF 1 LEMON

1700 ML OR 7 CUPS WATER

500 GRAMS OR 2½ CUPS BROWN SUGAR

25 GRAMS OR 2½ TABLESPOONS CREAM OF TARTAR

1–2 TEASPOONS BEER YEAST (AVAILABLE ONLINE)

Wash the dandelions well, place in a pan with the ginger root, lemon rind, and water. Boil for 15 minutes. Strain into a fermentation bin, add the sugar and cream of tartar, and stir until the sugar is dissolved. Add the rest of the water and the lemon juice. Sprinkle the yeast on top or according to manufacturer's instructions. Cover the bin and leave in a warm place for 5 days, stirring daily. Strain into screw-topped bottles. It is ready to drink in 4–7 days.

Dandelion Coffee

Pick as many roots as you wish and wash them thoroughly. Let them dry off overnight, then put them on a baking tray. Roast for around 45 minutes in a very low oven (100°C/200 F/gas mark ¼) until they are dark brown and completely dry, but take care not to let them burn. Cool the roots and then grind them in a coffee grinder or with a pestle and mortar. You are then ready to brew your natural caffeine-free dandelion coffee just as you would your usual ground coffee. This may help joints and stimulate the removal of acid deposits from them.

Dandelion Leaf Tea

250 ML OR 1 CUP BOILING WATER

2 TEASPOONS LEAVES

Pour the water over the leaves. Cover. Infuse 15 minutes. Strain and drink for rheumatism and arthritis.

. . . .

DANDELION TABBOULEH

JUICE OF 2 LEMONS

75 GRAMS OR ½ CUP CRACKED BULGUR WHEAT

HANDFUL YOUNG DANDELION LEAVES

HALF A HANDFUL FRESH MINT LEAVES

5 SPRING ONIONS (SCALLIONS), CHOPPED

80 ML OR 7 TEASPOONS OLIVE OIL

SEASONING TO TASTE

Pour the lemon juice over the wheat and leave for 90 minutes until the wheat has softened. Chop the dandelion and mint and add to the wheat along with the onions and oil. Season to taste before transfering to a serving dish.

. . . .

DANDELION TINCTURE

The whole plant can be tinctured, including the roots. To make a tincture, put 100 grams of dried or 200 grams fresh herbs into a clean jar and pour on 500 ml of vodka or brandy. Seal and keep in a warm place for 2–4 weeks, shaking daily. Strain through muslin and store in a dark bottle in a cool place for 2–6 years. Because a tincture is much stronger than an infusion or decoction, you only need a few drops in a glass of water as a medicinal dose. Take 10 drops in water twice a day. Alternatively, a few drops may be added to a salve or bath for external use.

. . . .

DANDELION FACIAL STEAM

Put a heatproof bowl on a mat and two-thirds fill it with boiling water and add 8 dandelion flower heads. Leave them to infuse for 5 minutes, then put a towel over your head and lean over the bowl for 10 minutes. This will help cleanse and brighten your skin. Wash your face with cool water and apply your usual moisturiser.

. . . .
Dandelion Vinegar

Gather fresh dandelion blossoms and leaves and pack them into a glass jar. Cover with white vinegar or cider vinegar. Put on the lid. Leave in a dark place for a month, shaking daily. Strain the liquid vinegar into a clean jar and put the leaves and flowers on the compost heap. Use as a salad dressing or diluted with water as a hair tonic.

. . . .
Dandelion Fritters

110 GRAMS OR 1 CUP PLAIN (ALL-PURPOSE) FLOUR

PINCH SALT

1 EGG

140 ML OR ½ CUP MILK

DANDELION LEAVES

Sift the flour and salt together, add the beaten egg and some milk. Beat well and stand for 30 minutes. Dip the leaves in the batter and deep-fry till golden brown.

. . . .
Dandelion "Honey" (Vegan)

500 ML OR 2 CUPS WATER

2-3 LARGE HANDFULS FRESH DANDELION FLOWER HEADS

2 CM OR 1 INCH CINNAMON STICK

½ LEMON, SLICED

SUGAR

Put the water, dandelion flowers, cinnamon, and lemon in a pan. Put a lid on and simmer 15 minutes. Take this off the heat and leave to infuse overnight. Strain and measure the liquid. For each 500 ml (2 cups) of liquid, add 500 grams or 2¼ cups + 1 tablespoon sugar. Bring to boil and simmer for around 15 minutes. Pour into clean jars.

. . . . .

· ·

Macerated Dandelion Flower Oil

Pick dandelion flowers. Put them on a tray and leave them overnight to wilt and lose some of their water content. Pack them into a glass jar and cover with vegetable oil. Fit a lid and leave this on a sunny windowsill for 3 weeks, shaking daily. Strain the oil into a clean jar.

Fuchsia

Fuchsia spp.

· · · · · · · · · · · · · · ·

PLANETARY RULER: Venus

ELEMENT: Water

ASSOCIATED DEITIES: Fairies, Virgin Mary, Inti

MAGICAL VIRTUES: Love, fairy magic, solar magic, blessing

Fuchsias are a genus of about 105 species of flowering shrubs and trees with many varieties and hybrids. They are mostly native to the tropical and subtropical regions of Central and South America, where they are pollinated by hummingbirds.

The Incas cultivated fuchsia for its edible berries, and it is still often found growing on terraces built by the Incas. Depictions sometimes occur on Inca pottery and painted wooden bowls, and they possibly had ritual and religious uses in connection with the sun god Inti.[59]

They first became known to Europeans when Charles Plumier (1646–1704), a French monk and botanist, discovered them on one of his three plant-hunting trips to the Caribbean and South America. During his third voyage in 1695 he described a new plant that he had found on the foothills of Hispaniola and named it *Fuchsia triphylla*, in honour of Leonhard Fuchs (1501–1566), a German physician and botanist. The first plants and seeds were lost at sea, and it was not until 1788 that fuchsias reached the UK. They soon became

---

59   https://fuchsiasinthecity.com/blog/files/Inca-and-the-fuchsia.php.

popular in gardens and greenhouses. Most fuchsias are not frost hardy; in my garden, they have to be grown under glass or in pots that can be taken into the greenhouse in the winter, though the *Fuchsia magellanica* is hardy outdoors and is naturalised in several places in the UK. You can even see it in hedgerows in some locations. I grow that in my garden too.

As usual with imported plants, Europeans soon sought to connect it with Christian lore, claiming that the fuchsia sprang from the blood of Christ dripping to the foot of the cross, and its pendant flowers dangle because it hangs its head from sorrow. In both Britain and Ireland its folk names include Lady's Eardrops, Lady's Earrings (of the Virgin Mary), and God's Teardrops.

A favourite pastime of British and Irish children used to be making a lady or flower fairy from fuchsia flowers by trimming the petals and stamens to make a skirt and legs, sometimes with a twig for the arms. They would also suck the sweet nectar from the flowers. However, in both Britain and Ireland it was considered unlucky to bring the flowers into the house, as was true of all flowers associated with fairies.

A few species of fuchsia come from New Zealand and have blue pollen, which was used by young Maori people to decorate their faces. Known as katukutuku, it was eaten, made into jams, used in tanning leather, and employed by Maori woman in vapour baths after childbirth.

MAGICAL USES

When fuchsias reached Europe, they were immediately marked out as fairy flowers. They can be used in all workings to contact fairies.

They are flowers of blessing. Plant in the garden, pots, and hanging baskets to bring luck to your home. Give them as gifts to friends. Include some in a wedding bouquet.

The delicate blossoms make them symbols of beauty and love. Use them in love spells, charms, herbal talismans, incense, and potions for love magic.

They may be dried and added to **Venus Planetary Incense** and water incense. They can also be added to incense for rituals celebrating the sun.

CULINARY USES

Many of us grow fuchsias in our gardens, but did you know that from the flowers to the berries, every part of the fuchsia is edible? You can add the flowers to salads or use them to decorate cakes, cheesecakes, in a salad, or frozen in an ice cube and added to drinks.

The berries are a revelation and full of vitamin C. However, some varieties have better-tasting berries than others with flavours from sweet or peppery to downright disappointing. One variety is even sometimes marketed as the "edible fuchsia," *Fuchsia splendens*, though all varieties are nontoxic and can be eaten. You can even use them in recipes in place of soft fruits like strawberries, raspberries, blackberries, blueberries, cranberries, and gooseberries. Use them in ice creams, jellies, **Fuchsia Berry Jam**, tarts, pies, cheesecakes, pavlovas, buns, cookies, trifles, and cakes.

COSMETIC USES

None.

MEDICINAL USES

The fuchsia was used in traditional medicine. In Transylvania the fresh leaves are applied to wounds and skin inflammations,[60] while in South America the flowers are used on bites, scratches, and grazes, and the berry juice is utilized to relieve itching and redness of the skin, inflamed blisters, and sunburn.[61] Use fuchsia leaves as a poultice for inflamed skin, bites, and stings.

> *Caution:* *None known for external medical use.*

---

60 https://www.ncbi.nlm.nih.gov/pmc/articles/PMC7070992.

61 https://academicjournals.org/journal/AJB/article-full-text-pdf/2AAF79325190.

Recipes

Fuchsia Berry Jam

450 GRAMS OR 2¼ CUPS SUGAR

2 TABLESPOONS WATER

1 TABLESPOON LEMON JUICE

680 GRAMS OR 3¾ CUPS RIPE FUCHSIA BERRIES

1 APPLE, PEELED, CORED, AND CHOPPED FINELY (FOR THE PECTIN)

Over a low heat, melt the sugar in the water and lemon juice. Add the berries and apple, bring to boil, and maintain a rolling boil until you reach the setting point on a sugar thermometer. If you don't have a sugar thermometer, spoon a little jam onto a cold saucer. Leave a minute and tip the saucer. If the jam is set, it will stay put and will not trickle away. Keep testing till you get to setting point. Pour into warmed, sterilised glass jars and seal.

Fuchsia Perisco Liqueur

225 GRAMS OR 1 CUP FUCHSIA BERRIES, JUICED

225 GRAMS OR 2 CUPS SUGAR

600 ML OR 2½ CUPS RUM OR BRANDY

RIND AND JUICE OF ½ LEMON

6 CM OR 2 INCH CINNAMON STICK

Strain the juice from the berries. Add it to the other ingredients in a large jar with a lid. Cover and leave for 7 days, stirring daily. Strain and bottle.

. . . .

Fuchsia Buns

110 GRAMS OR ½ CUP MARGARINE OR BUTTER

85 GRAMS OR ⅜ CUP SUGAR

2 EGGS, BEATEN

1 TEASPOON VANILLA ESSENCE

128 GRAMS OR 1 CUP PLAIN (ALL-PURPOSE) FLOUR

½ TEASPOON BAKING POWDER

PINCH SALT

50 GRAMS OR ¼ CUP FUCHSIA BERRIES

Cream the margarine/butter and sugar. Adding a little at a time, beat in the eggs. Add the vanilla essence, then fold in the flour, baking powder, salt. Add the fuchsia berries. Spoon into muffin cases. Bake at 220°C/425°F/gas mark 6 for 15 minutes.

. . . .

Venus Planetary Incense

1 PART RED ROSE PETALS

2 PARTS SANDALWOOD

½ PART FUCHSIA FLOWERS

½ PART BENZOIN

3 PARTS FRANKINCENSE

Blend together and burn on charcoal.

Scented Geranium

Pelargonium spp.

· · · · · · · · · · · · ·

PLANETARY RULER: Venus

ELEMENT: Water

ASSOCIATED DEITIES: None

MAGICAL VIRTUES: Fertility, love, health,
aura cleansing, protection, happiness

It turns out that most of the plants we called "geraniums" are not geraniums at all but pelargoniums, and the scented geranium is definitely a pelargonium. Confused? Let me try to explain. While true geraniums are native to Europe and frost hardy, pelargoniums come from the subtropical regions of South Africa (and elsewhere) and are tender, but both were originally classified in the genus *Geranium* by Linnaeus in 1753. Though the French botanist Charles L'Héritier had classified pelargoniums as a separate genus by the late 1700s, the confusion still continues, and pelargoniums are still called geraniums. The seed heads also differentiate them. The genus name *Pelargonium* comes from the Greek word *pelargos*, which means "stork," because the seeds look like a stork's beak and the genus has the common name Storkbills, while true geraniums are Cranesbills. I hope that's clear, but I am afraid I am probably going to use the terms scented pelargoniums and scented geraniums interchangeably in this piece since most people call them by the latter name.

Scented-leafed pelargoniums have smaller (sometimes furry) leaves and flowers than other pelargoniums like the bright red geranium so familiar on Mediterranean terraces, but they come in a wide variety of fragrances from lemon, lime, rose, mint, ginger, strawberry, apricot, and nutmeg to coconut and apple and a host of others.

There are around 280 pelargonium species, with most of them (71 percent) growing in South Africa, but a few species occur naturally in Australia, eastern Africa, New Zealand, the Middle East, and Madagascar. They were brought to Europe by plant collectors and introduced into the Americas by colonists. In both Europe and America they became extremely popular with all classes of society, grown from grand houses to humble cottage gardens.

The strongly scented leaves were put to a variety of uses. Pots of scented geraniums were placed around houses to freshen the air, wafted around by the sweeping long skirts of passing ladies. They were added to potpourris, ointments, and cosmetic preparations; fragranced the finger bowls used to cleanse hands between courses at banquets; and, of course, they were used for perfume. Rose geranium oil became an economic substitute for very expensive rose oil in the French perfume industry. Furthermore, scented geraniums are edible and were employed as a flavouring for food, especially desserts.

In the language of flowers employed by lovers, the different scented leaves had very precise meanings. While sending a rose geranium meant "preference" and the apple-scented leaves "present preference" (suggesting things might change), nutmeg-scented leaves meant "expected meeting" and lemon-scented leaves conveyed "unexpected meeting."[62]

In Poland, pelargoniums in the home are considered to be protective and a symbol of hope.

According to a Muslim legend, the rose geranium was created when the prophet Mohammed hung his shirt on a mallow branch after bathing in a river. The mallow plant was so honoured and happy that she slowly transformed herself into a lovely flower with leaves that were richly perfumed: the rose geranium.

All types of scented geranium leaves can be added to potpourri and blend well with lavender, rose petals, and cinnamon.

MAGICAL USES

Add the dried leaves and petals to incenses, spells, talismans, and sachets for love magic. Add to planetary Venus and water incenses.

Pelargoniums can be used in any spells, incense, talismans, oils, and potions related to happiness, prosperity, and fertility.

Scented pelargonium leaves and oil can be used for protection oils and charms.

---

62   Herb Society of America, https://www.herbsociety.org.

CULINARY USES

The leaves and flowers of scented pelargoniums are edible. The essential oils they contain add scent and flavour to a variety of dishes, though it must be said that some smell better than they taste. The rose-, lemon-, and mint-scented varieties are most often used for culinary purposes.

You can add apple-scented or rose-scented leaves to **Apple Geranium Jelly** or make **Rose-Scented Geranium Tea**. Add the leaves to cakes, jellies, fruit punches, syrups, iced tea, herb butter, baked puddings, pie toppings, cookies, rice dishes, cobblers and fruit crumbles, cheesecakes, sorbets, and ice cream or just use as a garnish. The flowers can be candied and used to decorate cakes. Freeze the flowers or leaves in ice cubes and drop one in a summer drink or cocktail.

Make a **Rose Geranium Sugar** and use this for baking or add it to cocktails and lemonades. Try a scented geranium vinegar as a salad dressing.

Try macerating a few leaves in wine overnight or infusing them in gin or vodka for a few days.

It is best to chop the leaves just before use, and—like other scented ingredients—use very, very sparingly or the taste will be unpleasant.

If you want to be really posh, don't forget the finger bowl! Add a few leaves of lemon-scented geranium leaves to individual bowls of water on your dining table so your guests can cleanse their fingers between courses.

COSMETIC USES

The use of pelargoniums in toiletries dates back centuries. They are still used commercially in perfumes, soaps, lotions, creams, and men's colognes.

Rose-scented geranium is very moisturising and good for mature skin, dry skin, acne, and dry eczema. Make a **Scented Geranium Cream**, use a **Scented Geranium Skin Toner**, or use a washcloth dipped in **Scented Geranium Infusion** to cleanse your face and body.

You can also make a **Heat Macerated Scented Geranium Oil** to add to your homemade skin-care products, pour it into the bath, or apply it directly to the skin. Rub the oil into your tired legs and feet to refresh them.

Add the dried leaves to homemade soap.

Combine the dried, powdered leaves with baking soda (bicarbonate of soda) and dab this beneath your armpits as a natural deodorant.

MEDICINAL USES

Pelargoniums have a history of traditional medicinal use in their native Africa, employed for intestinal problems, boils, wounds, burns, respiratory ailments, fevers, coughs, colds, kidney complaints, nausea, diarrhoea, and other conditions. Over-the-counter remedies for respiratory ailments containing *Pelargonium reniforme* and *Pelargonium sidoides* are available in parts of Europe and the USA.

Use **Scented Geranium Infusion** in the bath to treat cellulite and water retention, as well as stiff and sore muscles. Add it to a footbath to treat chilblains.

Take **Rose-Scented Geranium Tea** to soothe and relax you if you are feeling stressed.

For a headache, used a cloth soaked in cooled **Scented Geranium Infusion** on your temples or take a cup of **Rose-Scented Geranium Tea**.

As a first-aid remedy, if you are bitten by an insect in the garden or if you scratch yourself, just crush up a leaf and apply to the affected area. It has an antibacterial action and will help soothe any itchiness.

> **Caution:** *There have been some rare cases of contact dermatitis with scented geraniums (pelargoniums) or rose geranium essential oil. To be on the safe side, do not use medicinal amounts of any scented geranium if you are pregnant or breastfeeding, and do not consume the coconut-scented Pelargonium grossularioides at all if you are pregnant as it had historic use as an abortifacient.*

HEAT MACERATED SCENTED GERANIUM OIL

Crush a handful of scented geranium leaves in a pestle and mortar. Put them in a double boiler or slow cooker and just cover with vegetable oil. Simmer on a very, very low heat for 15–20 minutes. Turn off the heat and leave overnight. Strain into a clean glass bottle and label. Will keep around 6 months in a cool, dark place. This is a moisturising oil for your skin or rub it into tired legs and feet.

SCENTED GERANIUM SKIN TONER

Pack a sterilised glass jar with scented geranium leaves. Fill up the jar with witch hazel. Fit the lid. Leave in a dark place, shaking daily, for 3 weeks. Strain the liquid into a clean bottle and label. Will keep 6–12 months in a cool, dark place.

SCENTED GERANIUM WOOD OIL

FRESH LEAVES AND FLOWERS OF SCENTED GERANIUM

OLIVE OIL

WHITE VINEGAR

Half fill a jar with scented geranium leaves and flowers. Top up the jar with olive oil. Put on a lid and leave in a cool, dark place for 2 weeks, shaking daily. Strain the oil into a measuring jug. Mix three parts oil with one part vinegar—i.e., if you have 300 ml oil, add 100 ml vinegar. Pour into a clean jar, fit a lid, and label. To use, shake the jar and apply to your wooden furniture with a soft cloth.

. . . .
ROSE-SCENTED GERANIUM TEA

2 ROSE-SCENTED GERANIUM LEAVES

250 ML OR 1 CUP BOILING WATER

Pour the water over the *Pelargonium graveolens* leaves and infuse for 15 minutes. Strain and take one or two cups a day for anxiety.

. . . .
SCENTED GERANIUM BATH VINEGAR

Pack a jar with scented pelargonium petals. Pour in enough white vinegar or cider vinegar to cover. Fit the lid. Leave on a sunny windowsill for 2 weeks, shaking daily. Strain the vinegar onto fresh pelargonium leaves and repeat the process. You can repeat several times until you have the perfume strength you would like. Strain into a pretty bottle. To use, pour a couple tablespoons into your bath. Will keep 6–12 months in a cool, dark place.

. . . .
SCENTED GERANIUM WARDROBE SACHETS

DRIED FLOWERS AND PETALS OF SCENTED GERANIUM

SMALL CLOTH BAGS (WEDDING FAVOUR BAGS WORK WELL
OR MAKE YOUR OWN)

Put the herb in the bags and hang in your wardrobe or pop into your linen drawers to scent your clothes and deter moths.

. . . .
ROSE GERANIUM SUGAR

Place alternate layers of rose-scented pelargonium leaves and castor sugar (superfine sugar) in a dry glass jar until the container is full. Cover tightly and leave in a warm place for a week. Shake from time to time. Sift out the flowers and leaves. To use, substitute for plain sugar in white cakes and icings for a unique and subtle flavour.

. . . .

SCENTED GERANIUM COOKIES

170 GRAMS OR ¾ CUP MARGARINE OR BUTTER

280 GRAMS OR 2¼ CUPS PLAIN (ALL-PURPOSE) FLOUR

50 GRAMS OR 6½ TABLESPOONS CORNFLOUR (CORNSTARCH)

170 GRAMS OR ¾ CUP GERANIUM SUGAR (SEE ABOVE)

1 LEVEL TEASPOONS BAKING POWDER

2 EGG WHITES

Stir all the ingredients together to form a soft dough. Knead lightly and roll out to 3 mm (⅛ inch). Using a cookie cutter, cut into rounds. Put the cookies onto a baking sheet that has been sprinkled with flour. Bake for 10–15 minutes at 180°C/350°F/gas mark 4.

. . . .

APPLE GERANIUM JELLY

1.8 KILOS OR 4 POUNDS APPLES OR CRAB APPLES

12 APPLE-SCENTED OR ROSE-SCENTED GERANIUM LEAVES

SUGAR

Remove the stems and chop the apples roughly. You don't need to peel or remove the cores. Stew them in their own juice with the geranium leaves until soft. Strain through muslin and collect the juice. Discard the pulp. Add 500 gm or 1 pound or 2¼ cups + 3 tablespoons sugar for every 500 ml or 1 pint or 2 cups juice and boil together until the setting point on a sugar thermometer is reached. If you don't have a sugar thermometer, spoon a little jelly onto a cold saucer. Leave a minute and tip the saucer. If the jam is set, it will stay put and will not trickle away. Keep testing till you get to setting point. Pour into warmed, sterilised glass jars and seal. Yields about 2.5 kilos or 5 pounds.

. . . .
SCENTED GERANIUM INFUSION

Pour 1 cup boiling water over 4 rose-scented geranium (*Pelargonium graveolens*) leaves and infuse for 15 minutes. Strain.

. . . .
SCENTED GERANIUM CREAM

8 TABLESPOONS HEAT MACERATED SCENTED GERANIUM OIL

50 GRAMS EMULSIFYING WAX

5 TABLESPOONS SCENTED GERANIUM INFUSION

2 TABLESPOONS CALENDULA TINCTURE

Prepare the oil part and the liquid part separately before bringing them together. Combine the oil and emulsifying wax in a double boiler. The water part (the infusion and tincture) needs to be warmed in a separate pan but must reach the same temperature as the oils, as this will help the two elements combine when they come together. Then the water part is dripped into the oil part very slowly, whisking constantly with a wooden spoon, hand whisk, or electric whisk until they are fully combined and emulsified. Stir and quickly transfer to your storage jars before it thickens too much.

Heather

Calluna vulgaris

PLANETARY RULER: Venus

ELEMENT: Water

ASSOCIATED DEITIES: Aphrodite Erycina, Astarte, Attis, bee goddesses, Butes, Cybele, Dana, Isis, Nechtan Mac Labraid, Osiris, goddesses of high summer, Uroica, Venus Erycina

MAGICAL VIRTUES: Midsummer, fairy contact, protection, luck, money, death and mourning, regeneration, resurrection, community harmony, initiation

The common heather, also called ling or heath, is a low-growing evergreen shrub found widely in Europe and Asia Minor that was taken to America by Scottish settlers[63] as it is as much a symbol of Scotland as the thistle. Heather thrives on acidic soils in open situations and is often the dominant plant on most heathland and moorland in Europe. Great sweeps of naturally growing heather are even called heaths, though they are, in fact, the result of human activity, the clearance of trees on poor acidic soil for grazing animals, for which it provides a food source. It's also an important food in these situations for grouse, red deer, mountain hares, and bees, as well as providing an important habitat for birds, many insects, and small mammals.

---

63   Mabey, *Flora Britannica*.

For those living at subsistence level on heaths, heather was a useful resource, employed for thatching roofs, insulation, as an industrial packing material, and for rope making and basketry. The root stock could be made into musical pipes or the handles of knives, especially the Scottish dirk. A yellow-orange dye can be obtained from the plant, which was used for dying wool. One of its common names is ling, which derives from the old Norse *lyng* or the Anglo-Saxon *lig*, both meaning "fire." The dried branches make a good fuel, which was used extensively in Scotland and other areas and still is in some cases.

Heather flowers are slightly soporific (sleep inducing) and this, together with the softness of the flowering shoots, was put to good use for making mattresses and pillows. In the sixteenth century, George Buchanan, tutor to James VI of Scotland, recorded that a heather bed was "so pleasant, that it may vie in softness with the finest down, while in salubrity it far exceeds it…and restores strength to fatigued nerves, so that those who lie down languid and weary in the evening, arise in the morning vigorous and sprightly."[64]

Growing as it does on deserted moors, heather is very often a symbol of loneliness and melancholy; because of this, in some parts of the world, it is used as a graveyard plant.

There is a Welsh saying that runs "Gold under furze, silver under rushes and famine under heather," probably because it grows on soil so poor that it will support nothing else, and a superstition that bringing heather into the house would result in misfortune or death. In Germany it was said that if heather grows tall, there will be a harsh winter.

White heather has a lore all of its own. Heather flowers are usually pinky-purple or purple, and naturally growing white heather is very rare, the very scarcity making finding some lucky, like finding a four-leafed clover. There is a legend that when Malvina (daughter of the poet Ossian) learned that her betrothed, Oscar, had died in battle, sending her a spray of purple heather as the final token of his love, the tears that she shed upon it turned the flowers white, causing her to say that though it was a symbol of her sorrow, it would bring luck to any who found it. In 1884 Queen Victoria wrote that her servant Mr. Brown "espied a piece of white heather and jumped off to pick it. No Highlander would pass by it without picking it, for it was considered to bring good luck." In 1544 Clan Ranald attributed a victory to the fact they had worn white heather in their bonnets. Cluny of Clan MacPherson eluded his pursuers after Culloden and believed his escape was due to the fact that searchers had overlooked him whilst he slept on a patch of white heather. There was a belief that white heather grew on patches of ground where no blood had been shed in battle, a lucky thing indeed on an island where almost every inch must have seen a battle

---

64 Quoted in Mabey, *Flora Britannica*.

of some kind. In the Scottish Lowlands, however, it is said that where white heather grows, fairies tread, and maybe they are responsible for its magic.

The botanical name *Calluna* comes from the Greek meaning "to sweep," since heather twigs were commonly used to make brooms and besoms. Heather besoms have special protective powers; in Germany one placed by the cowshed door would repel evil spirits and witches, who would be forced to stop and count all the twigs before entering the shed, which would take them till dawn, when their powers naturally decreased. In Tuscany heather besoms were used to unmask witches trying to enter a church door—an ordinary woman would simply step over it, while a real witch would straddle the broom and try to fly away! In Brittany when people swept their homes, to ensure that luck was not swept out of the door, a sprig of heather would be placed in the window to retain it.

Heather had great protective powers. A German proverb says, "Marjoram, St. John's wort, and white heather cause the devil great pains." On Walpurgis Eve (May Eve), cows were given a drink of heather infusion to protect them from the attention of wandering witches, and in Switzerland heather gave protection to cows moving pastures. In Scotland farmers carried torches of burning heather around their fields before Midsummer to ensure good crops and around their cattle to guarantee the expulsion of negative influences and bring fertility. In Holland putting a sprig of heather beneath the pillow was believed to prevent convulsions.

The honey-scented heather flowers attract bees in the summer, who buzz from plant to plant, sipping the nectar and taking it back to the hive to make the delicious heather honey that is so prized. One of the epithets of Aphrodite, the Greek goddess of love, was Aphrodite Erycina ("Aphrodite of the Heather") who had a cult centre on Mount Eryx on Sicily, where the bees hummed amongst the wild heather. It was said to have been founded when Aphrodite saved Butes, one of the Argonauts, from the call of the siren-song and took him to Sicily, where he became her lover and where she gave birth to their son Eryx.[65] Some accounts make Butes a famous beekeeper.[66] So strong was the association between Aphrodite of the Heather and the bee that the legendary architect and inventor Daedalus crafted a honeycomb of pure gold, scarcely distinguishable from the real thing, and dedicated it at Aphrodite Erycina's altar.

---

65   http://www.perseus.tufts.edu/hopper/text?doc=Perseus:text:1999.01.0022:text=Library:book=1: chapter=9 and https://www.perseus.tufts.edu/hopper/text?doc=Perseus:text:1999.01.0160, and https://www.theoi.com/Olympios/AphroditeLoves2.html.

66   Diodorus Siculus, *Bibliotheca historica*, https://penelope.uchicago.edu/Thayer/e/roman/texts/diodorus _siculus/2a*.html.

The Greeks believed that bees reproduced asexually, spontaneously generating from corpses, life coming from death, making them a suitable symbol of a self-sufficient goddess who needed no outside agency to create life and who could regenerate nature after the winter death. Priestesses of various kinds were called *Melissae* ("bee"), a name which, according to Pindar, came from an association of the purity of the bee and the chastity of the priestesses.[67] The priestesses were maidens who served the queen bee, the Goddess herself.

Honey made by bees feeding on common heather has a jelly-like texture and strong taste. Ale and mead made from rich heather honey have a magical reputation. Robert Louis Stevenson even wrote a poem about it:

> *From the bonny bells of heather,*
> *They brew a drink Langsyn*
> *Was sweeter far than honey*
> *Was stronger far than wine.*[68]

Common heather is used as a flavouring agent for beer and wine. The flowers and the young shoots have been used instead of hops to flavour beer. Heather ale is believed to have been developed by the Picts over 4,000 years ago. There is evidence, on the Isle of Rhum, of Neolithic drinking vessels containing heather and other plant ales. A legend relates how in the fourth century the Vikings (some say the Scots) defeated a Pictish army. They slaughtered all but the king and his son, whom they cornered on a cliff top. From these two the victorious chieftain hoped to extract the secret recipe for heather ale. After torturing the pair for a short while, the Pictish king offered to reveal the recipe if his son died a quick death. The captors obliged and threw the prince from the cliff. The Pictish king then revealed that though he was sure he himself could keep the secret, he had had doubts about his son's ability. With that, he grappled with the Viking chief and hurled them both over the precipice. However, it was still reported as being made on Islay in 1772, when Pennant reported "ale is frequently made in this island from the hops of heath, mixing two thirds of the plant with one of malt."[69] In northern parts of Britain, people often added the tips of flowering heather shoots to herbal drinks and beer to purify the blood.

Despite being a lowly shrub, heather appears in the Celtic ogham tree alphabet, where it is Ura or Úr, one of the five vowels. The Druid author Colin Murray wrote that "Heather

67   Pindar, *Pythian Odes*, http://www.perseus.tufts.edu/hopper/text?doc=Perseus%3Atext
      %3A1999.01.0162%3Abook%3DP.

68   A *Galloway Legend*.

69   Watts, *Elsevier's Dictionary of Plant Lore*.

is the symbolic gateway linking the fertile earth and the spirit world…At the time of the Midsummer sunrise, the sun casts three spreading rays of light, which open the Gates of Annwn, the portal to the otherworld…"[70] This associates the heather, Midsummer, and the bee in modern Druid lore. The summer solstice is the peak of the solar year, the time of greatest light, when the sun shines the longest. The honeybee orientates itself on its journey by the angle and position of the sun, and the Celts regarded it as a messenger who travelled the paths of sunlight to the realm of the spirits. Being winged they share with birds the ability to carry messages from this world to the world of spirits, and the old practice of telling the bees all the family news means sending messengers to souls in the otherworld.

Because heather can survive the annual heath burnings that formerly took place and actually pushes out many fresh new shoots afterwards, it was a plant symbolic of regeneration and resurrection. The Egyptian death and resurrection god Osiris was boxed up in a coffin and washed up on Byblos, where heather grew over it. In legend Cybele imprisoned the vegetation god Attis in heather at Midsummer. Heather is dedicated to a number of Catholic saints who have their feast days in December; heathers are evergreen and survive the winter.

In Scotland the annual burning of heather in the spring was believed to bring the spring rains. In west Prussia, Finland, and Estonia, the blossoming of the flowers determined the timing of winter grain sowing—if it flowers high, sow rye early; if it blooms in the middle, sow at Michaelmas (September 29); if at the top, sow after Michaelmas.

Heather has a long history of use as a medicinal plant. Dioscorides discussed it in his first century CE *Materia Medica* as a treatment for snakebite, while Galen (131–200 CE) wrote that it could induce sweating. In the Highlands of Scotland, an infusion of heather tops was used to treat coughs, consumption, and soothe the nerves. Highlanders also made heather tea and ointments to treat arthritis and rheumatism. "Moorland tea," made from heather flowers, was a favourite of Robert Burns. Highlanders used a strong infusion of heather for coughs and colds.

MAGICAL USES

Heather is a plant of regeneration and renewal, of life through death, the resurrection of gods, the earth itself, and the human soul. Moreover, it is associated with the death and rebirth that comes through initiation. It may be used at rituals of death and mourning in the form of incense and funeral flowers, at Samhain, or planted on graves as a sign of the

---

70   Murray, *The Celtic Tree Oracle*.

continuation of the soul. Utilise as **Heather Mead**, **Heather Ale**, **Heather Tea**, incense and anointing oils at initiations. Heather flower essence can be taken in the days leading up to initiation.

Heather is a sacred herb of Midsummer, when the gates open to the otherworld and the earth is joined to the world of spirit. It may be thrown onto the Midsummer bonfire and used in incense, oils, teas, and wines.

It is sacred to the summer goddess, lush and fertile, sensuous and sexual. Use it to invoke her and honour her in all her rituals.

Heather provides food for bees, communal creatures who work together for the good of the whole hive. Taking **Heather Tea** or heather flower essence can help us take the needs of others into account and learn not to be self-centred. Use heather incense in communal spaces, particularly when there are conflicts to be resolved.

Heather is cleansing and purifying. Burn heather incense to clear negativity, and use a heather broom to sweep the circle or temple to clear away negative influences prior to ritual. Use at home to brush away negative influences after a disagreement. Use a bunch of heather twigs as an asperger to sprinkle water or a herbal infusion around your sacred space for the same purpose.

Heather contains the power of fire, which transforms, purifies, and regenerates. Use heather incense, wine, tea, or flower essence when these energies are needed.

Burning heather is said to call the cleansing and fertilising rain and can be employed to manifest these qualities both physically and spiritually.

Heather is a plant of protection. Carry it in a herbal talisman or pouch when you are in a difficult situation. Put a heather sprig in the window or a wreath of heather on the front door. Have heather plants in your garden. Take a cup of **Heather Tea** to align you with the plant's energies.

Plant heather around the house and garden to attract friendly spirits. Honour them with heather at Midsummer.

Carry white heather to attract positive energies and general good luck. Include white heather in bridal or handfasting bouquets to bring luck and blessings on the marriage.

CULINARY USES

Heather flowers can be infused in honey or made into herbal syrups, both of which can be used to flavour baked goods.

A pleasant **Heather Tea** is made from the flowers. Common heather is used as a flavouring agent for beer and wine. Try the **Heather Ale** or **Heather Mead** below.

COSMETIC USES

Heather is used commercially in shampoos, lotions, baths, and perfumes. It is cleansing, detoxifying, disinfecting, and anti-inflammatory as well as being nourishing, conditioning, and soothing for the skin. It has a strong antioxidant effect that reduces free radical damage to the skin.

The tannins in heather are astringent, so a **Heather Tea** makes a good tightening and cleansing face wash, or macerate heather flowers in witch hazel or rosewater to make your own skin toner. Grind dried heather flowers and mix them with a little honey and water to make a skin exfoliator.

Heather contains arbutin, which inhibits melanin production, making heather useful in your homemade cosmetics for treating uneven skin pigmentation, age spots, and freckles. It has a mild bleaching effect. Apply pads soaked in a weak **Heather Tea** to the under-eye area for dark circles.

Heather is anti-inflammatory and may be useful for irritated and itchy skin. Use **Heather Tea** as a wash or apply **Macerated Heather Oil**.

Make a **Heather Infusion** and add to your bath to cleanse and refresh your skin. Put heather flowers in a muslin bag and use in the shower as an exfoliating skin scrub.

MEDICINAL USES

The flowering tips are used medicinally. **Heather Tea** is a urinary antiseptic that disinfects the urinary tract and mildly increases urination. It is useful in the treatment of cystitis and inflammatory bladder conditions.

Useful for rheumatism, gout, arthritis, and chilblains, a heather salve or **Macerated Heather Oil** can be rubbed on affected joints or a poultice of the crushed flowers applied to the area. A **Heather Infusion** poured into a warm bath helps joint problems.

Heather Tea is mildly sedative and useful for insomnia and nervous exhaustion. Use a heather-stuffed pillow for a refreshing sleep.

Apply a compress dipped in **Heather Infusion** to the forehead to relieve headaches.

> *Caution:* Heather is generally considered safe when used topically or taken orally. However, to be on the safe side, avoid medicinal amounts if pregnant or breastfeeding.

Recipes

HEATHER MEAD

600 ML OR 2½ CUPS HEATHER FLOWERS

3½ LITRES OR 14 CUPS WATER

1.8 KILOS OR 4 POUNDS HONEY

WHITE WINE YEAST (AVAILABLE ONLINE)

YEAST NUTRIENT (AVAILABLE ONLINE)

Put the flowers in a pan with the water and simmer for 20 minutes. Turn off the heat. Add the honey and stir to dissolve. Cool to lukewarm and strain into a demijohn. Add the yeast and nutrient (check manufacturer's instructions). Top up with more lukewarm water if necessary. Fit an airlock and leave in a warm place to ferment out (until the airlock stops bubbling completely). Siphon off the mead into a clean demijohn, fit an airlock, and leave another six months before siphoning into sterilised bottles. Store as you would any wine.

HEATHER TEA

2 TEASPOONS FRESH OR 1 TEASPOON DRIED HEATHER FLOWERS

250 ML OR 1 CUP BOILING WATER

Pour boiling water over the herb and infuse for 10 minutes. Strain and drink to help induce natural sleep.

HEATHER INFUSION

4 TEASPOONS FRESH OR 2 TEASPOONS DRIED HEATHER FLOWERS

250 ML OR 1 CUP BOILING WATER

Pour boiling water over the heather and infuse for 10 minutes. Strain. Add to your bath to aid joint pain.

. . . .

Macerated Heather Oil

Chop up some heather tops, put them in a glass jar, and cover with vegetable oil (olive, sunflower, almond, etc.). Fit the lid. Leave on a sunny windowsill for 2 weeks, shaking daily. Strain into a clean jar. This will keep in a cool, dark place for up to 1 year. This is useful applied to irritated and itchy skin or arthritic joints.

. . . .

Heather Ale

1 LITRE OR 5 CUPS HEATHER SHOOTS

9 LITRES OR 38 CUPS WATER

500 GRAMS OR 2¼ CUPS + 3 TABLESPOONS SUGAR

500 GRAMS OR 1 POUND BREWING MALT (AVAILABLE ONLINE)

1 TEASPOON BEER YEAST (AVAILABLE ONLINE)

Put the heather in a large pan, cover with half the water and boil for 15 minutes. Strain into a fermenting bin and add the sugar and malt. Stir to dissolve. Add the rest of the water and cool to lukewarm. Add the yeast (check manufacturer's instructions) and cover. Stand for 5 days and bottle into screw-top bottles. Ready to drink after 7 days.

. . . .

Midsummer Incense

4 PARTS FRANKINCENSE

2 PARTS RED SANDALWOOD

1 PART HEATHER FLOWERS

½ PART CALENDULA PETALS

½ PART CHAMOMILE FLOWERS

Blend together and burn on charcoal.

Honeysuckle

Lonicera spp.

· · · · · · · · · · · · ·

PLANETARY RULER: Jupiter

ELEMENT: Earth

ASSOCIATED DEITIES: Ceridwen, fairies, Pan

MAGICAL VIRTUES: Binding, protection,
love, lust, counter magic

There are around 150 species of honeysuckle native to the northern latitudes of North America, Europe, and Asia. Most of them are hardy climbers, some evergreen, some deciduous, some with a compact growing habit, and some wildly rampant. They are found wild in many places and have even become an invasive nuisance in some areas. However, they are beautiful, come in a variety of colours, and most of them have deliciously scented tubular flowers, followed by orange or red berries.

Most of honeysuckle's folk names and folklore come from its climbing habit, winding itself around other trees, shrubs, fences, or walls in order to climb towards the light. The wild honeysuckle in the UK is called Woodbine or Woodbind for this reason. It always binds and grows in a clockwise direction, and this sunwise spiral growing habit gives it magical properties.

This winding and binding habit made honeysuckle a symbol of constancy and devotion, the bonds of love, or even of erotic desire. Honeysuckle was thought to give young girls sensual dreams, and concerned mothers in the English Fenlands banned it from the house "or a wedding would follow shortly."[71] Unsurprisingly, it was used in love spells and magic. In Sussex boys bound a growing hazel twig with honeysuckle, and after several months the wood would be found twisted like barley sugar, and when this was cut off the tree, it would provide a magic wand that would ensure success in love (and lust). Conversely, carrying honeysuckle is said to help you forget a lover.

It was very much associated with witchcraft, both protecting against the attentions of evil witches and being used by them. On the dangerous time of May Day, when witches, fairies, and all kind of sprites were believed to be abroad, it was placed on the cattle shed and dairy to protect the cows, butter, and milk. In Scotland it was a barrier to all witches and stopped them entering the house or cattle shed, as the Scots rhyme says:

> The ran-tree an' the widd-bin
> Haud the witches on come on in.[72]
> (The rowan tree and the woodbind
> Holds the witches coming in.)

The widd-bin (honeysuckle) twig would be wound round a ran-tree (rowan) and put over the cattle byre door.

The protective nature of honeysuckle also made it a cure for the evil eye, which would be effected by passing a wreath of honeysuckle over the body from head to foot. However, using such a charm could lay the user open to accusations of witchcraft. In 1597 Janet Stewart was charged with using witchcraft "by taking ane garland of green wood-bynd, and causing the patient to pas thyrsi throw it, thereafter she cut it in nine pieces and cast it into the fire."[73]

Not surprisingly, it was also used in binding spells. In *The Ballad of Willie's Lady*, it was used to stop the lady in question giving birth when a witch put woodbine outside her bedroom. Once the binding plant was removed, she gave birth naturally.[74]

Like other witch plants, it was unlucky to bring it indoors. From Scotland to Dorset, it was believed to bring sickness with it. However, grown in the garden, it brought luck and money.

---

71 Watts, *Elsevier's Dictionary of Plant Lore.*

72 J. M. McPherson, "Primitive Psychology," in Warren R. Dawson (ed.), *The Frazer Lectures* (Macmillan, 1923).

73 Rorie, *Folk Tradition and Folk Medicine in Scotland.*

74 Watts, *Elsevier's Dictionary of Plant Lore.*

The honeysuckle is very attractive to bees, and old lore has it that honeysuckle rubbed inside a hive will stop the bees from leaving. Country folk would use the juice to ease bee stings. Insects often burrow into the base of the flower tubes in search of honey.

MAGICAL USES

The sun-loving honeysuckle follows the path of the solar disc from east to west during the day. It is a herb that helps connect to the cycles of life, accepting change. **Honeysuckle Tea** or honeysuckle flower essence is taken to invite higher guidance and obtain a wider perspective, letting go of the past and what is no longer necessary.

Honeysuckle is a herb of spiritual immortality, reflecting the ebb and flow of life and death. Because of this, it can be used at various points of the wheel, from the celebration of lusty Beltane with aphrodisiac **Honeysuckle Wine** through to the fresh flowers used at Midsummer and Lughnasa and incense at the rite of the harvest and the underworld entrance of Samhain.

Honeysuckle can be used in incenses to invoke or honour the god Pan.

It is a herb of protection. Grow honeysuckle around your door, use in incense and protection oils, or carry a herbal talisman.

The stems are used in binding spells, wrapped around an image of the person you wish to bind from doing further harm; it is used for preventing harm only.

CULINARY USES

As children, we used to sneak into the garden and surreptitiously suck the "honey" from the honeysuckle as a tiny sweet treat. If you want to try it, pluck a flower, including its little green base (calyx). Holding the flower, tug on the calyx and pull, drawing the threadlike stamen backwards through the flower. There will be a tiny bit of "honey" on the tip.

The stems, leaves, and berries of most varieties of honeysuckle are slightly toxic and will give you a stomach upset if you try to eat them. However, all the flowers are edible.

The flowers can be made into **Honeysuckle Tea**, used as a garnish for salads and desserts, or made into honeysuckle syrup that can be added to cocktails and poured over desserts such as ice cream. They can also be made into **Honeysuckle Jelly**.

The flowers are used to flavour some botanical gins, and you can make your own **Honeysuckle Gin** or vodka. **Honeysuckle Wine** is fragrant and delicious—the perfect summer's evening tipple.

COSMETIC USES

Honeysuckle is antibacterial and anti-inflammatory and has long been used to treat irritated and reddened skin. It is rich in antioxidants that protect the skin against the free radical damage that causes signs of aging. Use **Honeysuckle Coconut Balm** or gently massage **Macerated Honeysuckle Oil** into your skin or add it to your homemade creams.

To improve the tone and texture of the skin and combat uneven tone and dullness, use a honeysuckle facial steam or a **Honeysuckle Exfoliant**.

Use **Macerated Honeysuckle Oil** as a warmed oil treatment for dry, flyaway hair, or rub **Honeysuckle Coconut Balm** into frizzy and split ends.

MEDICINAL USES

Only use the flowers internally. They contain salicylic acid (like aspirin) and have pain-killing and anti-inflammatory actions. **Honeysuckle Tea** may be taken for headaches. For rheumatism, drink **Honeysuckle Tea** or pour a stronger infusion of honeysuckle into a warm bath and soak away your aches and pains.

Honeysuckle is antispasmodic and helps with the coughing spasms of croup and bronchitis. It may be used as a treatment for coughs, colds, sore throats, and catarrh. Try a teaspoon of **Honeysuckle Glycerite** or **Honeysuckle Tea**. **Honeysuckle Electuary** is antiseptic, reduces coughing spasms, and is good for sore throats.

As a treatment for chilblains, gently warm some **Macerated Honeysuckle Oil** and rub it into your hands or feet to improve circulation.

Honeysuckle is antiseptic. As a first-aid treatment for bites and stings, crush up some honeysuckle leaves and flowers, apply them directly to the affected area, and cover with a clean cloth.

Honeysuckle Tea is cooling for menopausal hot flushes or try a spoonful of **Honeysuckle Electuary**.

Caution: Most varieties of honeysuckle berries, stems, and leaves are slightly toxic and if consumed in sufficient amounts will upset the gastrointestinal tract and induce vomiting and diarrhoea. Skin contact with honeysuckle can cause a rash in sensitive people. To be on the safe side, avoid medicinal quantities of honeysuckle during pregnancy and breastfeeding, and for two weeks before surgery.

Recipes

MACERATED HONEYSUCKLE OIL

Pack a clean glass jar with honeysuckle petals. Cover them with vegetable oil (use a light oil like almond, grapeseed, or jojoba). Fit the lid. Leave on a sunny windowsill for 4 weeks, shaking daily. Strain off the oil into a clean jar. If you like, you can strain this off onto fresh flowers and repeat the process for a stronger smelling oil. Will keep in a cool, dark place for 6–12 months. This is good for chilblains or can be used as a treatment for dry hair.

HONEYSUCKLE COCONUT BALM

HANDFUL OF HONEYSUCKLE FLOWERS
2 TABLESPOONS SOLID COCONUT OIL

In a double boiler or slow cooker, melt the coconut oil and add the honeysuckle flowers. Simmer gently for 40 minutes. Strain the oil off into wide-necked jars. Label. Will keep around a year. Good for irritated and reddened skin.

HONEYSUCKLE GLYCERITE

Half fill a glass jar with honeysuckle flowers, then slightly warm some glycerine in the microwave and pour it over the flowers. Leave for 2 weeks in a cool, dark place, shaking daily. Slightly warm the mixture again and strain the glycerine through a sieve into a clean jar. Will keep for 6–12 months. Take a teaspoon as needed for coughs, colds, sore throats, tonsillitis, bronchitis, and hot flushes.

. . . .
HONEYSUCKLE ELECTUARY

Pack a jar with fresh flowers. Slightly warm some honey in the microwave and pour it over the flowers. Leave for 2 weeks, slightly warm the honey again, and strain the honey through a sieve into a clean jar. Discard the flowers. Will keep 1–2 years. Take a teaspoon as needed for coughs, colds, sore throats, tonsillitis, bronchitis, and hot flushes

. . . .
HONEYSUCKLE WINE

2 LITRES OR 8⅓ CUPS COLD WATER

1 LITRE OR 5 CUPS HONEYSUCKLE BLOSSOMS

1.4 KILOS OR 6¾ CUPS SUGAR

1 LITRE OR 5 CUPS GRAPE JUICE

JUICE OF 2 LEMONS

300 ML OR 1 CUP BLACK TEA

1 TEASPOON WHITE WINE YEAST (AVAILABLE ONLINE)

1 TEASPOON WINE YEAST NUTRIENT (AVAILABLE ONLINE)

In a fermenting bin, pour cold water over the honeysuckle blossoms. Add the sugar, grape juice, and lemon juice and stir well. Fit the lid. The next day, add the black tea, the yeast, and nutrient according to manufacturer's instructions. Fit the lid and ferment for seven days in a warm place, stirring daily. Strain into a demijohn, fit an airlock, and leave in a warm place to ferment out (when the bubbling in the airlock stops completely—this may take several months). Siphon into a clean demijohn and leave to clear for 4–6 weeks. Siphon into sterilised bottles. Store as you would any other wine.

. . . .

Honeysuckle Tea

250 ML OR 1 CUP BOILING WATER

1 TEASPOON DRIED OR 2 TEASPOONS FRESH HONEYSUCKLE FLOWERS

Pour the water over the flowers and cover. Infuse 10 minutes, strain, and drink hot or cold. Drink for headaches or menopausal hot flushes.

. . . .

Honeysuckle Jelly

440 ML OR 1¾ CUPS APPLE JUICE

2 TABLESPOONS LEMON JUICE

225 GRAMS OR 1 CUP SUGAR

20 HONEYSUCKLE FLOWERS, PETALS ONLY

Put the apple and lemon juice in a pan. Add the sugar and stir until dissolved. Add the flowers and boil till setting point. Strain into sterilised, warm glass jars.

. . . .

Honeysuckle Gin

1 BOTTLE GIN (OR VODKA IF YOU PREFER)

HANDFUL OF HONEYSUCKLE FLOWERS

In a jug, pour the gin over the fresh honeysuckle flowers, cover, and leave to infuse for 24 hours. Strain and rebottle the gin.

. . . .

Honeysuckle Exfoliant

Use powdered dry honeysuckle flowers mixed with ground almonds and honey (or a little water) as a facial exfoliant scrub.

. . . . .

Horsetail

Equisetum arvense

· · · · · · · · · · · · · ·

PLANETARY RULER: Saturn

ELEMENT: Earth

ASSOCIATED DEITIES: Smith gods

MAGICAL VIRTUES: Survival, endurance,
protection, past-life work, magical smithcraft

Most people see horsetail as an intractable weed, and indeed, it is impossible to eradicate. However, the horsetail is an amazing ancient plant with some wonderful properties.

Horsetails have existed for more than 400 million years and have barely changed during that time. They are found on all land masses except Australia. Though the *Equisetum arvense* now grows between 20–40 cm (8–16 inches) high, millions of years ago its relatives grew up to 30 metres (100 feet) tall. Horsetails survived the Permian-Triassic mass extinction event, which took Earth 30 million years to recover from. We can learn a lot from its powers of survival and endurance.

Horsetail is a gymnosperm, or non-flowering plant, which spreads through spores released by fertile stems. These grow up in spring to be replaced later in the season by the distinctive segmented sterile stalks, which look like green bottle brushes; the name *equisetum* means "horse bristle," while the Romans called it "hair of the earth."

The mature plant contains high amounts of silica (about 30 percent), and the plant becomes very hard when dried. This has a number of uses. Cabinet makers used it as a very fine sandpaper. It was historically used for the polishing of tools, wood, and other utensils. This gave it its folk names Pewterwort, Shave Grass, or Scouring Rush. The burnt ash of horsetail contains 80 percent silica; made into a paste with a little water, it makes an excellent silver polish. The plants were sold on the streets of eighteenth-century London for polishing.

Horsetail infusions are fungicidal and effective in treating mildew and blackspot on roses. Its antiseptic properties make it valuable as a pan scourer, particularly useful when camping. Before the advent of detergents and disinfectants, horsetail ferns were gathered by dairymaids and used to scour milk pails and dairy equipment.

It has long been used as a healing herb. Ancient Greeks and Romans used it to staunch bleeding, heal ulcers and wounds, and treat tuberculosis and kidney problems.

MAGICAL USES

Horsetails shared the earth with dinosaurs and survived a mass extinction. That is powerful magic that teaches us about endurance and adaptability when facing difficult and trying situations. It can be employed in spells, incenses, amulets, and pouches for strength and protection. It can also be used in workings designed to connect with the long-distant past. Take **Horsetail Tea** prior to meditation or past-life work.

As a herb of Saturn, horsetail can be used in workings for endings and letting go.

Use horsetail to clean and polish magical tools, particularly metal ones, and give them magical strength and endurance.

CULINARY USES

Horsetail contains important vitamins and minerals. The young spore stems that appear in spring were eaten by the Romans as a tonic salad. They can be dressed like asparagus, boiled, or coated with flour and fried.

COSMETIC USES

Horsetail contains a large amount of bioavailable silica, which the body uses to build and maintain healthy collagen, connective tissue, and skin. It also contains smaller amounts of bioavailable calcium and other minerals such as potassium, manganese, sulphur, and magnesium. It stimulates hair growth and shine and boosts collagen and skin elasticity. It is a healing astringent when used in the bath or creams and lotions.

Try a rinse of **Horsetail Tea** for hair shine and strength, or massage **Horsetail Tincture** into your scalp to promote hair growth. As a split ends treatment, mix a few drops of tincture with coconut oil and brush it through your hair, leave it for 2–3 hours, and wash out.

Dab strong **Horsetail Tea** or use **Horsetail Nail Oil** on weak and split nails to strengthen them and help remove ridges. **Horsetail Bath** is good for reducing cellulite. Add some horsetail infusion or a few drops of **Horsetail Tincture** to your bath.

Medicinal Uses

The high silica content of horsetail is water soluble and readily available to the body. It is good for weak and broken bones, pulled tendons, osteoarthritis and rheumatoid arthritis weak skin, hair and nails, helps rebuild connective tissues and stimulates the production of bone cells. Take in the form of **Horsetail Tea**, **Horsetail Tincture** or horsetail syrup for no longer than one week.

Horsetail has some pain-relieving and anti-inflammatory effects and may help ease the pain of arthritis when taken in the form of **Horsetail Tea**, **Horsetail Tincture** or syrup, or applied externally as a fresh poultice.

Chemicals in horsetail have an astringent effect that may lessen bleeding when applied directly to minor injuries such as cuts and scrapes. You can apply **Horsetail Tea** to the affected areas or add a stronger infusion to the bath. When applied to infected wounds, in the form of a compress, it helps them release pus and damaged cells.

Horsetail has a mild diuretic action and helps cleanse the kidneys without exhausting them as it replaces the minerals it helps excrete. It has been used to treat bladder, kidney, and urinary tract infections. Taken for no longer than one week, **Horsetail Tea** may relieve swelling due to the excess accumulation of water in the body.

Macerated Horsetail Oil made may be used externally in the treatment of ear infections (otitis), with a few drops dripped into the ear.

Use **Horsetail Decoction** in baths and footbaths to treat sprains.

> *Caution:* *Do not use an incorrect species (the marsh horsetail, Equisetum palustre, contains poisonous alkaloids). The external use of horsetail is considered safe for most people, but there are some cautions for internal use. Horsetail is toxic to grazing animals if they eat very large amounts as it contains thiaminase. However, this is destroyed by heat. Do not eat large quantities of horsetail. Do not take for longer than two weeks. Horsetail is known to block the absorption of thiamine, one of the B vitamins. Do not take if you have low vitamin B levels; if it is taken for too long, a thiamine deficiency is possible. Horsetail increases urination; avoid if you are taking prescription diuretics. Do not take at the same time as herbal or prescription laxatives. Horsetail can lower blood sugar, so treat with caution if you are on diabetic medication. Do not take if you are on antiretroviral drugs. Avoid if you have heart or kidney problems. Do not use if you are an alcoholic. As with any herb, do not use medicinal amounts if you are pregnant or breastfeeding.*

• • • • •

Recipes

Horsetail Tea

250 ML OR 1 CUP BOILING WATER

1 TEASPOON DRIED OR 2 TEASPOONS FRESH HORSETAIL

Pour boiling water over the herb. Infuse 15–20 minutes. Strain. Take for arthritis for no longer than 2 weeks. Dab onto nails to strengthen them.

Horsetail Decoction

1 TABLESPOON DRIED HORSETAIL

2 CUPS WATER

Put in pan, bring to boil, then simmer until the liquid is reduced by half. Use in the bath to treat sprains.

Incontinence Tea

10 GRAMS OR 2 TEASPOONS DRIED HORSETAIL

10 GRAMS OR 2 TEASPOONS DRIED BORAGE LEAVES

25 GRAMS OR 5 TEASPOONS DRIED MALLOW LEAVES

Grind the herbs together but not to a powder. Store in an airtight container for one year. Allow 2 teaspoons per cup, infuse in a boiling water for 5 minutes, strain, and drink. Two cups a day will help strengthen the bladder. Do not take for more than one month.

. . . .

Horsetail Tincture

HORSETAIL STEMS

VODKA OR BRANDY

Put the stems and vodka into a blender and whizz them up. Pour into a clean glass jar, label, and place somewhere cool and dark for 4–5 weeks, shaking daily. Strain into clean dropper bottles. Label. Store in a cool, dark place for 2–4 years. Take for arthritis for no longer than 2 weeks.

. . . .

Horsetail Bath

1 LITRE OR 4 CUPS BOILING WATER

100 GRAMS OR 8 TABLESPOONS FRESH HORSETAIL

Pour the water over the herb and infuse for 60 minutes. Strain and add the liquid to a warm bath and soak for aches, pains, rheumatism, and gout, or to treat cellulite.

. . . .

Horsetail Foot Rub

100 GRAMS OR 8 TABLESPOONS FRESH HORSETAIL

100 ML OR 7 TABLESPOONS RUBBING ALCOHOL

Put the herb in a jar and pour the alcohol over it. Fit the lid. Infuse for 3 weeks, shaking daily. Strain the liquid into a clean bottle. This is good and cooling to rub onto sore and sweaty feet.

. . . .

Horsetail Skin Toner

HORSETAIL STALKS, FRESH

WITCH HAZEL

Put the crushed stalks in a jar and cover with witch hazel. Fit the lid. Leave 2 days and strain the liquid into a clean jar. Will keep 12 months.

. . . . .

. . . .

Macerated Horsetail Oil

Pack a glass jar with crushed horsetail stems. Cover with vegetable oil. Fit the lid. Leave on a sunny windowsill for 2 weeks, shaking daily. Strain the oil into a clean jar. Label. Will keep 6–12 months. Use to boost collagen and skin elasticity or on arthritic joints.

. . . .

Horsetail Nail Oil

HANDFUL OF FRESH HORSETAIL, CRUSHED

GRAPESEED OR ALMOND OIL

Pound the horsetail in a pestle and mortar, put into a glass jar, and cover with the oil. Fit the lid. Leave in a cool, dark place for 2 weeks, shaking daily. Strain the oil into a clean jar and label. Using a cotton pad, rub this into dry, flaking nails daily to strengthen them. Will keep 6–12 months.

Houseleek

Sempervivum tectorum

· · · · · · · · · · · · · · ·

PLANETARY RULER: Jupiter

ELEMENT: Air

ASSOCIATED DEITIES: Jupiter, Thor, Zeus

MAGICAL VIRTUES: Protection, luck, love, aphrodisiac

The houseleek is a hardy evergreen perennial succulent thought to be a native of the Greek islands. It has a fibrous root that will cling to many surfaces, including roofs. The house-leek grows in rosettes with fleshy wedge-shaped leaves with red-brown tips. The plant produces numerous rosettes that develop roots and later become separate plants. Some of the rosettes are extended outwards by smooth runners. Very occasionally pinky-purple flowers are borne on an erect stem that is covered with scale like leaves. Its common name is derived from the Anglo-Saxon word *leac*, meaning "leek"—a name given to all members of the onion family by the Saxons (though it is not a member of this family).

According to legend, the houseleek was *diopetes*, a gift from the god Zeus/Jupiter as a protection against thunder, lightning, and fire, properties that also brought it under the protection of the Norse god Thor and earned it the folk name Thor's Beard. The emperor Charlemagne (748–814 CE) said that every dwelling must have one to protect it. He demanded that all farmers and tenants on the imperial estates should grow houseleek on their roofs as a protection against evil, pestilence, fire, and war. It was this command that spread the houseleek throughout Europe. In France it brings luck to the house if it grows on the roof. In Sussex it was unlucky to remove a houseleek from a roof, as that would bring trouble. During the Middle Ages the belief persisted that a houseleek growing on the roof would keep the home safe from lightning. In Wales it was understood that a houseleek grown in the garden will protect the home from violent storms. Culpeper said it preserved whatever it grew upon from thunder and lightning and was "as good as a fire insurance."[75] The poet John Clare declared that "no cottage ridge about us is without these as Superstition holds it out as a charm against lightning."[76] In Ireland, if it grows on a thatch, it will protect the occupants from fire, burns, and scalds, as long as it is not touched. Because of these associations, it was a sovereign remedy against burns and scalds. In Scotland it was put on burns as a poultice.

In Somerset houseleek was believed to protect against witches. On the Isle of Man, it was encouraged to grow near the door for the same reason. It is a symbol of domestic industry, vivacity, and long life for the inhabitants. The flowering stalks hung over stable doors in the form of a cross would protect the animals within.

The Greek botanist Theophrastus recorded the presence of the houseleek in the fourth century BCE. It was regarded by the ancient Greeks as an aphrodisiac. A Breton belief was that if a man put a houseleek in his pocket and a girl smells it, she will desire him. To attract love, carry the leaves of the houseleek about the person and renew every few days.

Magical Uses

The houseleek can make a good plant friend and ally and will give protection to those in its sphere of influence. You can grow it on the roof of the house, shed, or garage, cracks in pavements, rock gardens, or in pots and baskets by the front door.

Use it in incenses, oils, and workings for thunder gods such as Jupiter, Zeus, and Thor to invoke their protection.

Houseleek can be used in love spells and herbal talismans, added to incense and oils, and used to anoint candles.

Culinary Uses

The fresh leaves and young shoots can be eaten in salads. Use in a drinking water infusion for a refreshing taste.

---

75 Culpeper, *Culpeper's Herbal.*
76 Watts, *Elsevier's Dictionary of Plant Lore.*

Cosmetic Uses

Houseleeks provide a healing gel that has many similar properties to aloe vera and makes a viable alternative. Houseleek gel helps skin repair and regeneration, moisturises and firms the skin, and can be used in anti-aging preparations. It also has a mild skin-lightening effect and can be used in creams to treat age spots on the hands. Try the **Houseleek Coconut Balm** below.

Houseleek leaves are cooling and astringent. **Houseleek Tea** may be used as a skin toner or houseleeks may be added to your homemade skin toners. Add the leaves to a facial steam or to your bath.

Medicinal Uses

The houseleek is regarded by herbalists as one of the safest treatments for inflammations, burns, scalds, swellings, bruises, cuts, stings, bites, and ulcers, with similar properties to aloe vera. The bruised leaves of the fresh plant or its juice can be applied as a poultice to burns, scalds, bruises, and inflammatory conditions of the skin. Choose a thick, fleshy leaf and remove it from the plant. It can be peeled or pressed and applied directly to the affected area. Treat cysts and corns with crushed leaves applied directly to them.

Drink or gargle with **Houseleek Tea** for sore throats, mouth ulcers, mouth infections, and bronchitis. Try a houseleek electuary for oral thrush. Use in a salve for burns, scalds, and skin inflammations.

Caution: Large doses taken internally are emetic.

Recipes

HOUSELEEK TEA

1 TEASPOON FRESH HOUSELEEK LEAVES

250 ML OR 1 CUP BOILING WATER

Pour boiling water over the herb and infuse for 10 minutes. Strain and drink for sore throats, mouth ulcers, mouth infections, and bronchitis.

HOUSELEEK COCONUT BALM

2 TABLESPOONS COCONUT OIL

1 TABLESPOON CRUSHED HOUSELEEK LEAVES

In a double boiler or slow cooker, simmer the oil and leaves for 40 minutes. Strain the oil into a clean glass jar and label. Use for scalds, bruises, and inflammatory skin conditions. Keeps around a year.

English Ivy

Hedera helix

. . . .

PLANETARY RULER: Saturn

ELEMENT: Water

ASSOCIATED DEITIES: Ariadne, Arianrhod, Attis, Bacchus,
Bran, Ceridwen, Christ, Cissia, Cronos, Dionysus, Feronia,
Gorgopa, Hercules, Hymen, Isis, Kundalini, Lakshmi, Mars,
Osiris, Pan, Persephone, Priapus, Psyche, Rhea, Saturn, Zeus

MAGICAL VIRTUES: Changing consciousness, prophecy,
vision, rebirth, regeneration, initiation, Yule

Scrambling up walls, trees and the faces of houses, ivy is a tenacious climbing plant that attaches itself very firmly to whatever it grows up, producing aerial roots along its stems that change shape to fit the surface of whatever it climbs. Tiny root hairs grow out from the root with hook-like structures on the ends and fit themselves into any tiny cavities within the climbing surface. There, they dry out, scrunching into a spiral shape that locks the root hair into place. They will stay attached even when the plant dies.[77] No wonder ivy was an ancient symbol of loyalty, devotion, undying desire, and friendship beyond the grave.

Most of ivy's other symbolic associations come from the fact it is an evergreen, flowering late in the year and staying alive and vibrant throughout the winter while other plants

---

77   http://news.bbc.co.uk/earth/hi/earth_news/newsid_8701000/8701358.stm.

around it lie dead or dormant. This made it a sign of life continuing and hope for the future. The ancients thought that evergreens had magical powers that enabled them to withstand the cold and dark, and they were used in rituals and decorations around the winter solstice to encourage the return of light, warmth, and life. At the Roman Saturnalia, a winter solstice festival of peace and joy that temporarily re-created the Golden Age when the god Saturn ruled on earth, holly and ivy were employed for decorations, rituals, and gifts. The early Christian author Quintus Tertullian (155–220 CE) tried to ban the practice as a Pagan custom. When that didn't work, the church was forced to reinterpret it by making the holly a Christian symbol of the crown of thorns, though it continued to try prohibiting ivy from decorations as being too Pagan.

That obviously didn't work either, as we still use holly and ivy in our decorations today, and one of our oldest and best-known carols is "The Holly and the Ivy." The pairing of the holly and ivy was seen in the old Christmas custom of the Holly Boys and Ivy Girls, who played games of forfeits and sang uncomplimentary songs about each other in a good-natured battle of the sexes. However, there were taboos remaining. Holly and ivy were only brought in on Christmas Eve; in Guernsey it invited disaster for any ivy to come into the house before then. In Cambridgeshire it was even unlucky to accidentally bring in ivy with the firewood at any time other than Christmas Eve. As an ornament, ivy was only placed in out-of-the-way parts of the house such as passageways or it would bring bad fortune. The ivy was never to be left up after Twelfth Night, and it was always burned to dispose of it, as any other method of clearance would court catastrophe.

The ivy was an important sacred plant for our Pagan ancestors. It begins to grow on the ground but then climbs the nearest tree, spiralling around it, heading towards the light. This associates the plant with the path of the sun since the path of the sun during the year appears to be a spiral one. Any plant with a spiral growth pattern was thus considered a plant that reflected the immortal nature of the sun, which goes into the underworld at night but is reborn each morning and which dwindles in the winter but is reborn at the winter solstice.

As a plant of the sun, ivy was used to make fire. The Greeks thought that fire should come from an ivy stick struck into a laurel groove, a union of the two genders, the active male (ivy) being brought into the passive female (laurel). Pliny wrote of ivy as a warm wood suitable for fire.

The ivy was especially sacred to death and resurrection vegetation gods such as Dionysus, Bacchus, Attis, Liber, and Osiris; in Christian allegory it symbolised the eternal life and the resurrection of Christ. For this reason, ivy is sometimes included in the costumes of the Jack in the Green figures that appear in folklore festivals in spring or the green men carved in churches. Ivy leaves were depicted on the sarcophagi of early Christians as a symbol of eternal life. On All Souls' Day, Catholics lay ivy on the tombs of the dead to signify the immortality of the soul as well as love and friendship beyond the grave.

Ivy was a plant of fertility. It has five-pointed leaves representing the creative hands of the earth goddess Rhea. Its connection with fecundity persisted in popular belief right into the early twentieth century. Because of its special powers, church ivy saved from Christmas was a fertility charm, fed to ewes to induce the conception of spring lambs, or a woman might keep an ivy leaf from the Christmas decorations to encourage the birth of twins.

In classical mythology the ivy and the grapevine were often paired. The Greeks viewed ivy as a kind of primordial grapevine.[78] Though they are both climbing plants, with similar shaped leaves and closely related mythologies, the grapevine causes drunkenness, while wearing ivy was believed to prevent it. The ivy was beloved of the god Zeus, whose priests avoided wine and instead consumed ivy in order to prophesy. The wine god Dionysus wore a crown of ivy, and the Maenads ("Raving Ones"), his female votaries, carried the thyrsus (an ivy-entwined staff) and draped in the skins of animals, abandoned themselves to orgiastic dancing and singing during their celebrations. At the revels of Thrace and Thessaly, drunken Maenads, wreathed in ivy, would rampage in the mountains, tearing animals and sometimes people apart in their intoxication, having eaten ivy leaves and berries to heighten the state of ecstasy. The legendary musician Orpheus was torn to pieces by the Maenads, who had drunk a concoction of ivy and toadstool. However, all this is a bit of a mystery, as ivy is not psychoactive and to date, no inebriating substances have been found in ivy. The gods and Maenads were certainly depicted wearing the kind of ivy we recognise, so perhaps taking a sacrament of the god was enough for the Maenads, without any chemical stimulation from the ivy, to believe that he was within them, "nor need its possession be considered something detrimental, like drugged, hallucinatory, or delusionary: but possibly instead an invitation to knowledge or whatever good the god's spirit had to offer."[79] All else was beer, wine, and mushrooms.

---

78   Troy Markus Linebaugh, "Shamanism and the Ancient Greek Mysteries: The Western Imaginings of the 'Primitive Other,'" https://etd.ohiolink.edu/apexprod/rws_etd/send_file/send?accession=kent1512462129881859&disposition=inline.

79   Ruck and Staples, *The World of Classical Myth*.

In England, right up to the time of Shakespeare, an ivy bush was the sign of a tavern. Wearing ivy leaves as a garland was thought to prevent the ill effects of drunkenness. An old hangover cure was made by simmering ivy leaves in wine and drinking the mixture.

Ivy's strength, durability, and immortal nature made it a suitable plant to form the crowns of victors in ancient Greece. Alexander the Great returned from his victory in India wearing an ivy crown. Many deities were depicted wearing ivy crowns, including Pan, Hercules, Feronia, Priapus, and Chiron. Calliope, the muse of epic verse, wore an ivy wreath, suggesting a connection between the inspirational nature of the plant and poetry. Classical poets wore ivy garlands to signify everlasting fame. Even in the twentieth century, crowns of ivy were presented to the winners of the first revived Eisteddfods, the festivals of bards that still takes place in Wales.

Ancient Greek newlyweds wore wreaths of ivy, as the clinging nature of the plant and the evergreen leaves made it a symbol of constancy and eternal love. It was used to decorate the altars of Hymen ("joiner"), the Greek god of marriage. In the Victorian language of flowers, ivy signified "I choose thee above all" and was featured in popular love spells and divinations right into the twentieth century. To find whom she would marry, a girl might use the following charm:

> *Ivy, ivy, I love you*
> *In my bosom I put you*
> *The first man who speaks to me*
> *My future husband he will be.*

Its use in love charms may stem partly from the fact that the juvenile leaves are heart shaped, only developing into five lobes as they grow.

Because of its magical nature, ivy featured in many charms. In Shropshire, for example, children with whooping cough drank from ivy wood cups to cure them, and at least one wood turner did a roaring trade in vessels for the purpose. Wreaths of ivy with rowan and woodbine were placed near milk containers to protect the contents from invading sprits. In Germany, when the cows were put out to their summer pastures, they were each given wreaths of ivy. It was believed that anyone who wore ivy on May Eve would have the power to recognise witches. However, it was very unlucky to pluck an ivy leaf from a church wall and invited illness.

Ivy leaves were used in divination. In Cornwall on Twelfth Night, an ivy leaf was passed through a ring for each member of the family, then put in water. The next day the leaves were examined and the future of each person judged from their condition; a stain on the leaf in the shape of a coffin meant death. In a similar practice, an ivy leaf was placed in water on New Year's Eve and left till Twelfth Night. If the leaf stayed green, it meant the year would be happy. If the leaf turned black, it indicated illness; if decayed, it foretold death. At Halloween in Wales, ivy leaves were gathered, the pointed ones considered males and rounded ones, female. One of each would be named for a couple. When they were thrown into the fire, if they jumped together, the parties would be married; if they jumped apart, it meant antipathy. In Wales the state of ivy growing on the wall was also significant. If it withered, it meant that the property would pass into the hands of strangers through lack of heirs.

The ivy is sometimes seen as the female companion to the male grain spirit at harvest time. In England the last sheaf to be cut was bound with ivy and called the Ivy Girl. The farmer who was last in with his harvest was given the Ivy Girl as his penalty and it represented bad luck until the following harvest.

Though ivy worries some gardeners and homeowners, it is not parasitic and will not damage a healthy tree. On a house it does not damage the fabric of the building but can provide a natural insulation that has the added benefit of removing toxins from the air. Try to appreciate the benefits of ivy: its nectar-rich flowers feed bees and other insects late in the season, and its berries provide food for birds throughout the winter.

Magical Uses

Ivy is protective. Grow ivy up your garden walls or on the house to safeguard your property. Have a hanging basket with ivy near your front door or hang an ivy wreath on it.

At the Autumn Equinox, the invoking priestess might wear a chaplet of ivy and the cut corn be tied with strands of the plant.

Decorate your altar with ivy during the dark time between the Autumn Equinox and Yule to house the continuing life force of the spirits of nature.

Ivy is a traditional decoration at Yule time. At Yule it represents the power of rebirth and the sun god reborn at the winter solstice. He might be called forth with a wand entwined with ivy and topped with a fir cone.

At Ostara ivy can be used in incenses and in rituals of death and resurrection vegetation gods such as Osiris, Bacchus, and Dionysus.

At Beltane it is used on Green Man masks and figures of the God are crowned or wreathed in ivy and new greenery.

Ivy represents the path of the sun and the labyrinthine dance of life with its spiral growth and the spiral arrangement of leaves. In the journey of initiation, the spiral is a double one; inward towards the self, then outward to share the knowledge amongst the others we meet in the dance. Ivy is also the change of consciousness that takes place at initiation, bringing with it the gifts of prophecy and vision. It teaches the lesson of sacrifice; the old self must be left behind or "die" before a spiritual rebirth can take place. Use it in chaplets, decorations, and incense.

Culinary Uses

None.

Cosmetic Uses

Ivy is used in commercial bath preparations and massage creams. At home the primary cosmetic use of ivy is in the treatment of cellulite, the orange peel appearance of skin that dimples thighs and other body parts. Ivy can be used in poultices, compresses, creams, and lotions to treat the condition. Use **Ivy Infusion** in your bath. The macerated oil or an ivy ointment can also be used with massage to help disperse the toxins and accumulated fluid that accompanies cellulite.

Ivy tightens the skin of your face too. Try using the **Ivy Skin Tightening Wash** and follow with the **Ivy Skin Toner**.

The leaves may be made into a soothing ointment to relieve sunburn—make a macerated oil and thicken with wax.

Medicinal Uses

Though ivy featured in ancient and mediaeval herbalism for breathing problems and is still used by the pharmaceutical industry in some cough remedies, it is not recommended in internal preparations at home because of its slight toxicity. Stick to using ivy for external remedies only.

The leaves may be made into a soothing lotion or salve for tired muscles. Pour some **Ivy Infusion** into a warm bath and soak. A poultice or compress of ivy leaves has some pain-relieving qualities when applied to the affected part in cases of neuralgia, rheumatism, and neuritis.

An ivy leaf poultice applied to an infected wound will draw the pus from it.

An **Ivy Infusion** may be used as a hair rinse for treating headlice.

Ivy Skin Toner can be rubbed on your temples to relieve headaches.

If you have mould growing inside your home and it is causing you problems, wash the paintwork and walls with an **Ivy Infusion** and grow ivy as a pot plant, as it will reduce the incidence of mould by as much as 78 percent, according to research presented to the American College of Allergy, Asthma & Immunology.[80]

> **Caution:** *For external use only. Ivy is mildly toxic when eaten and can cause vomiting, abdominal pain, and diarrhoea. The berries are more poisonous than the leaves, but both contain toxic compounds. Contact with ivy can cause skin reactions in those who are sensitive.*

---

80   https://www.webmd.com/allergies/news/20051107/english-ivy-fix-allergies.

Recipes

Ivy Infusion

12 FRESH IVY LEAVES

250 ML OR 1 CUP BOILING WATER

Pour boiling water over the leaves. Cover and leave to infuse for 20 minutes. Strain. NB: Not for internal use.

Ivy Skin Tightening Wash

8 FRESH IVY LEAVES OR 2 TABLESPOONS DRIED IVY LEAVES, CRUMBLED

2 TABLESPOONS BOILING WATER

3 TEASPOONS ROSEWATER

1 TABLESPOON LINSEED SEEDS

Pour the water over the leaves and infuse for 2 hours. Strain and reserve. Meanwhile, warm the rosewater in a double boiler. Turn off the heat. Add the linseed and leave 2 hours. Strain and combine both liquids. Pat on the skin of the face and neck. Leave 15 minutes. Rinse off with clean water.

Ivy Skin Toner

125 ML OR ¼ CUP ROSEWATER

5 IVY LEAVES, CRUSHED

Make a cold infusion by putting the crushed ivy leaves in a bowl and covering them with rosewater. Leave overnight, then strain the liquid into a clean bottle. Keep in the fridge for up to 10 days.

. . . .

IVY LAUNDRY LIQUID

A FEW HANDFULS OF IVY LEAVES, CHOPPED

WATER TO COVER

Put the ivy in a large pan and cover with water. Simmer, with the pan lid on, for 20–25 minutes. Strain off the liquid. Discard the leaves. You can use the ivy liquid for handwashing clothes or simply add a cupful to your washing machine. Ivy contains saponins (soap) and will make a good job of washing your clothes without the nasty chemicals of washing powder. NB: Do not wash your dishes with this as, if ingested, ivy is slightly toxic and may upset your stomach.

. . . .

CELLULITE WRAP

HANDFUL FRESH IVY LEAVES

HANDFUL FRESH HORSETAIL SHOOTS

Mash the fresh herbs, apply directly to the skin, and cover with a warm cloth.

. . . .

CELLULITE OIL

75 ML OR 5 TABLESPOONS GRAPESEED OIL

10 LARGE IVY LEAVES

FEW DROPS GRAPEFRUIT ESSENTIAL OIL (OPTIONAL)

Put the ivy into a glass jar and cover with the oil. Fit the lid. Leave on a sunny windowsill for 2 weeks, shaking daily. Strain into a clean jar and add the essential oil. Massage the oil into the affected areas of your skin daily, after your shower or bath.

. . . . .

Jasmine

Jasminum spp.

· · · · · · · · · · · · ·

PLANETARY RULER: Moon/Jupiter

ELEMENT: Water

ASSOCIATED DEITIES: Artemis, Diana, Ganesha,
maternal aspects of the Goddess, Quan Yin,
Virgin Mary, Vishnu, Zeus, Kamadevi

MAGICAL VIRTUES: Positivity, sensuality,
aphrodisiac, luck, love, beauty

Jasmine is a name that covers many tropical and subtropical plants of the genus *Jasminum*, mostly native to the Himalayas, Iran and northern India. The most commonly grown in gardens are *Jasminum officinale* with fragrant white blossoms, and the larger flowered *Jasminum grandiflorum*.

The name jasmine derives from the Persian word *yasmin*, meaning "gift from God," indicating just how highly the plant is valued for its intoxicating, heady perfume. In China the scent is thought to be that of heaven. The Persians used jasmine oil to fragrance the air at banquets, and the ancient Egyptians employed the scent in cosmetics and baths. Arab traders introduced jasmine to Europe's budding perfume industry, where it soon became very popular. Perfumers and aromatherapists call jasmine "the king of flowers" (as opposed to the rose, which is "the queen") as the dark essential oil has a faintly animal scent, classified as male.

The perfume is sensual and often claimed as an aphrodisiac; for this reason, it has many connections with love and marriage. In folklore to dream of jasmine is good fortune for lovers. In India it is sacred to Kamadevi, the god of human desire, particularly sexual desire. At Hindu weddings the bride-to-be wears a garland of jasmine and roses around her neck as a symbol of purity and passion. In some Indian wedding traditions, the groom wears a veil of jasmine in front of his face. In Italy jasmine is often woven into bridal wreaths.

In the Western symbolism of flowers, jasmine represents purity, modesty, amiability, and virginity, which might seem strange given its aphrodisiac reputation, but the white flower is small and of modest size. In Renaissance Italy the pure white jasmine blooms became associated with the purity of the Virgin Mary, and jasmine flowers are shown in many religious paintings. It has a similar reputation in China, where it is associated with the feminine and womanly sweetness. In Thailand jasmine represents motherhood and signifies love and respect.

MAGICAL USES

Though modern Pagans generally place jasmine under the dominion of the moon, the famous seventeenth-century astrologer herbalist Culpeper describes it as a "warm, cordial plant, governed by Jupiter in the sign of Cancer."

Divination by smoke (capnomancy) is performed by throwing jasmine seeds into fire and watching the direction of the smoke. A thin, straight plume of smoke indicates a good omen whereas large plumes of smoke are a bad sign. If the smoke touches the ground, immediate action must be taken to avoid catastrophe.

The incense smoke of jasmine flowers can be directed around the aura, boosting it after depletion incurred during illnesses or emotional stress. It also gives psychic protection to the aura.

The intoxicating scent of the flowers is most powerful in the evening and is said to be even stronger during a waning moon. The exotic, heady scent not only lifts the spirits but helps to dissolve emotional barriers. Jasmine has a reputation as an aphrodisiac, and the oil or incense can be used for creating a relaxed, romantic, sensual atmosphere. Use the oil for a couples' massage.

Add the dried flowers to love sachets and incenses. Use **Macerated Jasmine Oil** to anoint a pink candle for a love spell. Dreaming of jasmine portends good fortune, especially in love.

Take **Jasmine Tea** before meditation or drink before bed to promote psychic dreams. Apply **Macerated Jasmine Oil** to the third eye to open the Sight.

Culinary Uses

A syrup made of jasmine flowers is used as a flavouring agent in the food industry. At home jasmine flowers can be used to flavour beverages, ice cream and sorbets, sweets, cakes, cookies, jellies, and puddings.

Perhaps the best-known culinary use of jasmine is the delicate aromatic **Jasmine Tea**.

For jasmine rice, add **Jasmine Tea** or a jasmine tea bag to the water your rice is cooked in.

Cosmetic Uses

Jasmine is wonderful for the skin, increasing its elasticity, softening and moisturising, and decreasing the appearance of wrinkles. It is suitable for all skin types but especially sensitive and aging skin. Add a **Macerated Jasmine Oil** to your homemade skin preparations such as moisturising creams and lotions or apply it neat to your face and allow it to absorb for 10 minutes before wiping off with a cotton cloth.

Use **Jasmine Hydrosol** as a skin toner or substitute it for the water part of a homemade cream.

To relax and nourish the skin of your body, rub in **Macerated Jasmine Oil** or use it in a sensual body massage. It will also help relieve conditions like sunburn and skin rash.

Indian women often use jasmine oil to scent and condition their hair. Give your hair a treat and use **Macerated Jasmine Oil**, slightly warmed and brushed through the length of your hair. Wrap your head in a warm towel and leave for 30–60 minutes before washing and conditioning as usual. If you have dry hair or frizzy ends, brush a little jasmine oil through.

Medicinal Uses

The flowers and sometimes the leaves are used to make medicine.

Jasmine is antispasmodic. A cup of **Jasmine Tea** aids digestion and may help relieve flatulence, abdominal pain, diarrhoea, dyspepsia, and irritable bowel syndrome.

Jasmine Tea has sedative effects on the nervous system and promotes peaceful sleep. Take a cup when you are feeling stressed or before bed.

Jasmine is also antiseptic and used in the treatment of cuts and wounds. Use a decoction of the leaves or apply the bruised fresh leaves directly as a poultice. **Jasmine Tea** can also be used externally as a wash to treat cuts and scrapes.

Jasmine Tea has anti-inflammatory properties that help reduce aches and pains related with arthritis or joint pain. Massaged into the affected area, **Macerated Jasmine Oil** can be used for treating rheumatism.

Jasmine flowers can be soaked overnight in cold water and the strained water used as eyewash to treat swelling, inflammation, and reddening of the eye.

A compress dipped in jasmine infusion and applied to the forehead can be soothing for headaches.

> **Caution:** *Make sure you identify your species of jasmine correctly. Some plants are called jasmine but are not members of the* Jasminum *species at all, and some of these are toxic. Jasmine is an emmenagogue (stimulates menstruation) and therefore should not be used during pregnancy. The scent of jasmine can worsen some migraines.*

Recipes

Aura Protection Incense

1 PART DRIED JASMINE FLOWERS

2 PARTS FRANKINCENSE

Combine the ingredients and burn on charcoal. Direct this into the aura of the subject with a feather.

Jasmine Face Pack

4 TEASPOONS AVOCADO OIL

6 TEASPOONS COSMETIC CLAY

4 TEASPOONS ALOE VERA GEL

6 FRESH JASMINE FLOWERS

Put all ingredients in a blender and whizz up. Apply as a face pack. Leave 20 minutes and rinse off with warm water. Finish with a cold rinse and moisturise as usual. Will keep for one week in the fridge.

Macerated Jasmine Oil

Pack a clean glass jar with fresh jasmine flowers and cover with a fine vegetable oil such as grapeseed. Fit a lid. Leave on a sunny windowsill and shake daily for 2 weeks. Strain off the oil to a fresh jar packed with jasmine flowers and repeat the process. This can be repeated several times until you have the strength of perfume you require. Finally, strain the scented oil into a clean bottle and label. Will keep 6–12 months. Use for a sensual massage.

. . . .

JASMINE TEA

1 TEASPOON JASMINE FLOWERS

½ TEASPOON GREEN OR BLACK TEA

250 ML OR 1 CUP BOILING WATER

Using *Jasminum officinale*, *Jasminum sambac*, or *Jasminum polyanthum* flowers, infuse together with tea and water in a covered pot for 10 minutes. Strain and drink.

. . . .

JASMINE BODY SCRUB

200 GRAMS OR 1 CUP GRANULATED SUGAR

15 GRAMS OR 3 TEASPOONS DRIED JASMINE FLOWERS

10 DROPS JASMINE ESSENTIAL OIL (OR OTHER OIL OF YOUR CHOICE)

120 ML OR ½ CUP GRAPESEED OIL

1 TABLESPOON VEGETABLE GLYCERINE

Combine all the ingredients and spoon into a pretty jar. Massage into your skin well and rinse off in the shower. Will keep 12 months.

. . . .

JASMINE HYDROSOL

To make a homemade distilled jasmine hydrosol, take a large pan and put a metal trivet on the bottom of it. Pack your flowers around it (but not on it) and add just enough distilled water to cover them. Put a small heatproof bowl on top of the trivet. Bring the water to boil. Now place a large heatproof bowl on top of the big saucepan and fill it with ice cubes. This will cause the rising steam to condense back into water droplets and drop back down onto the small bowl. (Add more ice if it starts to warm up.) Simmer for a while before carefully removing the pan from the heat and taking out the small bowl—there will be some condensed liquid in it. Allow it to cool. The condensed water is jasmine hydrosol (flower water).

Lavender

Lavendula spp.

PLANETARY RULER: Mercury

ELEMENT: Air

ASSOCIATED DEITIES: Cernunnos,
Circe, Hecate, Medea, Saturn

MAGICAL VIRTUES: Midsummer, love, apotropaic

In summer my front garden is covered in fluffy mounds of blooming purple lavender, welcoming visitors to my door with their sweet scent and attracting thousands of busy bees to their nectar. I love to stroke the flower heads to release the perfume, and I know these plants are going to supply me with many useful products when I harvest them.

The genus name *Lavendula* comes from the Latin *lavare* and means "to wash," which explains its ancient purpose. The Greeks, Romans, and Carthaginians all used lavender in bathing water for both its scent and its therapeutic properties. By the early Middle Ages, washerwomen were known as "lavenders" for their practice of spreading clothes to dry upon lavender bushes and for scenting the clean clothes in storage with dried lavender flowers. The fragrance and insect-deterring properties made it a popular household herb. Throughout the Middle Ages it was a common strewing herb (fragrant herbs scattered onto the floors of rooms to perfume the air and keep down dust and pests). Lavender flowers were also placed in linen cupboards to deter moths and keep away flies. In 1387 Charles VI of France had lavender-stuffed cushions. Today we still use the dried flowers in sachets to freshen stored linen and deter moths and insects from attacking it or we use it as a general air freshener in potpourri.

Lavender has been used in medicine since ancient times. The physician to the Roman army, Dioscorides, wrote that lavender taken internally would relieve indigestion, sore throats, and headaches, while externally it cleansed wounds. During the thirteenth and fourteenth centuries it was grown extensively in monastery gardens for its medicinal properties. The mediaeval glove makers of Grasse used liberal amounts of lavender oil to scent leather, and it was rumoured that they seldom caught the plague, so people began to carry posies of lavender to ward off disease. Lavender was a component of the legendary Four Thieves Vinegar, which was alleged to prevent plague. According to the story, four thieves claimed the vinegar they had invented allowed them to burgle the houses of plague victims without catching the infection themselves.

Lavender was strewn on the floors of churches to ward off the plague and protect churchgoers. In the seventeenth century lavender was found in most herbals as a cure-all. The great English herbalists of the time, Gerard, Parkinson, and Culpeper, all wrote about lavender and the treatments that could be made from it, making medical knowledge available not just to the wealthy but to anyone who could afford to buy a book. Many country homes kept a bottle of lavender oil for aches and pains, bruises and burns. Lavender flowers soaked in gin or brandy were a popular farmhouse remedy for many ailments, while harvesters wore a sprig of lavender in their hats to prevent headaches caused by the sun. During the Second World War, lavender oil was still being used as an antiseptic swab on wounds in hospitals.

Lavender was widely used in love magic. The Bible tells us that Judith wore perfume containing lavender to seduce Holofernes before killing him. Prostitutes wore lavender to arouse sexual desires in men, and lavender was used in love spells and divinations. In Tudor times, young girls would sip lavender tea and chant, "St. Luke, St. Luke, be kind to me; in my dreams let me my true love see." Alpine girls would tuck some lavender under their sweetheart's pillow to make their thoughts turn to romance, and wives would secrete lavender under the mattress to ensure marital passion and harmony.[81] On the other hand, a sprig of lavender carried along with a sprig of rosemary preserved chastity.

As well as averting disease, lavender was used to avert evil. Crosses of lavender could be hung over the door for protection, while in Spain and Portugal lavender was included in bonfires on St. John's Day (Midsummer's Day) to ward off wicked spirits. In Tuscany a

---

81   https://yourehistory.wordpress.com/2014/07/19/folklore-in-my-garden-lavender.

sprig of lavender pinned to one's shirt warded against the evil eye. In Sardinia lavender was combined with rue in small bags of fabric and worn around the neck, next to the skin, for protection.[82] In Wales wearing a sprig of lavender drove off witches and ghosts.

Sacred to the Greek witch goddess Hecate and her witch daughters Medea and Circe, lavender also played its part on magic and witchcraft. Carrying or inhaling the scent of lavender was said to enable one to see ghosts.

MAGICAL USES

Lavender is a potent magical plant that purifies and cleanses. A lavender infusion may be used in the washing of ritual robes and equipment, added to the pre-ritual bath, or used for cleaning down the temple. This will remove negative influences and attachments.

Lavender Tea, incense, or oil brings inner stillness and peace during meditation.

Burn lavender incense or have **Lavender Wands** or bowls of lavender around to bring about peace and harmony during meetings and gatherings.

Dried lavender flowers may be burned as an incense in workings and rituals that explore the element of air, to develop the intellect and powers of logical thought. Dab the oil on the forehead or inhale the scent from the flowers for the same purpose.

Lavender can be thrown onto the solstice fire as an offering to the Old Gods and drive off negativity, as it is one of the sacred aromatic herbs of Midsummer.

It may be added to love incense, oils, sachets, charm bags, or love spells. Lavender posies are given to newly married couples to bring luck for the future and make pretty handfasting gifts. A posy of lavender may be carried by the handfast bride. Lavender is a good addition to the handfasting cake.

Lavender attracts fairies, elves, and nature spirits. Plant lavender in the garden or have lavender potpourri in the house.

Lavender is worn in charm bags as protection against the evil eye. For protection, hang an equal-armed lavender cross over your door. Wipe **Macerated Lavender Oil** around your door and window frames.

Lavender has underworld connections and may be used to honour underworld Cernunnos and crone/witch aspects of the Goddess, including Hecate, Circe, and Medea.

---

82 Sabina Magliocco, "Witchcraft, Healing and Vernacular Magic in Italy in Witchcraft Continued," https://doi.org/10.7765/9781526137975.00012.

CULINARY USES

Lavender can be used in cooking, especially cakes, biscuits, ice creams and desserts such as creme brulée, but the secret is to be very, very sparing with it. Rather than added lavender flowers, try using **Lavender Sugar** instead, as this will be much more subtle.

Try using a lavender syrup in cocktails and smoothies, lemonade or in vodka. Try **Lavender Gin** for an interesting floral tipple.

COSMETIC USES

A bathing herb since Roman times, lavender is still used commercially in perfumes, cosmetics, and soaps. Lavender is a gentle ingredient that helps skin heal and renew itself, fights wrinkles, and promotes the production of collagen. Its antibacterial properties help prevent acne. Add **Macerated Lavender Oil** to your homemade cosmetics or use lavender in skin washes, toners, lotions, and creams. Use **Lavender Hydrosol** as a skin toner.

Lavender is a natural deodorant. Make a lavender bath bag by putting lavender flowers into a muslin bag and dropping it into the water. Or, after washing them, rub **Macerated Lavender Oil** on feet that tend to sweatiness.

Using a lavender infusion as a final rinse for your hair or rubbing **Macerated Lavender Oil** or **Lavender Tincture** into your scalp may help prevent hair loss.

MEDICINAL USES

For centuries lavender has been used as a treatment for inflamed skin and skin conditions such as eczema, dermatitis, psoriasis, rashes, and irritation. Try **Lavender Salve** or **Macerated Lavender Oil** to protect the skin and provide deep moisture to cracked and red skin while reducing inflammation.

Lavender is an antiseptic that also aids wound healing whilst minimising scarring. For minor cuts, wash with a lavender infusion. Apply **Lavender Salve** to cuts, bruises, burns, and skin irritations.

Lavender has a soothing effect on the central nervous system, combined with mild pain relief. Take **Lavender Tincture** or **Lavender Tea** to sooth nervous tension, mild depression, tension headaches, nervous debility, exhaustion, stress, and insomnia or to act as a mild sedative before bedtime.

Lavender is antifungal. A strong lavender infusion can be used as a mouthwash for oral thrush. A lavender infusion douche can be used as a treatment for vaginal infections, especially Candida-type yeast infections.

Lavender is antispasmodic and helps promote the production of bile needed for digestion. **Lavender Tea** can help some digestive issues, such as bloating, indigestion, flatulence, and colic.

Drink **Lavender Tea** or use a lavender steam treatment for respiratory disorders like throat infections, cough, cold and flu; just put a few flowers in a bowl of boiling water and inhale the steam. This helps open up the airways while the antibacterial and anti-inflammatory properties of lavender treat the problem.

Lavender Tea can be taken as a general tonic and immune booster to fight off colds and flu, as it contains antioxidants and antibacterial compounds as well as vitamin C, calcium, and magnesium.

Caution: Lavender is considered safe for most adults in food amounts and probably safe when taken orally, applied to the skin, or inhaled in medicinal amounts, though it can cause irritation and headaches in some individuals. Do not use medicinally or use the essential oil if you are pregnant or breastfeeding, for two weeks before surgery, or if you are taking barbiturates. Do not use lavender essential oil on prepubescent boys. People with sensitive skin may find it irritating. Do not take in combination with other sedative or anticonvulsant drugs.

Recipes

Lavender Biscuits

115 GRAMS OR ½ CUP BUTTER

200 GRAMS OR 1 CUP SUGAR

2 EGGS

½ TEASPOON DRIED LAVENDER FLOWERS, GROUND

200 GRAMS OR 1¼ CUPS PLAIN (ALL-PURPOSE) FLOUR

2 TEASPOONS BAKING POWDER

½ TEASPOON SALT

Preheat the oven to 190°C (375°F). Cream the butter and sugar. Gradually add the eggs a little at a time. Fold in the lavender, flour, baking powder, and salt. Drop a teaspoonful at a time onto a baking sheet. Bake for 10 minutes.

Lavender Sugar

To make lavender-flavoured sugar, layer dried lavender buds and sugar in a jar and let it sit in a dark place for about a month. Sift out the lavender buds and enjoy your sugar in delicately flavoured cakes, custards, and tea.

Macerated Lavender Oil

This is simply made by placing fresh or dried lavender flowers in a jar, covering them with oil, and leaving for a couple of weeks in a dark place, shaking daily. Strain the oil onto fresh flowers and repeat. You can do this several times until the scent is as strong as you would like it, then strain into a clean bottle, label, and keep in a dark place. Will keep for 6–12 months. Use directly on your skin or add to homemade cosmetics.

. . . .

LAVENDER SALVE

Once you have your macerated oil (see above), turn it into a salve by adding beeswax or soy wax. In a double boiler, gently warm the oil. Add the wax and melt. The more wax you add, the firmer the set will be. Pour into warm glass jars. Apply to cuts, bruises, and skin irritations.

. . . .

LAVENDER COCONUT SALVE

Put some solid coconut oil and fresh or dried lavender flowers into a double boiler and simmer very gently for an hour (or you can use a slow cooker for this). Strain into clean jars and label. Apply to cuts, bruises, and skin irritations.

. . . .

LAVENDER GIN

500 ML OR 2½ CUPS GIN

3 SPRIGS LAVENDER

Pour the gin into a bottle and add the fresh lavender. Seal and leave at room temperature for 1–4 days, depending on how strong you would like the lavender flavour. Strain into a clean bottle, discarding the lavender.

. . . .

LAVENDER TINCTURE

Pack a jar with lavender flowers, covering them with vodka or brandy. Fit the lid. Leave for 2–3 weeks, shaking daily. Strain the liquid off into a clean bottle and label. This will keep 2–5 years. May help nervous tension. Take a few drops in a glass of water as a medicinal dose. Alternatively, a few drops may be added to a salve or bath for external use.

. . . .

LAVENDER TEA

250 ML OR 1 CUP BOILING WATER

2 TEASPOONS FRESH LAVENDER BUDS

Put in a teapot (or covered cup) and leave to infuse for 10 minutes. Strain and drink for nervous tension and before bed to aid natural sleep.

. . . . .

. . . .

LAVENDER HYDROSOL

To make a homemade distilled lavender flower hydrosol, take a large pan and put a metal trivet on the bottom of it. Pack your flowers around it (but not on it) and add just enough distilled water to cover them. Put a small heatproof bowl on top of the trivet. Bring the water to boil. Now place a large heatproof bowl on top of the big saucepan and fill it with ice cubes. This will cause the rising steam to condense back into water droplets and drop back down onto the smaller bowl. (Add more ice if it starts to warm up.) Simmer for a while before carefully removing the pan from the heat and taking out the small bowl—there will be some condensed liquid in it. Allow it to cool. The condensed water is lavender hydrosol (lavender water). You can use this as a skin toner, to cleanse small wounds, or add to homemade cosmetics.

. . . .

LAVENDER AFTERSHAVE

Pack a clean jar with lavender flowers and cover them in witch hazel. Leave for 2 weeks, shaking daily. Strain the liquid into a clean bottle. Add a teaspoon of vegetable glycerine. You can add a drop or two of essential oil of your choice if you wish. This makes a soothing, healing aftershave.

. . . .

LAVENDER & ROSE POTPOURRI

1 PART DRIED LAVENDER FLOWERS

1 PART DRIED ROSE PETALS

½ PART DRIED SCENTED GERANIUM LEAVES

½ PART ORRIS ROOT POWDER

FEW DROPS LAVENDER ESSENTIAL OIL

GROUND CINNAMON

WHOLE CLOVES

Dry your flowers on paper for a few days. Mix the ingredients and seal together in a large jar for at least one month before using.

. . . . .

Lavender Shoe Deodoriser Bags

1 TABLESPOON BICARBONATE OF SODA (BAKING SODA)

1 TABLESPOON ARROWROOT POWDER

6 TABLESPOONS DRIED LAVENDER FLOWERS

SMALL CLOTH BAGS (SUCH AS WEDDING FAVOUR BAGS)

Mix the soda and arrowroot powder. Add the lavender flowers and mix well. Fill the bags with the mixture and pop one into smelly trainers, shoes, and boots. NB: Instead of purchased bags, you could use old stockings and socks.

Lavender Reed Diffuser

1 TABLESPOON LAVENDER FLOWERS

2 TABLESPOONS ISOPROPYL ALCOHOL

10 DROPS CEDAR ESSENTIAL OIL

10 DROPS CYPRESS ESSENTIAL OIL

1 TABLESPOON DEIONISED WATER

NARROW-NECKED BOTTLE

RATTAN REED STICKS

Put the lavender flowers in a jar with the isopropyl alcohol. Fit a lid. Infuse on a sunny windowsill for 3 weeks, shaking daily. Strain into your narrow-necked bottle with the rest of the ingredients. Put in the reed sticks.

Lavender Linen Bags

COTTON FABRIC

NEEDLE AND THREAD

DRIED LAVENDER FLOWERS

Cut an oblong of fabric and fold it over. Sew up two sides. Fill the cavity with dried lavender flowers and sew up the remaining side. You can make these any size you wish. Small ones are good placed in linen and underwear drawers to freshen your laundry and deter insects, while a larger one can be used as a sleep pillow.

. . . .

Lavender Heat Wrap

Lavender Flowers, Dried

Cotton Fabric

You can make this any size or shape you wish. Sew up the lavender in the fabric. Place the bag in the microwave for 1½–2 minutes (be careful not to overheat) and apply to any painful area of your body.

. . . .

Lavender Wands

Long Lavender Stalks

Narrow Ribbon

Strip the leaves from lavender stalks. Tie the stalks together just below the heads. Holding the flower heads in one hand, bend the stems back down over the flower heads, covering them. These will form a basket over the top of the flowers, encasing them and keeping them in. Take the ribbon and begin to weave it in and out of the basket, over and under the stems, until the basket of stems and ribbon completely encloses the flowers. Wrap the rest of the ribbon around the stems and tie it off. Trim the end of the ribbon and the stalks.

. . . .

Lavender Bath Bombs

1 TABLESPOON DRIED LAVENDER FLOWERS

1 TABLESPOON CITRIC ACID POWDER

3 TABLESPOONS BICARBONATE OF SODA (BAKING SODA)

FEW DROPS LAVENDER ESSENTIAL OIL

SPRAY BOTTLE OF WATER

In a bowl, mix the dry ingredients and essential oil with a metal spoon. Spray in water a tiny bit at a time until the mixture just sticks together (this will take less than you think). Shape into balls or put in moulds and leave overnight to dry out.

Lilac

Syringa spp.

. . . .

PLANETARY RULER: Venus

ELEMENT: Water

ASSOCIATED DEITIES: None

MAGICAL VIRTUES: Renewal, apotropaic,
warding, banishing, death, mourning

The sweet scent drifting across the evening air in the garden tells me that my lilacs are starting to bloom—a brief gift, as they only flower for two or three weeks. To me there is something in it that stirs the blood, for the lilacs are a sign of renewal and the year opening up, and the perfume carries with it the promise of things to come—the drone of humming bees, lazy, balmy days, and the taste of heady lilac wine.

Lilacs (*Syringa* spp.) are found in old gardens all across Britain, America, and Europe, so we think they have always been with us, but both the common lilac (*Syringa vulgaris*) and the smaller Persian lilac (*Syringa persica*) were only introduced into northern European gardens in the sixteenth century from Ottoman gardens, and the name *lilac* comes from the Arabic word *lilak*, which means "dark blue." The plant was certainly not known by the Celts and Greeks, despite what I occasionally read on the internet, and even in sixteenth-century Europe it was a rarity, though the English herbalist John Gerard was able to obtain some specimens and wrote about them in 1597. Lilacs quickly became immensely popular and were carried by colonists to the Americas in the eighteenth century.

The genus name *Syringa* comes from the Greek word *sirinx*, which means a "pipe," referring the pith-filled stems—pipes and flutes used to be made by hollowing out the stems of wood or reeds, and our word *syringe* (another hollow tube) comes from the same root. In 1753 the botanist Carl Linnaeus bestowed the genus name on the plant based on this attribute of pith-filled stems. Sadly, it doesn't come from an ancient association of lilac and the Greek nymph called Syrinx who was transformed into reeds to save her from the amorous attentions of the god Pan, from which he created his famous Pan pipes, the syrinx. This story refers to reeds, and there is no ancient association of Pan, Syrinx, and the lilac, as lilacs were unknown in classical Greece. It turns out that the lilac is not good for making flutes either as the limited size of the shrub makes it only suitable for making very small woodwork projects, and even then the wood has a tendency to twist and crack as it dries.

The lilac has heart-shaped leaves, and this, along with the sweet scent, associated it with love. In the Victorian language of flowers, by which sweethearts could pass coded messages to each other, the giving of a lilac was meant to be a reminder of an old love; widows often wore lilacs. In modern lore, each lilac colour has its associations. According to the International Lilac Society, white is purity, innocence, and childhood; violet is spirituality; blue is happiness and tranquillity; a pale purple is first love; magenta is love and passion; pink is love and friendship; and a dark purple is for mourning.

However, the older folklore is somewhat different. In Britain taking lilac flowers indoors was considered unlucky and meant to "take death into the house" from its association as a funeral flower since strong-scented flowers and herbs were often used to cover up the scent of death and decay. The colour purple associates it with mourning.

It was used for apotropaic (evil repelling) purposes in many places. In Bulgaria it was included in wedding bouquets to protect the bride, and in Russia it was hung above cradles to safeguard infants.[83] In New England lilacs were planted to keep evil away from properties or used to drive out ghosts.

MAGICAL USES

Lilac is used by modern witches for warding magic. To protect your home, plant a lilac near your door, place vases of lilac flowers in the windows, or use **Macerated Lilac Oil** as a pro-

---

83   Zoja Karanovic and Jasmina Jokic, "Plants and Herbs in Traditional Serbian Culture," *Handbook of Folk Botany*, https://www.scribd.com/document/353639787/Zoja-Karanovic-Jasmina-Jokic-Plants-And-Herbs-In-Traditional-Serbian-Folk-Culture-I-pdf.

tective barrier smeared around the beading of your window frames. To prevent negativity entering your door, scatter lilac petals on the doorstep.

Just as the energy of spring drives away the gloom of winter and brings regeneration to the land, the spring-blooming lilac drives away negative energies, replacing them with the power of renewal and new beginnings. When you are trying to shake off situations and feelings that drag you down or hold you back, the energy of lilac can help. Take **Lilac Flower Essence** or a cup of **Lilac Tea** to unblock stuck energies, shake off your hibernation, and move into new growth and self-realisation.

CULINARY USES

While lilac flowers are edible, they are astringent, so eating too many will dry your mouth out and taste slightly bitter. If you want to use them, as with all perfumed flowers, they can be overwhelming, and a little is better than a lot. Use as an edible garnish on cakes, ice cream, and cocktails. You can also add a small number of fresh flowers into the batter of cakes, scones, and cookies, but too much may be unpleasant. One of the best ways to use them is to make **Lilac Sugar** to add to your baking, a **Lilac Syrup** to pour over ice cream or use as a base for cocktails, or make **Lilac-Infused Honey** to use in baking, teas, and drinks. You can crystallize the flowers for later use as a decoration on biscuits and cakes.

COSMETIC USES

The delicious scent of lilacs is often found in cosmetics, soaps, and toiletries. Sadly, it is usually a synthetic perfume that is used since a true lilac flower essential oil is not available. This is a great shame because lilac has wonderful benefits for the skin and hair. It contains antimicrobial substances, antioxidants, has anti-inflammatory effects, stimulates cell regeneration, and helps repair oxidative damage.

To combat skin aging, slow the development of age spots and hyperpigmentation, and stimulate cell renewal, add some **Macerated Lilac Oil** to your homemade moisturiser recipes or apply the oil directly to your skin.

Lilac flowers and leaves are astringent, tightening and slightly drying the skin, which can be useful for oily, acne-prone skin. Make the **Lilac Toner** below or just cleanse your face with **Lilac Infusion**.

Lilac is a great tonic for your hair and scalp. Massage **Lilac Infusion** into your scalp to strengthen your hair at the roots and help eliminate dandruff.

Medicinal Uses

Lilac is rarely used in modern herbalism, though in the past it was used for digestive problems such as dyspepsia, flatulence (excess gas), and diarrhoea, parasitic worms and malaria, and by folk herbalists for headaches, cough, colds, and skin diseases.

Lilac Tea makes a good after-dinner digestive.

A **Lilac Compress** can be applied to sprains and bruises.

Lilac flowers are very soothing—to de-stress and unwind, just add a few flowers to your bath (pop them into a muslin bag to save mess), inhale the released perfume, and relax.

> **Caution:** *Do not use internally if taking medicines that alter blood coagulation or during pregnancy or lactation. Do not use the bark as it can be toxic.*

Recipes

LILAC TONER

LILAC BLOSSOMS

WITCH HAZEL

Fill a glass jar with lilac blossoms that have been picked on a dry, sunny day. Cover the flowers with witch hazel. Allow to infuse for 2 weeks, shaking daily. Strain into a clean jar and label. Will keep at least 6 months. After cleansing your skin, apply your lilac toner on a cotton pad. Follow with your usual moisturiser. This is good for oily and acne-prone skin.

LILAC INFUSION

2-3 LILAC FRESH FLOWER HEADS, FLOWERS ONLY

250 ML OR 1 CUP BOILING WATER

Put boiling water over the flowers. Infuse 15 minutes. Strain. Add it to your bath or massage into your scalp to stimulate hair growth.

MACERATED LILAC OIL

Pack a glass jar with lilac flowers. Cover with vegetable oil (sunflower, olive, etc.). Leave to infuse for 2–3 weeks, shaking daily. Strain into a clean bottle. You can make the scent stronger by infusing the oil a second, third, and fourth time. Use as a facial, body, or hair oil or add to any of your homemade bath or skin recipes that call for a carrier oil. It is regenerative for the skin and combats age spots and uneven pigmentation.

Lilac Infused Honey

Half fill a clean jar with freshly picked flowers. Warm your honey a little and pour over the flowers. Fit the lid. Infuse for a month. You can strain this by warming the honey a little again and pouring the honey through a sieve into a clean jar. Use this for baking, in tea, or take a spoonful as an after-dinner digestive.

Lilac Sugar

To make lilac-flavoured sugar, layer fresh lilac flowers and sugar in a jar and let it sit in a dark place for a day. Sift out the flowers. Use the sugar for baking.

Lilac Wine

3½ LITRES OR 14¾ CUPS LILAC FLOWERS

4 LITRES OR 16¾ CUPS WATER

1100 GRAMS OR 5½ CUPS GRANULATED SUGAR

YEAST NUTRIENT (AVAILABLE ONLINE)

JUICE OF 2 LEMONS

WHITE WINE YEAST (AVAILABLE ONLINE)

Put the flowers into a fermenting bin or plastic bucket with a lid. Boil the water and pour over the flowers. Cover and infuse for 48 hours. Strain the infused liquid into a demijohn. Add the sugar, yeast nutrient, and lemon juice and stir until completely dissolved. Sprinkle the yeast on top or according to manufacturer's instructions. Fit an airlock and leave to ferment out (until the airlock stops bubbling completely) before siphoning off into a clean demijohn. Leave this to clear for at least 6 months. Siphon off into bottles and store as you would any other wine.

· · · · · ·
Lilac Tea

2 TEASPOONS FRESH LILAC FLOWERS

250 ML OR 1 CUP BOILING WATER

Pour boiling water over the flowers. Infuse 15 minutes, strain, and drink, adding a little honey if desired. This makes a good after-dinner digestive.

· · · · · ·
Lilac Gin

Fill a large jar with lilac flowers. Cover with gin. Infuse for 24 hours only, as your gin will take on an unpleasant taste if left for longer. Strain into a clean bottle.

· · · · · · · · · ·
Lilac Compress

For bruises, strains, and muscle aches, make a lilac infusion as above. Prepare a clean cotton cloth and soak it in the hot herbal infusion. Use this as warm as possible on the affected area (take care and do not burn yourself). Cover with a warm towel, leave for 30 minutes, and change the compress as it cools down. Use 1–2 times a day.

· · · · · · · ·
Lilac Syrup

1 LITRE OR 4 CUPS WATER

250 ML OR 1 CUP LILAC FLOWERS (FLOWERS ONLY)

50 GRAMS OR ¼ CUP SUGAR

Pour the water over the lilacs and stand overnight. Strain, discarding the flowers, and add the sugar to the retained liquid. Heat gently for 20 minutes (do not boil) and strain again. Keep refrigerated and pour over fruit salads, puddings, and ice cream.

· · · · ·

. . . .

LILAC FLOWER ESSENCE

To unblock stuck energies and move into new growth, gather a few mature lilac flowers. Float them on the surface of 150 ml spring water in a bowl and leave in the sun for 3–4 hours. Make sure that they are not shadowed in any way. Remove the flowers. Pour the water into a bottle and top up with 150 ml brandy or vodka to preserve it. This is your mother essence. To make up your flower essences for use, put 7 drops from this into a 10 ml dropper bottle, and top that up with brandy or vodka. This is your dosage bottle. The usual dose is 4 drops of this in a glass of water 4 times a day. When making flower essences, it is important not to handle the flowers—it is the vibrational imprint of the flowers you want to be held by the water, not your own imprint.

Mallow

Marshmallow (Althaea officinale)
Common Mallow (Malva sylvestris)

. . . .

PLANETARY RULER: Venus, Moon

ELEMENT: Water

ASSOCIATED DEITIES: Venus, Aphrodite

MAGICAL VIRTUES: Lughnasa

While the marshmallow is usually used in medicine and cooking, the common mallow shares many of its qualities and makes an effective alternative. Both plants belong to the *Malvaceae* family, whose members all contain a healing mucilage. The genus name of marshmallow, *Althaea*, is believed to come from the Greek *altho*, meaning "to cure."

Both the common mallow and the marshmallow are tall, hardy, herbaceous perennials, with large velvety leaves. The marshmallow has pink flowers, while the common mallow has slightly larger purple flowers. Both have light brown disk-shaped seeds that are found slotted upright in a ring called a "cheese."

Did you know that the sweet called marshmallow was once made from the candied roots of the marshmallow plant? The kind we buy in the shops is now made from starch, gelatine, and sugar, but real marshmallow roots used to be boiled in sugar and made a chewy sweet, as the root itself contains starch, albumen, sugar, and gelatinous matter. In Lincolnshire it was thought to cure rheumatism. The roots would be collected from the wild along the coast by fishermen's wives to sell at the market. In France the dried roots were sold in pharmacies to be used as teethers for babies—they soften as they are chewed.

On the Isle of Man, mallow was believed to remove illness caused by walking "on bad ground," i.e., walking on ground that belonged to the fairies and thereby invoking their curse. In Germany an ointment of mallow was used to remove "the ill effects of any malicious influence,"[84] meaning a hostile spiritual influence.

A species of althaea was among flower pollens found scattered around the grave of a Neanderthal man who had been buried in a cave in Iraq over 60,000 years ago. Archaeologists speculate that it was placed there to strengthen the man on his journey to the next world.

MAGICAL USES

Mallow has long been associated with love. Mallow root is used in love spells and charms and can be added to love incenses. It can be used in incenses or added to the ritual cup at occasions such as handfastings. The seeds, gathered at the full moon, can be made into an ointment for use in the Great Rite or in tantric magic, or use macerated mallow oil.

A protection salve is made by steeping the leaves in vegetable oil and setting with wax. Rub this onto the skin to dispel negativity and protect from black magic.

The seed should be gathered during the full moon and added to incense for exorcism, protection, and to aid in otherworld journeying.

Marshmallow can be added to the ritual food for the feasting at Lughnasa.

CULINARY USES

Mallow was eaten by the Syrians and mentioned by the ancient writers Pythagoras, Plato, and Virgil. The Romans used it in barley soups and in stuffing.

The young leaves, tops, and flower petals can be added to salads. The leaves can be steamed and served as a vegetable. You can make a soup with mallow leaves, but it is too gloopy for most people. Try **Deep-Fried Mallow Leaves** or add a couple leaves to a bottle of vinegar, infuse for 48 hours, and strain out the vinegar (discarding the leaves) to make your own mallow vinegar.

The seed capsules, called "cheeses," can be nibbled as a snack or added to salads. They have a nutty flavour.

---

84 Watts, *Elsevier's Dictionary of Plant Lore*.

The sweets we call marshmallows once contained marshmallow root. The mucilage contained in the root was thickened in water and heated with sugar to produce a sweet paste. Today these products are artificially made. See below for a recipe for **Real Marshmallows**.

Fresh marshmallow roots can be eaten raw in salads or made into tea. The root can be boiled to soften it and then fried.

COSMETIC USES

Marshmallow is a safe and gentle cosmetic ingredient suitable for all skin types. It is anti-inflammatory, so it is especially good for sensitive, itchy, and irritated skin. It stimulates tissue regeneration. The flowers, leaves, and roots can all be used, though the root has a higher concentration of active ingredients. Add the roots, flowers, or leaves to creams and lotions to moisturise and improve the skin.

Use a marshmallow infusion as a final hair rinse to detangle and nourish hair.

A salve or cream made from the roots is good for chapped hands.

MEDICINAL USES

All parts of the plant can be used. Pick the flowers and use fresh. Pick the leaves before the plant flowers. Roots are harvested from three- to five-year-old plants. While marshmallow is used by herbalists, many of the qualities of the marshmallow are shared by the common mallow, which can provide an effective alternative.

The leaves and roots contain a high level of mucilage, a gelatinous substance that soothes and reduces inflammation throughout the body, internal and external, making it useful for coughs, colds, gastric upsets, dry skin conditions, urinary infections, stomach ulcers, and urinary tract infections. Take **Mallow Leaf Tea** for indigestion, IBS, a dry sore throat, a dry cough, and mild constipation.

Marshmallow root is used in cough sweets and syrups for sore throats—in France it was taken in a sweet paste called pâté de guimauve—and in herbal preparations for peptic ulcers and gastric inflammation.

Applied externally as poultice or salve, mallow root reduces inflammations in infected skin complaints such as boils, ulcers, and abscesses.

The leaves are also a demulcent but less so than the roots. They are slightly astringent and can be used for rashes, boils, bites, and stings. Boil them in water for 5 minutes, then lay over the skin and cover with a warm cloth. You can mash up the leaves and flowers for a poultice.

Use a mallow infusion in hand or foot baths following fractures.

Caution: *Marshmallow or mallow is considered safe for most people when used internally or externally. To be on the safe side, avoid medicinal doses when pregnant or breastfeeding. If you are taking mallow internally, take it for 2 hours before other food or medicine as it may decrease their absorption. Large doses can be a laxative and purgative. It may affect blood sugar levels, so exercise caution if you are diabetic. Avoid for two weeks before surgery or if you take lithium.*

Recipes

Mallow Flower Tea

1 TEASPOON FRESH OR DRIED FLOWERS

250 ML OR 1 CUP BOILING WATER

Infuse together for 5 minutes, covered. Strain and drink as a pleasant floral tea that may aid a sore throat.

Mallow Leaf Tea

2 FRESH OR DRIED LEAVES

250 ML OR 1 CUP BOILING WATER

Infuse together for 5 minutes. Strain and drink for indigestion, IBS, a dry sore throat, a dry cough, and mild constipation.

Mallow Cough Syrup

1 TABLESPOON DRIED MALLOW ROOT

450 ML OR 2 CUPS WATER

340 GRAMS OR 1⅔ CUPS SUGAR

4 TABLESPOONS LEMON JUICE

Simmer the root in the water for 40 minutes. Strain and retain the liquid. Discard the root. Add the sugar to the liquid and simmer for a further 5 minutes. Remove from the heat and add the lemon juice. Pour into a sterilised glass bottle. Will keep in the fridge for 1 month.

. . . .

Real Marshmallows

LARGE HANDFUL FRESH MARSHMALLOW ROOTS, WASHED AND CHOPPED

250 ML OR 1 CUP WATER

400 GRAMS OR 2 CUPS SUGAR

SPICES TO TASTE (GINGER, CINNAMON, CLOVES, ETC.)

Put the roots in a pan and cover them with water. Boil to soften them (about 30 minutes). Drain them and discard the water. Next, mix the 250 ml or 1 cup water and the sugar. Gently heat in a pan until the sugar dissolves. Add the roots and spices and boil until the liquid is reduced and absorbed by the roots. Spoon the roots out onto a drying rack to set. Store in a sealed container.

. . . .

Mallow Gin

600 ML OR 2½ CUPS GIN

100 GRAMS OR ½ CUP SUGAR

600 ML OR 2½ CUPS LEAVES, BRUISED

Mix together the gin, sugar, and mallow leaves in a glass jar. Fit a lid and leave in a dark place for 2 weeks, shaking daily. Strain the liquid over a fresh jar of leaves. Leave 2 weeks, shaking daily. Strain into a clean bottle. Will keep indefinitely.

. . . .

Mallow and Chamomile Compress

10 GRAMS OR 2 TEASPOONS DRIED MALLOW LEAVES

10 GRAMS OR 2 TEASPOONS DRIED CHAMOMILE FLOWERS

100 ML OR 3 TABLESPOONS BOILING WATER

For rashes, boils, bites, and stings, pour the water over the herbs. Infuse until the water goes cold. Strain. Prepare a clean cotton cloth and soak it in the herbal infusion. Use this on the affected area. Cover with a warm towel and leave for 30 minutes, changing the compress as it cools down.

. . . .
Mallow Hand Gel

20 GRAMS OR 4 TEASPOONS DRIED MALLOW ROOT

20 GRAMS OR 4 TEASPOONS DRIED MALLOW LEAVES

200 ML OR ¾ CUP WATER

150 ML OR 10 TABLESPOONS WITCH HAZEL

15 GRAMS OR 3 TEASPOONS GELATINE (AGAR)

Chop the root and put in a pan with the leaves. Add the water. Soak for 4 hours, then turn on the heat and simmer for 10 minutes. Strain. In a double boiler, warm the witch hazel. Add the agar to it. Remove from the heat. Add the mallow liquid and stir. Put in a jar and label. This is very soothing and moisturising for the hands, especially after working in the garden.

. . . .
Mallow Foot Bath

2 LITRES OR 8⅓ CUPS WATER

1 TEASPOON MALLOW FLOWERS

2 TEASPOONS MALLOW LEAVES

1 TEASPOON LAVENDER FLOWERS

½ TEASPOON SAGE LEAVES

Bring the water to boil. Remove from the heat. Add the herbs and cover. Infuse for 15 minutes. Strain the liquid into a bowl large enough to bathe your feet. Soak your feet for at least 15 minutes, adding more hot water as it cools. This soothes, softens, and deodorises.

. . . .
Deep-Fried Mallow Leaves

Simply deep-fry the leaves in hot oil, drain, and serve.

. . . .

Mallow Hand Cream

5 GRAMS OR 1 TEASPOON DRIED MALLOW LEAVES

150 ML OR 10 TABLESPOONS WATER

20 GRAMS OR ¾ OUNCE EMULSIFYING WAX

50 ML OR 3½ TABLESPOONS VEGETABLE OIL

10 GRAMS OR 1-3 OUNCES COCOA BUTTER

Put the mallow in a pan with the water. Simmer 10 minutes. Strain, retaining the liquid. In a double boiler or slow cooker, melt the wax, vegetable oil, and cocoa butter. Add the mallow liquid a little at a time, whisking. Put in a jar and label.

. . . .

Mallow Face Mask

5-6 FRESH MALLOW LEAVES

30 ML OR 2 TABLESPOONS WATER

2 TEASPOONS HONEY

1 TEASPOON ALMOND OIL

1 TEASPOON CORNFLOUR (US CORNSTARCH)

Simmer the leaves in the water for 10 minutes or until the water reduces by about one third. Put this (leaves and water) in a blender with all the other ingredients. Whizz up and spread on the face and neck. Will store for 2 days in the fridge.

Nasturtium

Tropaeolum majus

· · · · · · · · · · · · · ·

PLANETARY RULER: Mars

ELEMENT: Fire

ASSOCIATED DEITIES: None

MAGICAL VIRTUES: Vitality, positivity,
strength, recovery, protection, victory

I love nasturtiums: they grow quickly and provide a riot of hot-coloured flowers and juicy round leaves throughout my garden in pots and containers and trailing over walls and fences all summer long. They are good value too, for the thrifty gardener, as a single plant can cover three square yards, as well as being one of the easiest plants to cultivate, thriving on neglect and not even minding whether they are in the sun or the shade. In the autumn I save the seeds they produce for next year's crop.

Nasturtiums are native to South America, the seeds taken to Europe by Spanish conquistadors and explorers in the sixteenth century. The plants quickly became widespread around Europe and Britain. The English herbalist John Gerard reported having received seeds of the plant from Europe in his 1597 book *Herball, or Generall Historie of Plantes*. They became especially popular after being displayed in the Versailles palace flowerbeds of Louis XIV of France.[85]

---

85 Alice Formiga, "A Brief History of Nasturtiums," https://nasturtiums.wordpress.com /2008/10/31/a-brief-history-of-nasturtiums.

Gerard considered it a kind of cress because it has a spicy, peppery taste and grows in a similar way, and he described it alongside common watercress (*Nasturtium officinale*), though the plants are unrelated. This is where it gets its common name nasturtium (literally "nose-twister" from the spicy taste); it is sometimes still called Indian Cress.

Nasturtium was classified in the botanical family *Tropaeolaceae* by the Swedish botanist Carl Linnaeus as the shape of the flowers and leaves reminded him of the ancient Roman victory custom of erecting a trophy pole (*tropaeum*) hung with the weapons and armour of the vanquished enemy; the round leaves of the plant reminded Linnaeus of shields, and the flowers of blood-stained helmets.

Much of the modern lore surrounding the nasturtium seems to come directly from this fancy: it is associated with patriotism, protection, strength, conquest, combat, and war. The Jesuit poet Paul de Rapin (1661–1725) even invented a myth about the flowers having sprung from the body of a fallen Trojan hero, his shield the leaves and his blood the flowers, though, of course, the plant was unknown in the Old World:

> *Shield-like Nasturtium, too, confusedly spread,*
> *With intermingling trefoil fills each bed—*
> *Once graceful youths, this last a Grecian swain,*
> *The first a huntsman on the Trojan plain.*

Because of its peppery taste, the astrologer herbalists placed nasturtium under the rulership of the planet Mars and the element of fire. Linnaeus's daughter Elizabeth-Christine, a botanist herself, noticed that on hot summer days at dusk, the stamens and styles at the heart of nasturtium flowers emit a spark.

MAGICAL USES

The flowers and leaves can be dried and added to incenses or made fresh into oils of Mars and fire. The plant may be used in spells, rituals, incenses, oils, and potions for vitality, positivity, strength, and recovery after depletion of mental and physical energy. A **Nasturtium Flower Essence** is used to aid recovery from fatigue after mental exertion and overuse of the intellect.

The plant has a strong protective reputation, perhaps partly from the symbolic shield shape of the leaves, although gardeners know that it is a useful companion plant that helps repel bugs from the vegetable patch and orchard; it is said that woolly aphids and white fly are repelled by nasturtiums. Plant a red nasturtium by your front door (or have one in a hanging basket) to deter unwanted visitors and keep negative influences from your home. Use macerated nasturtium oil as a protection smeared around your door and window frames. Carry some dried flowers and leaves in a pouch for protection.

CULINARY USES

The Incas used nasturtiums as a salad crop, and when the Spanish shipped plants back to Europe, it wasn't as a pretty flower but as a vegetable, along with tomatoes and potatoes.[86] Indeed, all parts of *Tropaeolum majus* are edible—the flowers, leaves, and seeds, while T. *tuberosum* produces an edible underground tuber that is a major food source in parts of the Andes.[87] Nasturtium leaves are rich in vitamin C and contain flavonoids, iron, sulphur, manganese, and amino acids, while the flowers contain vitamins B1, B2, B3, and C as well as manganese, iron, phosphorus, and calcium.

The pretty flowers have become quite a fashionable garnish for salads today, though this is merely a modern rediscovery of an old practice. In *Acetaria* (1699), the first-ever book devoted entirely to salads, John Evelyn recommended adding its shredded flowers to salads as a way of providing a spicy flavour. The flowers taste slightly peppery, rather like a mild watercress or rocket. For an attractive addition to a posh afternoon tea party, try chopping them into some soft butter, whisking it with a fork, then chilling it in a mould in the fridge before turning out to serve. Freeze the flowers in ice cubes to add to cocktails. The fresh blossoms can be stuffed with soft cheese, such as ricotta.

The leaves have a stronger, more piquant taste and can really enliven a salad. Thomas Jefferson planted large areas of them every year at his country home so that his summer salads could be garnished with flowers and flavoured by nasturtium leaves.[88] If you want to follow his example, pick the leaves young and add them chopped or shredded to salads. You can also pop them directly into a sandwich instead of mustard; add to soups, stews, and rice dishes for added zest; wilt them into stir-fries; or chop into soft cheese or egg dishes. Try **Nasturtium Pesto** for a taste sensation. The leaves are large enough to be used as a substitute for vine leaves, stuffed and baked with a filling of your choice. Use **Nasturtium Vinegar** as a salad dressing.

During World War II, when imported spices became scarce in Britain, nasturtium seeds were ground and used as a pepper substitute. If you want to try it, allow the seeds to ripen

---

86 "Plant of the Week: Nasturtium (Alaska)," The University of Arkansas System Division of Agriculture, https://www.uaex.edu/yard-garden/resource-library/plant-week/nasturtium-alaska-6-30-06.aspx.

87 https://www.cookipedia.co.uk/recipes_wiki/Nasturtium_(Tropaeolum).

88 Allen Lacy, "A Gardener's World: Nasturtiums, An Old Friend," *New York Times* (May 10, 1990).

on the plant, but do pick them as soon as they mature, as they can become bitter if left too long. Roast gently in the oven on a low heat, then grind.

Pickled unripe nasturtium seeds have long been used as **Poor Man's Capers**. Early in the nineteenth century, Bernard McMahon wrote in *The American Gardener's Calendar* that "the green berries or seeds of this plant…makes one of the nicest pickles that can possibly be conceived; in the estimation of many, they are superior to capers."[89]

COSMETIC USES

Nasturtium is a natural antibiotic and contains lots of sulphur, both of which help clear problem skin. Try a **Nasturtium Infusion** as a skin wash or use a nasturtium facial steam for acne and skin breakouts.

The high sulphur content makes it a beneficial plant for the hair; it helps prevent dandruff, slows hair loss, promotes hair growth, and tones the scalp.[90] Make a **Nasturtium Infusion** and apply to the hair and scalp or use the **Nasturtium Hair Tonic** below. For alopecia, juice the plant and rub into the scalp to stimulate hair growth.

MEDICINAL USES

The flowers, leaves, and seeds are all used medicinally. All parts of the plant have strong antibiotic and antimicrobial properties. Use a **Nasturtium Infusion** as an antiseptic wash for cuts and grazes.

Take **Nasturtium Infusion** to increase resistance to bacterial infection. It is an excellent source of vitamin C and may be sipped as a natural remedy for helping the body overcome catarrh due to colds and flu.[91] The juiced leaves (put the leaves through your juicer) may be of benefit in chronic lung conditions such as emphysema.

For mild muscular pain, pour a strong **Nasturtium Infusion** into a warm bath and soak.

Caution: Nasturtium contains mustard oil and when used topically can cause skin irritation. Avoid ingesting medicinal amounts if pregnant or breastfeeding, or if you have stomach ulcers or kidney disease.

---

89   Allen Lacy, "A Gardener's World: Nasturtiums, An Old Friend," *New York Times* (May 10, 1990).
90   de Bray, *The Wild Garden*.
91   Steel, *Neal's Yard Remedies*.

Recipes

Nasturtium Infusion

8 NASTURTIUM LEAVES

250 ML OR 1 CUP BOILING WATER

Infuse the leaves in boiling water, covered, for 15 minutes. Strain. Massage into the scalp to promote hair growth. Use as an antiseptic wash for cuts and grazes. Pour it into the bath and soak for muscular pain.

Poor Man's Capers

4 HANDFULS UNRIPE (GREEN) NASTURTIUM SEEDS

560 ML OR 2⅓ CUPS WHITE WINE OR CIDER VINEGAR

½ TEASPOON SALT

1 SMALL ONION, THINLY SLICED

JUICE OF ½ LEMON

1 TEASPOON PICKLING SPICE *

1 CLOVE GARLIC, CRUSHED

4 PEPPERCORNS, CRUSHED

Pick the half-ripened (still green) nasturtium seed pods. Put the seed pods to one side and combine the other ingredients in a pan. Simmer gently for 15 minutes. Allow to cool and strain. Place the nasturtium seeds in a jar and pour the vinegar over them. Fit a lid and label. Keep in the fridge after opening.

*If you can't get this where you live, it is a blend of mustard seed, bay leaves, cloves, allspice, ginger, peppercorns, chilli, coriander seeds, and mace.

Nasturtium Flower Essence

To aid recovery from mental fatigue, gather a few mature nasturtium flowers. Float them on the surface of 150 ml spring water in a bowl and leave in the sun for 3–4 hours. Make sure that they are not shadowed in any way. Remove the flowers. Pour the water into a bottle and top up with 150 ml brandy or vodka to preserve it. This is your mother essence. To make up your flower essences for use, put 7 drops from this into a 10 ml dropper bottle, and top that up with brandy or vodka. This is your dosage bottle. The usual dose is 4 drops of this in a glass of water four times a day. When making flower essences, it is important not to handle the flowers—it is the vibrational imprint of the flowers you want to be held by the water, not your own imprint.

Nasturtium Hair Tonic

200 ML OR ¾ CUP VODKA

5 TEASPOONS FRESH NASTURTIUM FLOWERS AND SEEDS

5 TEASPOONS FRESH NETTLE LEAVES

5 TEASPOONS FRESH BOX LEAVES (OR ROSEMARY LEAVES)

ROSEMARY ESSENTIAL OIL

Put the vodka and leaves in a blender and whizz up. Pour everything into a clean glass jar and leave for 2 weeks, shaking daily. Strain into a clean bottle and add a few drops rosemary essential oil. Use this tonic for a brisk scalp massage and sprinkle a few drops on your hairbrush before brushing.

. . . .
Nasturtium Pesto

50 GRAMS OR ½ CUP WALNUTS, ROASTED

80 GRAMS OR 2 CUPS NASTURTIUM LEAVES

50 GRAMS OR ½ CUP PARMESAN (OR VEGETARIAN OR VEGAN ALTERNATIVE)

150 ML OR 10 TABLESPOONS OLIVE OIL

2 GARLIC CLOVES

SALT TO TASTE

SQUEEZE OF LEMON JUICE

Put everything into a food processor and whizz until smooth. Spoon over cooked pasta.

. . . .
Nasturtium Vinegar

HANDFUL OF NASTURTIUM FLOWERS

HANDFUL OF NASTURTIUM LEAVES

2 TEASPOONS BLACK PEPPERCORNS, CRUSHED

WHITE WINE VINEGAR OR CIDER VINEGAR

Half fill a glass jar with the flowers, leaves, and peppercorns. Fill the rest of the jar with the vinegar. Fit a lid. Steep for 2–3 weeks, shaking daily. Strain through muslin into a clean bottle. Store in a cool, dark place for 6–12 months.

Nettle

Urtica dioica

PLANETARY RULER: Mars

ELEMENT: Fire

ASSOCIATED DEITIES: Agni, Blodeuwedd, Cernunnos, Donar, Hades, Horus, Jupiter, Osiris, Pcuvus, Pluto, Thor, Vishnu, Vulcan, Yama

MAGICAL VIRTUES: Protection, counter magic, love, fidelity, divination

The stinging nettle certainly has a bad reputation, and I've lost count of the times a hidden nettle has stung me in the garden. The genus name of this plant probably comes from the Latin *uro*, meaning "I burn," which is obviously a reference to the sting. No wonder they are a symbol of spitefulness and in the language of flowers mean "you are hateful." In the Highlands of Scotland, they were said to have sprung from the Devil himself when he and all his angels fell to earth. Many of their folk names associate them with the Devil, such as Devil's Apron, Devil's Leaf, and Naughty Man's Plaything (Naughty Man is a euphemism for the Devil). Others say they spring from dead men's bones. In Demark the presence of nettles indicated ground where innocent blood had been shed, while in Lincolnshire they were thought to grow from human urine.[92]

---

92   All this is explained by the fact nettles like a nitrogen-rich soil.

However, this dark reputation is more than a little unfair, as they are actually one of the most useful plants in the whole garden. They provide medicine, food, a natural vitamin and mineral supplement, potent magical ingredients, rope, cloth, nets, paper, dye, insect repellent, vegetable rennet, and a green manure. Pliny the Elder wrote that nettle was regarded as a sacred plant that maintained good health, for the Anglo-Saxons it was a holy herb called *wergula*, while St. Patrick blessed them as being useful to man and beast alike. Bearing all this in mind, who wouldn't tolerate a few nettles in their garden?

Like other plants with stings or thorns, they were considered protective. To prevent the enchantment of dairy equipment, a nettle root would be placed in the milk and then buried in the dunghill at the Epiphany. In Cornwall May 1 was sometimes called Stinging Nettle Day, when a nettle leaf was wrapped in a dock leaf and eaten as a charm to protect the consumer from harm until the next Stinging Nettle Day. In Flanders they were a protection against witchcraft. In Russia and Hungary farmers hung nettles outside the stable door to keep the animals from evil. To hold a nettle in the hand is a protection against ghosts.

The protection extended to thunderstorms. Nettles were thrown onto the fire during a thunderstorm to defend the house from lightning. In Hungary the plant kept lightning away. In Germany nettles were placed on the rim of beer barrels to stop lightning striking them. The connection may come from the fact that in Pagan times they were dedicated to the thunder gods Donar and Thor, who perhaps imbued the nettle plant with some of their lightning sting.

They were also used as a remedy against demons and in counter magic. In Germany nettles gathered before sunrise would drive evil spirits from cows. In the Carpathians a nettle put into the milk cask would ensure that the sheep would not fall ill. In the dairy, if the butter refused to form, the churn was struck with nettles to drive out the evil. A spell against crows raiding the fields was to put a besom and a bunch of nettles in each corner of the field and say: "There you go, crow; that is for you, and what I plant is mine!"

Nevertheless, witches were known to use nettles in their potions, and nettles growing at a crossroads meant that witches met there. According to the Romany people, nettles grow mostly in places where there are subterranean passages to the dwelling places of the earth fairies or *Pcuvus*, and nettles are dedicated to them.

In Germany nettles were a symbol of love and fidelity. They have been considered an aphrodisiac and fertility aid since ancient times. They were an ancient Greek remedy for impotence, used in the form of an ointment, while the Romans brushed the stems on frigid animals and women. Eating nettles was believed to lead to sex, and nettle root to stimulate pregnancy. The seeds were thought to stimulate sexual function.

They were also plants of omens. To dream of nettles means good health, but to dream of being stung indicates vexation and disappointment. To dream of gathering nettles means that someone has a good opinion of you. A white leaf appearing on a nettle is an omen of death. They even predicted the weather:

> If nettles flower early, sow early.
> If nettles grow extra high, a hard winter is ahead.

The common name *nettle* comes from the Anglo-Saxon *noedl*, meaning "a needle," which may be a reference to the sting or possibly to the fact that a sewing thread was once made from nettle fibre. Nettles yield a strong fibre that can be made into thread, linen, ropes, sailcloth, twine, fishing nets, and paper. The use of nettle for these purposes was widespread before the introduction of flax. Shortages during the First World War forced manufacturers to use nettle fibre for army clothing. The German name for muslin, *nessel-tuch*, refers to the manufacture of a fine muslin-like cloth from nettle, while in Russia nettles were used commercially to make dyes for wool. I am reminded of the Hans Christian Anderson fairy tale of the maiden who had to spin twelve nettle shirts to free her brothers from enchantment.

Nettles were a common folk remedy for rheumatism. In many rural areas the practice of thrashing afflicted joints with stingers was said to relieve the pain. There are several anecdotes about the success of nettles as a cure for rheumatism after the patient has stripped naked and rolled in a nettle patch. A more palatable remedy might be the nettle ale brewed in mediaeval times that was drunk as a cure. The preacher John Wesley recommended a nettle poultice as a remedy for sciatica.

Nettles were once very popular in the kitchen. In seventeenth-century Britain, nettle pottage was a favourite dish, while nettle soup and pudding were common in Scotland. Nettles provided a vegetable rennet used in cheese making. Nettle leaves brought fruit to ripening and were used as a packaging for plums.

Harvest the top few inches, wearing gloves. If you do get stung, remember the old injunction "Nettle out, dock in / Dock remove the nettle sting."

MAGICAL USES

Nettle is a herb of protection and may be used in rituals, talismans, incense, oils, and charm bags to ward off negative energies, as well as protect the home from the effects of storms.

It is a "venomous" plant with a fierce sting and may not be plucked easily, but though it appears antagonistic, once assimilated it is totally beneficial. Nettle teaches us that those spiritual and life experiences that are the most difficult and testing are those that make us grow most. The power of the nettle demonstrates that all things have their place in creation, and those things which may be experienced as painful can be integrated and transmuted. **Nettle Tea** or nettle flower essence may be taken when working through spiritual or emotional ordeals.

Nettle may be used in incense when undertaking underworld journeys or to ward off negativity. **Nettle Infusion** or macerated nettle oil can be used to consecrate the dowsing rod and align it to the guardians of underworld treasure.

Nettle Beer or **Nettle Wine** may be taken sacramentally at the rites of passage of birth, initiation, and death.

Nettle is especially sacred to thunder gods and may be added to incense dedicated to them.

CULINARY USES

Nettle leaves are very nutritious, with high levels of vitamins and minerals, especially vitamin C. Our ancestors utilised nettles as a spring tonic after subsisting on stored and dried food for months over the winter. The young leaves can be made into delicious soups or the young shoots cooked like spinach. You can make **Nettle Pesto** or eat a puree of the young leaves.

Only the young leaves should be eaten. It is said that the Devil gathers nettles to make his shirts on May Day, and after that they become unfit for eating.

The aerial parts can be made into **Nettle Wine** or **Nettle Beer**.

You can freeze nettles for future use. Blanch two minutes before putting in containers and freezing.

When picking nettles, wear gloves. The sting disappears as soon as the plant wilts even slightly, and certainly when they are mashed or cooked, so you don't need to worry about being stung when eating them.

COSMETIC USES

A hair rinse of **Nettle Infusion** helps treat dandruff and oily hair as well as adding shine; massage it into the scalp to promote hair growth. A decoction made from the root may also be used as a general hair tonic.

Nettles improve the complexion and circulation. The fresh young leaves can be used in facial steams or added to the bath as a cleanser (put them in a muslin bag and suspend it under the tap as it runs). They are particularly good for oily skin.

Medicinal Uses

The fresh and dried aerial parts, along with the fresh and dried roots, are used medicinally.

The leaves contain natural anti-inflammatories and compounds that reduce the feeling of pain or interfere with the way that nerves send pain signals. A **Nettle Infusion** wash, compress, or lotion can be applied externally to relieve sore joints in cases of arthritis and rheumatism, or a cup of **Nettle Tea** can be drunk regularly to reduce pain and stiffness. Taken internally, nettle helps to detox the blood, which can help with gout and arthritis.

The root is diuretic and is used to improve urine flow and frequency, which may be useful in some prostate conditions, as well as helping to lower high blood pressure.

Nettle has long been used to treat allergy symptoms as it seems to reduce the amount of histamine produced by the body in response to an allergen. Drinking **Nettle Tea** or taking a tincture of the roots may be useful for hayfever and allergies and may decrease the severity of an asthma attack.

Externally, the plant is used to treat skin complaints such as eczema (make an ointment of the leaves) and minor cuts (dab on **Nettle Infusion**). It is helpful for haemorrhoids as the astringent properties of the plant reduce swelling and irritation (use a **Nettle Infusion** in the bath).

A **Nettle Infusion** also makes a good gargle for mouth ulcers and sore throats.

Nettle enhances immunity. Drink **Nettle Tea** at the start of a feverish illness.

It stimulates the circulation and dilates the peripheral blood vessels.

Nettle Tea or eating nettles is useful in the treatment of iron deficiency anaemia as it is high in iron and chlorophyll. The iron in nettles is readily bioavailable and easily absorbed.

Grind nettle seeds, mix to a paste with honey, and eat a spoonful for coughs.

Caution: *Use gloves when collecting the plant as touching it causes temporary skin irritation. Stinging nettle has been found safe for most people when used internally or externally for up to two years. However, it may lower blood sugar levels and blood pressure, so monitor carefully if you are diabetic or hypertensive. It increases urine flow, so avoid if you have kidney problems. To be on the safe side, avoid medicinal amounts if you are pregnant or breastfeeding, and do not use if you take lithium, sedatives, or blood thinning and anti-clotting medications.*

Recipes

NETTLE TEA

1 TEASPOON DRIED OR 2 TEASPOONS FRESH NETTLE LEAVES

250 ML OR 1 CUP BOILING WATER

Infuse together for 10 minutes. Strain and drink for arthritis and rheumatism.

NETTLE INFUSION

2 FRESH NETTLE TOPS

250 ML OR 1 CUP BOILING WATER

Infuse 10 minutes. Strain. Use as an anti-dandruff hair tonic rinse. Use to clean cuts and irritated skin. Add to the bath to reduce skin swelling and irritation, or for arthritis pain.

NETTLE WINE

2 LITRES OR 8½ CUPS NETTLE TOPS

5 CM OR 2-INCH PIECE GINGER ROOT

JUICE AND GRATED ZEST OF 1 LEMON

1.4 KILOS OR 11 CUPS SUGAR

250 ML OR 1 CUP BLACK TEA

WHITE WINE YEAST (AVAILABLE ONLINE)

YEAST NUTRIENT (AVAILABLE ONLINE)

Wash the nettle tops and remove any stalks. Put the nettles in a pan with the ginger and juice and grated zest of the lemon. Add enough water to cover and boil, then simmer for 30 minutes. Strain into a demijohn. Dissolve the sugar in a little hot water and add the tea. Add this to the demijohn. Top up to the gallon mark with water and add the yeast and nutrient according to manufacturer's instructions. Fit an airlock. Leave in a warm place. When it has stopped fermenting completely (when the airlock has stopped bubbling), siphon off into a clean demijohn to clear for at least 6 months. Siphon into sterilised bottles. Store as you would any other wine.

. . . .
Nettle Beer

225 GRAMS OR 1⅛ CUPS SUGAR + 4 TEASPOONS

450 GRAMS OR 1 POUND BREWING MALT EXTRACT

1.4 KILOS OR 3 POUNDS NETTLE TOPS

4½ LITRES OR 19 CUPS WATER, DIVIDED

BEER YEAST (AVAILABLE ONLINE)

Mix the sugar and malt extract with 500 ml or 2 cups warm water and stir until dissolved. Wash the nettles and boil in the rest of the water for 30 minutes. Allow to cool and strain onto the malt mixture in a fermenting bin. Add the yeast (check manufacturer's instructions), cover, and leave in a warm place, stirring daily, skimming off any scum as it appears. Continue until fermentation finishes; this should take about a week. Stand in a cool place for 48 hours to settle and siphon into a clean container. Add 4 teaspoons sugar and stir well. Decant into beer bottles. Make sure you leave an air space at the top of 4 cm/1½ inches. Seal tightly and leave in a warm room for a week before drinking. Some sediment may collect at the bottom of the bottle, so pour gently so as not to disturb this. Store any bottles remaining in a cool place. Serve chilled.

. . . .
Nettle Anti-Dandruff Tonic

10 ML OR 2 TEASPOONS NETTLE TINCTURE

15 ML OR 3 TEASPOONS WITCH HAZEL

Mix together and bottle. Massage a few drops of this into the scalp.

. . . . .

. . . .

Nettle Pesto

50 GRAMS OR ½ CUP PINE NUTS, TOASTED

80 GRAMS OR 2 CUPS NETTLE LEAVES

50 GRAMS OR ½ CUP PARMESAN (OR VEGETARIAN OR VEGAN
ALTERNATIVE), GRATED

125 ML OR 9 TABLESPOONS OLIVE OIL

2 GARLIC CLOVES

SALT AND PEPPER TO TASTE

Put everything into a food processor and whizz till smooth. Season to taste.
Spoon over cooked pasta.

. . . .

Nettle Powder

Grind dried nettle leaves in a coffee grinder. Use the powder added to food and
smoothies as a tonic and vitamin and mineral supplement, or add to water for
gout, anaemia, and allergies.

. . . .

Nettle Root Decoction

Cover the washed and chopped roots with water in a pan. Simmer 20 minutes.
Strain and bottle. Take for inflammation and bacterial and fungal infections.
Take 2 cups a day. Will keep for 3–4 days refrigerated. Take as a urinary tonic.

. . . . .

Passionflower

Passiflora spp.

· · · · · · · · · · · · · · ·

PLANETARY RULER: Venus

ELEMENT: Water

ASSOCIATED DEITIES: Tonantzin, Krishna, Christ

MAGICAL VIRTUES: Love, calm, peace, friendship

There are around 550 species of passionflower, a type of woody vine. Some are grown purely for ornamentation, others for medicine, and some are edible. Passionflowers are native to the southeastern United States and Central and South America.

We don't know much about the lore of the passionflower before the arrival of Christian colonialists, except that passion fruits were grown as a semi-domesticated crop by the Aztecs, Incas, and other indigenous South Americans for centuries, and passionflowers are known to have been cultivated in the gardens of Aztec priests and kings, probably for medical and ritual use, and possibly for offerings. One of the sun god myths of the Aztecs alludes to the healing properties of the "snake vine," a vine guarded by a serpent. This has been variously identified with different plants, but the passionflower is certainly one of the candidates. The rayed flower would identify it with the sun.[93]

When Spanish colonialists in South America learned of passionflower, they fancied they had discovered a perfect symbol of Christ's passion. Jacomo Bosio, in his treatise on

---

93   "The Symbolism of the Passion Flower," https://www.paghat.com/passiflorasymbolism.html.

the Cross of Calvary (1609), related every part of it to the mysteries of the Passion: "It would seem as if the Creator of the world had chosen it to represent the principal emblems of His Son's Passion; so that in due season it might assist, when its marvels should be explained to them, in the condition of the heathen people, in whose country it grew."[94] The crown of thorns was represented by the corona filaments, the three nails by the stigma, the petals were the scourge, and the five stamens the five wounds of Christ. There are seventy-two corona filaments, which, according to tradition, is the number of thorns in the crown of thorns set upon Christ's head. The lance-shaped leaves represented the spear that pieced Christ's side, and the marks on the undersides of the leaves signified the thirty pieces of silver that Judas was paid to betray Christ. Furthermore, the flower's five petals and five petallike sepals represented the ten apostles who remained faithful to Jesus throughout the Passion (excluding Judas, who betrayed him, and Peter, who denied him). The 1633 edition of *Gerarde's Herball* remarked sceptically: "The Spanish friars for some imaginary resemblances in the flower first called it *Flos Passionis*, The Passionflower, and in a counterfeit figure, by adding what was wanting, they made it as it were an Epitome of our Saviour's passion."[95]

Elsewhere, the appearance of the flower reminded people of a clock face. In Israel they are known as "Clock-Flower" and in Greece and Japan as "Clock Plant." In Turkey they seemed to represent the wheel of fortune and are called *çarkıfelek*.

In India blue passionflowers are attributed to the blue-skinned god Krishna, the five anthers interpreted as the five *pandavas* (brothers) in the Hindu epic the Mahabharata, with Krishna at the centre.

In Japan the passionflower is a symbol of homosexuality in some urban areas. This may be because the lilac colour of the flower identified it with the Gay Liberation movement or because the plant is double sexed or because early in the Tokugawa period homosexual youths called *wakashu* wore flowery purple garments.[96]

MAGICAL USES

Passionflower Tea may be taken prior to meditation to help calm an overactive mind and find inner peace. It may also be used for dream work; take a cup before bed or before settling down to a trance induction.

---

94   Quoted in Thiselton-Dyer, *The Folk-lore of Plants*.
95   Gerard, *Gerard's Herbal*.
96   "The Symbolism of the Passion Flower," https://www.paghat.com/passiflorasymbolism.html.

Dried passionflowers can be used in incense, added to potpourri, or hung in a sachet in the home to calm problems and troubles and bring peace and harmony. Use in home blessing spells and rituals.

Passionflower works well in love magic or friendship workings. If you carry some with you, it can attract friends and popularity.

Meditate with the rayed flower on the turning of the wheel of the year.

CULINARY USES

Not all passion fruits are suitable for humans to eat, but many species of passionflowers have edible round or oblong fruits that range from yellow to purple in colour and contain many edible seeds. They can taste slightly sour or very sweet, depending on the variety. P. *edulis* is cultivated extensively for its fruit, which is used as a source of juice. Sweet granadilla (P. *ligularis*) is another widely grown species, and Maypop (P. *incarnata*) is a common species in the southeastern US. Other edible passionflowers include P. *quadrangularis*, P. *laurifolia*, P. *foetida*, and Banana passion fruits (P. *tripartita* var. *mollissima* and P. *tarminiana*).

Passion fruits can be eaten whole or used to make juice, marmalade, ice cream, jams, jellies, and desserts.

The flowers can be made into tea or used to decorate cakes and other dishes.

COSMETIC USES

The flowers contain antioxidants that benefit all skin types. Passionflower hydrates and is a natural anti-inflammatory. Use **Macerated Passionflower Oil** in your DIY beauty concoctions or apply it as a serum to your face after cleansing and before moisturizing.

The fruit is known to boost circulation and has anti-inflammatory properties. It's rich in omega-6 essential fatty acids. Use it in a **Passionfruit Gelatine Face Mask**.

MEDICINAL USES

Passiflora incarnata is used medicinally (do not use other varieties) and has a long history of traditional use. The upper parts of passionflower—the leaves, stems, and flowers—are used.

It is perhaps most well-known for its calming influence on the nervous system. Herbalists use the plant for anxiety, tension, and nervousness. It is a remedy for insomnia and sleep issues, acting as a mild sedative in the form of **Passionflower Tea**.

Likewise, because of its calming and anti-spasmodic properties, **Passionflower Tea** is often used for tension and pain. It can be particularly useful for menstrual cramping and PMS.

Apply **Macerated Passionflower Oil** or use the fresh flowers and leaves in a poultice to help relieve minor skin conditions such as burns, cold sores, insect bites, razor burn, scrapes, and sunburn.

Passionflower has also been used to alleviate the itching and burning pain of haemorrhoids. Add double strength **Passionflower Tea** to your bath or use it in a compress.

> *Caution:* Pregnant and breastfeeding women should avoid taking passionflower by mouth. Do not take with antiplatelet or anticoagulant drugs, or blood-thinning herbs such as danshen, devil's claw, eleuthero, garlic, ginkgo, horse chestnut, panax ginseng, papain, red clover, or saw palmetto. Do not take if you are using prescription sleep medication, antidepressants, or tranquillisers.

Recipes

PASSIONFLOWER TEA

1 TEASPOON DRIED OR 2 TEASPOONS FRESH PASSIONFLOWERS

250 ML OR 1 CUP BOILING WATER

Infuse *Passiflora incarnata* and water together for 10 minutes, covered. Strain and drink for anxiety, insomnia, and menstrual cramping.

PASSIONFLOWER SCRUB

4 TABLESPOONS DRIED PASSIONFLOWERS

4 TABLESPOONS SUGAR

4 TABLESPOONS FINE OATMEAL

1 TABLESPOON VEGETABLE OIL

Whizz all the ingredients up in a food processor. Put in a jar. Use in the shower as an exfoliating body scrub, mixed with a little water. Rinse off and apply a moisturiser. Will keep around 12 months.

PASSIONFRUIT GELATINE FACE MASK

Take two passionfruit, mash them, and then push through a sieve into a double boiler. Mix in one or two sachets of vegetable gelatine. Heat, stirring, until it forms a thick paste. Allow the mixture to cool and then apply the mask to your face, avoiding the eye area. Add a little olive oil or honey to the pulp if you wish. If the fruit seems too slippery to stick to your face, add a little fine oatmeal. Leave on for 15–30 minutes and rinse well with warm water. The mixture will keep in the fridge for 2 days.

. . . .

MACERATED PASSIONFLOWER OIL

Pack a glass jar with passionflowers. Pour on vegetable oil to cover. Put on a lid and leave on a sunny windowsill for 2 weeks. Strain into a clean jar. Label. Will keep 6–12 months. Apply to mild burns, sunburn, and insect bites, or add to your homemade cosmetics.

Peony

Paeonia sp.

PLANETARY RULER: Sun

ELEMENT: Fire

ASSOCIATED DEITIES: Paeon, Apollo, Aesculapius,
Leto, gods of healing, moon goddesses

MAGICAL VIRTUES: Healing, warding,
protection, counter magic, exorcism

As I write, the peonies are starting to come out in my garden this week, and I know from experience that this heralds a period of early summer storms—every year, my poor red peony gets its petals bashed off by thunderstorms and torrential rain as soon as it flowers! Luckily, the storms have usually passed by the time the slightly later pink and white varieties open. They have a short blooming period in early summer, lasting only 7–10 days, but their beauty and usefulness make them well worth the space.

Peonies have been used medicinally since ancient times. In Chinese traditional herbalism, peony root (Bai Shao) is still used in the treatment of a variety of conditions, including gout, menstrual cramps, migraines, and hepatitis.

In Europe the mediaeval monks grew them in their herb gardens, while the seventeenth-century English herbalist Culpeper stated that the "male" peony could cure falling sickness and the "female" could drive away nightmares.

Its connection with healing goes deep. It was named by Theophrastus in honour of Paeon, who is said to have used it to cure wounds in the Trojan War. He received the flower on Olympus from Leto, the mother of the god Apollo, and used it to cure Hades of a wound received in a fight with Herakles. Paeon was a pupil of Asclepius, the Greek god of medicine. However, Asclepius became jealous of his clever pupil and sought to kill him, but Zeus rescued the youth by changing him into a peony flower. Sometimes Paeon is used as an epithet of the sun god Apollo, who had aspects as a healer god himself, dispelling sickness just as he dispelled darkness when he rose as the sun each day. However, sometimes Paeon is used as a sobriquet of Asclepius himself.

The ancient Greeks believed that the peony was an emanation of the moon that glowed at night to drive away evil spirits, give protection to horses wherever it grows, safeguard shepherds and their flocks, keep the harvest from injury, and prevent storms. However, much like the mandrake, its collection was surrounded by taboos and danger. Pliny said, "That of necessity it must be gathered in the night for if any man shall pluck the fruit in the daytime being seen of the woodpecker he be in danger of to lose his eyes."[97]

In the mediaeval period, the peony was used to ward off evil in its various guises. Culpeper said it was an antidote to any sickness caused by demonic possession, such as epilepsy. Gerard said it healed those who had been bewitched. The seeds steeped in hot wine were believed to prevent nightmares or were strung onto a necklace to protect children from convulsions, ward off evil spirits, and prevent madness. Pennsylvanian Germans also used it to prevent fits, washing with a rag that had been tied to a peony. The plants were often grown near the door of cottages as they were considered to be able to drive away witches and storms, fairies and goblins. Peonies were widely believed to prevent nightmares, advocated as such by Pliny, and even Francis Bacon said that it protected against "the incubus we call the mare (nightmare)."[98] It protected against lightning.

One superstition held that if you count the petals on a flower and they come out odd, there will be a death in the family. Pennsylvanian Germans said that if you gave peony as a gift, someone in your family will die.

MAGICAL USES

The peony is an ancient plant of protection, its power bringing all within its sphere into the care of the moon goddess and the sun god, particularly all living and growing things.

---

97 Pliny the Elder, *Natural History.*
98 Watts, *Elsevier's Dictionary of Plant Lore.*

The petals may be scattered around the edge of the circle and the dried petals and powdered root used in protective incenses. Grow peony in your garden, put the dried petals in potpourri or charm bags, or carry on the person in a herbal talisman. Place a peony charm bag under the pillow to prevent nightmares. Peony is used in exorcism rituals and incense.

The peony makes a suitable incense to honour and invoke the god of medicine and invoke healing energies. Use peony in incenses, potions, and spells of healing.

CULINARY USES

Did you know that peonies are edible? The petals, seeds, and roots can all be eaten and were a popular ingredient in mediaeval cookery for those that could afford it. The seeds were used as a spice, and peony water (an infusion of the petals) was drunk.

Make some delicious and colourful peony petal tea or add the petals to salads, punches, lemonades, cocktails, use as a garnish, or use to colour jams and jellies.

COSMETIC USES

Peonies have become a buzz ingredient in commercial skin formulas, especially those for mature skin. They contain a chemical called paeoniflorin, which reduces wrinkles. You can try making your own **Macerated Peony Petal Oil** to use neat on your skin or add it to your homemade moisturisers.

Alternatively, make a **Peony Skin Exfoliant Scrub**, wet your skin with water, and massage the scrub very gently into your face or body to remove dead cells and leave your skin cleansed and glowing.

Drop a few fresh or dried peony petals into your bath for a relaxing soak that will soothe your skin.

MEDICINAL USES

The dried and powdered root is used medicinally. All peony species contain high amounts of anti-inflammatory glucosides, but paeoniflorin is the most abundant one, and it is largely responsible for peony's medicinal actions, though other compounds likely play a role as well. A decoction of the dried and powdered roots may be used to treat rheumatoid arthritis, muscle spasms, menstrual cramps, mild depression, and anxiety.

Peony has mildly sedative effects, so you could try a cup of peony flower tea.

Try **Peony Cough Syrup** for a cough.

Caution: *Peony is generally considered safe, though an overdose can lead to a stomach upset. It should not be taken by pregnant or lactating women as peony is an emmenagogue (i.e., it is capable of stimulating menstruation). Do not take if you are on blood-thinning medication or for two weeks before a scheduled surgery.*

Recipes

PEONY COUGH SYRUP

600 ML OR 2½ CUPS BOILING WATER

2 FRESH PEONY FLOWERS

450 GRAMS OR 2¼ CUPS SUGAR

½ TEASPOON CLOVES

Pour boiling water over the peony flowers and leave for 48 hours, covered. Strain. Add the sugar and cloves to the liquid and boil for 40 minutes. Bottle and keep in the fridge for 2–4 months.

PEONY BATH BOMBS

300 GRAMS OR 1½ CUPS BICARBONATE OF SODA (BAKING SODA)

150 GRAMS OR ¾ CUP CITRIC ACID

4 TABLESPOONS DRIED PEONY PETALS

FEW DROPS ESSENTIAL OIL SUCH AS JASMINE, ROSE, OR LAVENDER

SPRAY BOTTLE OF WATER

Combine the dry ingredients and essential oil in a bowl. Very carefully, a tiny bit at a time, spray water into the mix. You need to add just enough to make the mixture stick together, and this will be less than you think. Fashion into balls or press into moulds and dry overnight.

. . . .

PEONY SKIN EXFOLIANT SCRUB

Put some sugar or salt in a blender with a few peony petals and give them a short blend. You can add a few drops of your favourite skin oil to this if you like. Rub into your skin and rinse off with clean water to leave your skin exfoliated and glowing. Follow with your usual moisturiser.

. . . .

MACERATED PEONY FLOWER OIL

Pack a clean glass jar with peony flowers. Cover them in vegetable oil and fit a lid. Leave on a sunny windowsill for 2 weeks, shaking daily. Strain into a clean jar. You can use directly onto your skin or add to your homemade cosmetics for superb hydration and anti-wrinkle effects.

Red Poppy

aka Corn/Field Poppy
Papaver rhoeas

. . . .

PLANETARY RULER: Moon

ELEMENT: Water

ASSOCIATED DEITIES: Agni, Aphrodite, Artemis, Ceres,
Cybele, Demeter, Diana, Great Goddess, Hades, Harvest,
Hera, Hermes, Hypnos, Jupiter, harvest goddesses,
Mercury, Morpheus, mother goddesses, Persephone, Pluto,
Proserpine, Somnus, Venus, Vulcan, Yama, Thanatos, Nyx

MAGICAL VIRTUES: Fertility, death,
mourning, dreamwork, meditation

❦❦❦❦❦❦❦

Poppies are popular garden plants and come in many varieties. The genus *Papaver* contains about fifty species, from the oriental poppy (*P. orientale*) and the opium poppy (*P. somniferum*) to the small red field poppy, which grows wild in cornfields and wasteland. I remember being pleased to have the latter self-seeding in my garden, though my elderly neighbour dismissed them as weeds. I don't care. I encourage them because they are magical.

In Greek myth, Persephone was picking poppies when she was abducted by Hades, the god of the underworld. Her mother, the goddess Demeter, sought her all over the length and breadth of the land. At last, weary, she sat down for nine days and nights, and Hypnos, god of sleep, caused poppies to spring all around her feet. Breathing in the soporific perfume, she fell asleep and rested. Poppies, which grow along with corn, are an emblem of Demeter, goddess of the harvest, while Persephone is the seed in the earth that grows in the spring. She is depicted with a crown of poppies.

Poppies almost always accompany grain crops—or at least they did until the widespread use of herbicides—and a cornfield without poppies was unthinkable for the ancients. The Greeks called the poppy "the companion of the corn," and its presence was deemed vital for the health of the crop, the visible lifeblood of the harvest goddess Demeter nourishing the fields. They were offered, together with some symbolic grain, to the goddess.

The connection between poppies and the harvest continued right into the early twentieth century. In Britain the harvest lord (the foreman in charge of the workers) had red poppies and bindweed woven around his rush hat as his badge of office.

In Greece the poppy was also a plant of Hypnos, the god of sleep, and his son Morpheus, the god of dreams. Poppies have long been associated with sleep, dreams, and death, which is the final sleep. Ancient Egyptians, Greeks, and Romans presented poppies as offerings to the dead to ease the transition between life and death. Reclining figures were depicted on the sides of sarcophagi holding poppies.

In the ancient Greek mysteries of Eleusis, which celebrated the myths of Persephone and Demeter and promised eternal life to its initiates, poppies were a symbol of the life-giving earth and the short oblivion of death before resurrection.

Poppies sprang up after the Battle of Waterloo (1815) and on the battlefields of France in the First World War, growing profusely and rapidly. This is due to the seed's ability to germinate within twenty-four hours on recently disturbed soil. Each plant can produce around 17,000 seeds, which can remain dormant for up to 50 years. Soil disturbance can wake them up. After World War I, the poppy became the symbol of both the tragedy of war and of the renewal of life.

They are such magical plants that they are surrounded by superstition and taboos. Irish women had a dread of touching them. Picking or otherwise disturbing poppies was generally forbidden, perhaps because they were bound up with the fertility of the harvest. In Britain children were warned that picking poppies would cause storms and lightning (hence its folk name Thunderflower) and that putting one close to the ear would cause a headache or that wearing them caused blindness (thus another folk name, Blind Man). It was unlucky to bring them indoors, as it would cause illness. In Liege it was thought it would make children wet the bed, while in Warwickshire children would get warts on their hands.

Carrying poppy seeds was said to promote fertility. To become pregnant, a woman should add poppy seeds to all her food. Poppy seed cakes were eaten as luck and fertility charms at Christmas, New Year, Whitsun, and Easter in Germany and the Czech Republic. In Poland hens were fed with poppy seeds on Christmas Eve to encourage them to lay.

They were also plants of protection. Poppy seeds were eaten to ward off evil spirits and witches, especially in Slavic regions. It was the custom to put a freshly cut turf before the stable door and scatter poppy seeds on it. In Poland scattering poppy seeds on a coffin warded off vampires.

The opium poppy is a symbol of medicine, but field poppies were also used in country cures, used to treat headaches or, in Norfolk, a hangover. In south Uist a flower infusion was used for teething babies and earache. In Wales a decoction of poppy heads was boiled in ale as a sleeping draught. In the Highlands poppy juice was put in children's food to make them sleep.

MAGICAL USES

Poppies are used in harvest rituals at Lughnasa and the Autumn Equinox. Decorate the harvest loaf with poppy seeds to remember the cycles of the year—the planting of the seed, growth, harvest, death, and the seed in the earth awaiting new birth. At the Autumn Equinox we mark the sacrifice of the God as he dies with the grain, the death that comes before resurrection.

Poppies are sacred to the goddess of the harvest. They spring from her earth womb, the flowers are her blood, and the white poppy juice is the nourishing milk from her breasts. Together they symbolise fertility, plenty, and abundance.

As flowers of death and mourning with the promise of rebirth, use poppies in funeral flowers and memorial rituals.

As a plant of fertility, poppy seeds are used in spells and rituals of fertility. Carry poppy seeds in a sachet. Use them in incense, charm bags, amulets, and talismans, as well as add them to food.

The seed and flowers are added to love spells and rituals, incense, oils, talismans, and charms. Poppy can be added to the handfasting cup or used in love magic and incense.

The seeds and dried petals can be added to divination incense and potions.

CULINARY USES

The Romans and Greeks ate the fresh young leaves in salads and used poppy seeds as a condiment. The seeds are nutritious and often used today in baked goods. Poppy seeds can be scattered on bread, cakes, buns, and rolls, a practice that goes back to the ancient Greeks.

Red poppy petals were used to colour medicine, wines, sweets, herbal teas, and ink. The red flowers will add a red colour to syrups and beverages. **Poppy Petal Syrup** can be used in desserts, soups, and stews. Add the petals to summer salads.

The new leaves can be eaten raw or cooked but are best picked before the plant flowers.

COSMETIC USES

Soothing and refining poppy petals can be used in homemade skincare products or try the **Poppy Petal Face Wash**.

MEDICINAL USES

Poppy Petal Tea, **Poppy Glycerite**, or **Poppy Petal Syrup** made from red poppy petals may be used to ease coughs and respiratory catarrh, soothe respiratory passages, and remove excess mucus to soothe sore throats and hacking coughs.

The flowers of the red poppy are very mildly sedative and soothing. **Poppy Petal Tea** or poppy seed tea, **Poppy Glycerite**, or **Poppy Petal Syrup** may also be used as a sedative in cases of insomnia.

The seeds can be ground and made into a paste with a little water to apply to swollen and painful joints. Put a warm cloth over the area to keep them in place. **Poppy Seed Paste** can be taken internally to treat diarrhoea.

Red poppies contain pain-relieving qualities. A tincture of poppy petals is most quickly absorbed, but you could also try a **Poppy Seed Paste** or **Poppy Petal Tea**. The leaves can be warmed and used as a poultice for neuralgia.

NB: The California poppy (*Eschscholvia californica*) can be used in the same way as the corn poppy (red poppy). Like the corn poppy, there are no addictive opiates, and the flowers can be used as a mild sedative tea for insomnia and nervous tension. The petals can be made into a glycerite for coughs, and this will also help prevent the muscle spasm of coughing.

Caution: Unlike their cousin the opium poppy, red poppy flowers do not contain morphine, but they do contain some alkaloids and are sedative, so exercise caution and do not drive or operate machinery after taking. Do not use if you are pregnant or breastfeeding or taking other sedatives. They can be slightly toxic to some mammals. The seed contains no alkaloids and is considered safe to eat.

· · · · ·

Recipes

Poppy Petal Tea

1 TEASPOON POPPY PETALS

250 ML OR 1 CUP BOILING WATER

Infuse together for 10 minutes. Strain and drink for a mild painkilling and sedative effect.

Poppy Petal Syrup

1 LITRE OR 4¼ CUPS WATER

40 FLOWERS (PETALS ONLY)

50 GRAMS OR ¼ CUP SUGAR

Pour the water over the poppies and stand overnight. Strain, discarding the flowers; add the sugar to the retained liquid. Heat gently for 20 minutes (do not boil), strain again. Keep refrigerated for around a month. Use poured over desserts or in drinks or take a spoonful to treat coughs and sore throats.

Poppy Glycerite

RED POPPY PETALS

WATER

GLYCERINE

Fill a jar with poppy petals. Pour on a solution of 60 percent glycerine and 40 percent water. Stir. Sit in a sunny spot on the windowsill for 2 weeks, shaking daily. When the liquid goes red, strain out the petals. Will keep 12 months. Take a spoonful as required for coughs and sore throats.

. . . .

POPPY PETAL FACE WASH

HANDFUL POPPY PETALS

250 ML OR 1 CUP BOILING WATER

100 ML OR 7 TABLESPOONS ROSEWATER

4 TABLESPOONS LIQUID CASTILE SOAP

2 TABLESPOONS ALOE VERA GEL

1 TABLESPOON VEGETABLE GLYCERINE

Put the petals in a heatproof bowl and pour boiling water over them. Leave to infuse for 4 hours. Strain the liquid into a clean bottle. Add the other ingredients. Shake before use. Keeps 2 weeks in the fridge. Use as a skin-refining facial wash.

. . . .

POPPY SEED PASTE

1 TEASPOON POPPY SEEDS

1 TEASPOON HONEY

Crush together and take a spoonful as required to treat diarrhoea.

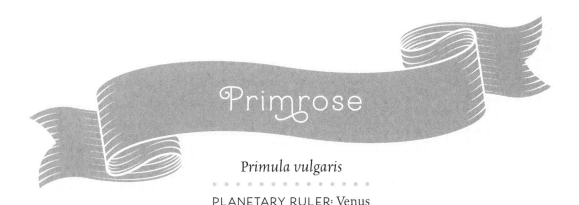

Primrose

Primula vulgaris

PLANETARY RULER: Venus

ELEMENT: Earth

ASSOCIATED DEITIES: Blodeuwedd, Freya,
spring goddesses, Virgin Mary

MAGICAL VIRTUES: Spring, youth, beauty, love, lust

The name *primrose* comes from the Latin word *prime*, meaning "first," as it is the first flower of the year. Every spring women and children sold bunches of primroses on the streets of London to celebrate the coming of spring. In the Victorian language of flowers, it signifies the joys of youth, in line with the youthful year.

This was the time of year when old varieties of chickens started laying, and the yellow flowers and yellow chicks were associated in sympathetic magic. If you take a bunch of primroses indoors, count the flowers; each of your hens will hatch that many fluffy chicks. As a spring flower it had magical powers and brought good luck into the house in Germany.

In Ireland they are called "fairy flowers." It is said that eating them is a sure way to see fairies or if you touch a fairy rock with the right number of primroses in a posy, it will open to fairyland and fairy gifts, but the wrong number opens the door to doom.

In the UK and much of Europe, primrose was used to protect the house and cattle on May Day. In Ireland they were tied to cow's tails. In Buckinghamshire on May Eve, primrose balls were hung over the house and cowshed door for protection from fairies and witches. In Somerset thirteen primroses were laid under a baby's cradle to stop the child from being kidnapped by fairies.

It was traditionally a herb of immortality, supposedly holding within it the secret of eternal bliss. When its lore was Christianised, the primrose was said to grant access to heaven.

The primrose was a plant much prized by the Druids. The poem "The Chair of Taliesin" describes the initiation of a bard with a drink made from primrose and vervain.

The primrose has associations with lust, "the primrose path of dalliance" from Shakespeare's *Hamlet* and "the primrose of her wantonness" from Braithwait's *Golden Fleece*, denoting an illusory sensual path of pleasure. If you presented a woman with a bunch of primroses, you were adversely commenting on her morals.

Primroses were carried by women to attract love or added to bathing water to increase beauty. In Britain, till the nineteenth century, it was used for love divination.

In old herbals primrose is recommended as a cure for rheumatism, paralysis, and insomnia. The sixteenth-century herbalist Gerard recommended that primrose tea should be taken in May to cure "the phrensie" and as a wound salve.

Magical Uses

Primrose is a herb of spring, used at Ostara and Beltane, and associated with new beginnings, the lusty currents of the season, growing life, and fertility. It can be used in garlands and incense or added to the ritual cup. **Primrose Tea** can be taken to attune to the season. At the feast the flowers can be eaten raw in salads, used as decoration in fruit drinks, or crystallised and used as embellishment on desserts and cakes.

Primrose is used in the initiation of a bard or as a drink to gain poetic inspiration. Try the **Primrose Tea** or **Primrose Mead** below.

In the Nordic tradition the primrose is sacred to the goddess Freya and can be used in rituals and incense dedicated to her.

Use the flowers in spells, talismans, and charm bags to attract love. Add the flowers to your bath to increase your beauty.

For protection, plant primroses in the garden or add the flowers to protection charms and incense. Use a **Macerated Primrose Oil** for sealing doors and windows against negative influences. Have pots of growing primroses in the house or add the flowers to potpourri. Carry primrose flowers in a talisman for protection.

Use **Primrose Tea**, primrose incense, **Macerated Primrose Oil**, or carry primrose to make contact with fairies and devas and gain access to the otherworld.

Culinary Uses

The leaves and flowers should be picked as they open and may be added to salads. The leaves can be added to soups and stews. **Crystallised Primrose Flowers** may be used for cake decorations. The flowers make one of the best country wines or can be made into **Primrose Mead**. Both the flowers and the leaves can be made into a syrup or **Primrose Tea**. The leaves of the primrose can be boiled and eaten as a vegetable.

Cosmetic Uses

Primrose Infusion may be used as a wash or made into a cream for acne, spots, wrinkles, and other skin complaints. A primrose cream or lotion or **Macerated Primrose Oil** will help fade age spots and freckles and treat sunburn. Add the oil or some fresh primrose petals to a luxurious beauty bath.

Medicinal Uses

The flowers, roots, and leaves are all used medicinally. The whole plant can be infused and used for the treatment of nervous headaches, insomnia, and as a cough medicine.

An infusion or decoction of the roots is slightly sedative and good for nervous headaches, as well as bronchial problems and coughs. An infusion of the leaves and flowers is a mild painkiller, useful for headaches and rheumatism.

A salve made from the flowers or **Macerated Primrose Oil** may be used on skin wounds.

> *Caution:* Avoid medicinal use if you are pregnant or breastfeeding, sensitive to aspirin, or taking anticoagulant drugs.

Recipes

Macerated Primrose Oil

Pack a jar with fresh flowers and fill with sweet almond oil. Leave for 14 days, shaking the jar daily. Strain into a clean, dark bottle and add a few drops of vitamin E oil. Keep tightly stoppered in a dark place for 6–12 months. Smoothed on your skin, this will help prevent wrinkles and fade age spots and freckles and treat sunburn.

Primrose Tea

250 ML OR 1 CUP BOILING WATER

2 TEASPOONS PRIMROSE FLOWERS AND YOUNG LEAVES

Pour boiling water over the herb and infuse for 15 minutes. Strain and drink for nervous headaches and insomnia.

Primrose Infusion

25 GRAMS OR 5 TEASPOONS DRIED PRIMROSE FLOWERS AND LEAVES

500 ML OR 2 CUPS BOILING WATER

Infuse together for 15 minutes. Strain and use as a face wash for acne, age spots, wrinkles, and other skin complaints.

· · · · · · · · · · ·
Primrose Mead

4½ LITRES OR 18¾ CUPS BOILING WATER

85 GRAMS OR 3 OUNCES PRIMROSE FLOWERS

900 GRAMS OR 2½ CUPS HONEY

250 ML OR 1 CUP COLD BLACK TEA

WHITE WINE YEAST (AVAILABLE ONLINE)

WINE YEAST NUTRIENT (AVAILABLE ONLINE)

SPICES TO TASTE (CINNAMON, NUTMEG, MACE, GINGER, ETC.)

Pour boiling water over the primrose flowers. Leave for 20 minutes. Strain, reserving the liquid. In a large pan, add the primrose infusion to the honey and bring to boil, skimming off any scum. Remove from the heat. When cooled to lukewarm, add the black tea, yeast, and nutrient according to manufacturer's instructions, plus spices to taste. Pour into a demijohn, fit an airlock, and leave in a warm place until the mead has finished fermenting completely. Siphon into a clean demijohn to clear for a few weeks, then siphon into sterilised bottles and cork. Store as you would any other wine.

· ·
Crystallised Primrose Flowers

1 LARGE EGG WHITE

FEW DROPS OF WATER

PRIMROSE FLOWERS

CASTER (SUPERFINE) SUGAR

Combine the egg white with the water and beat lightly. Dip a paint brush into the egg white and paint the flower. Sprinkle sugar evenly all over on both sides. Place the flower or petal on greaseproof paper to dry. Allow to dry for 12–36 hours. Store in an airtight container. Use for cake decorations.

· · · · ·

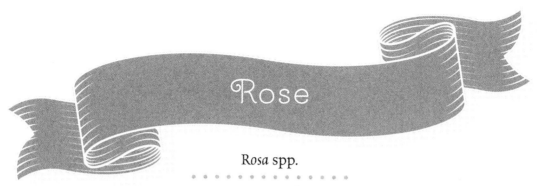

Rose

Rosa spp.

· · · · · · · · · · · · · ·

PLANETARY RULER: Red roses—Jupiter,
damask roses—Venus, white roses—Moon

ELEMENT: Water

ASSOCIATED DEITIES: Adonis, Aphrodite, Aurora,
Bacchus, Blodeuwedd, Christ, Cupid, Demeter, Dionysus,
Eros, Flora, Freya, Hathor, Horus, Hulda, Hymen, Hecate,
Inanna, Ishtar, Saule, Isis, Nike, Venus, Vishnu

MAGICAL VIRTUES: Love, peace, lust, beauty,
healing, health, anointing, psychic awareness,
initiation, union, marriage, death, sacrifice

The rose is known as the Queen of the Flowers, and it is inextricably linked to the feminine, the Goddess, romance, sexuality, and love. "The rose each ravished sense beguiles" wrote Sappho, the female poet of ancient Lesbos. It is easy to understand why these voluptuous and sensuously perfumed flowers are sacred to so many goddesses of love—Isis, Aphrodite, Venus, Inanna, and Ishtar, to name just a few. In one Greek tale, roses were created when Aphrodite first arose from the ocean and stepped onto the shore; the sparkling sea foam fell from her body in the form of pale white roses and took root. Later, as she pursued the beautiful youth Adonis, she caught herself on a thorn, and her blood dyed the roses crimson red, symbolising innocence turned to desire and maidenhood turned to womanhood. Eros, the son of Aphrodite and god of sexual desire, is also frequently depicted wearing a wreath of roses, further associating the flower with lust. Roman brides and bridegrooms were crowned with roses, and in Greece rose petals were scattered before the altars of Hymen, god of marriage. We still give bouquets of red roses to convey romantic love, and in Britain rose petals used to be scattered at weddings to ensure a happy marriage.

At Roman gatherings when a rose was hung on the ceiling it meant that nothing said at the meeting should be repeated outside—it was *sub rosa*, or "under the rose." Even now the plaster ornament on the centre of the ceiling is known as a ceiling rose and signified the same. The rose was a symbol of secrecy in the mystery religions of the classical world. In Graeco-Egyptian myth Harpocrates (the Greek name for the Egyptian god Horus) was bribed by Eros with a rose not to betray the secrets of Aphrodite. Horus/Harpocrates is his father, Osiris, reborn and stands as an emblem of the initiate reborn through the mysteries. Many later mystery sects took the rose as their symbol. The Rosicrucians have the rose joined to the cross, for example. The twelfth-century Sufi Abdul Qadir Gilani established a path of practical mysticism called Sebil-el-Ward (the Path of the Rose).

There are several treatises on alchemy called the Rosary of the Philosophers. In alchemy the rose is primarily a symbol of the mystical marriage of opposites and their rebirth into a new level of existence.[99] The white rose is the feminine, the moon, purity, perfection, innocence, and virginity, while the red is male, the sun, earthly passion, and fertility. Red and white roses together signify the union of opposites, and since the blending of two opposites into one means the death of individual ego, any red and white flowers together symbolise death. In *The Practice of Psychotherapy*, psychologist Carl Jung discussed the archetypal underpinnings of love between people in terms of the rose: "The wholeness which is a combination of 'I and you' is part of a transcendent unity whose nature can only be grasped in symbols like the rose or the *conjunctio* (Conjunction)."[100] Conjunction is the turning point in alchemy, the mystical marriage of the masculine sun (red rose) and feminine moon (white rose), or the union of Spirit with Soul.[101] Mystical poets have used the rose to symbolise the yearnings of the soul to be united with the divine.

In the Christian era, the rose was taken from the Goddess and given to the Virgin Mary, the Christian model of union with God, with the rose and the rosary becoming symbols of the union between God and humankind. Scenes of Mary in a rose garden or under a rose

---

99   http://alchemyguild.memberlodge.org/page-311919.
100   Jung, *The Practice of Psychotherapy.*
101   https://fd11-11ministries.org/2019/08/12/roses-the-spiritual-alchemical-practical.

arbour or before a tapestry of roses reinforce this idea. The rose garden in alchemical draw-ings is a symbol of sacred space, paradise itself, or the mystical bridal chamber, the place of the mystic marriage between the human and the divine.[102] The word *rosary* originally referred to an enclosed rose garden and hints at the much older feminine mysteries of the Goddess that Harpocrates was bribed to keep secret, with the walled garden standing for the secret place that every woman possesses. The Catholic rosary beads we know today originally consisted of strings of beads made from pressed rose petals.

The rose is often a sun symbol—anything round and rayed suggests the sun. The south-ern Ukrainians used the rosette as a solar emblem, and their designs suggest the ever-renewing strength of the sun, life, death, and rebirth. This makes the rose a symbol of immortality through death. There are many rosette symbols on Celtic tombstones in Alsace. In ancient Egypt roses were used in funeral wreaths. The Romans used roses at funerals, garlanded tombs with them, and planted graves with roses. Rose buds were offered to the dead at the festival of the Rosalia, and this may be the origin of the custom of having rose gardens in graveyards. The underworld goddess Hecate is sometimes portrayed wearing a crown of roses.

The rose can represent the opposites of life and death. In spring it is a symbol of resur-rection, love, and fecundity, while the faded flower represents the transience of life and beauty, sorrow and mortality. While the flower of the rose is beautiful, soft, and yielding, signifying love, beauty, and passion, the rose has thorns, which mean pain, blood, and sac-rifice. It is the blood and sacrifice of Osiris, Adonis, and Christ. In Christian lore it was Christ's death that re-dyed the white roses red.

Naturally, roses were deemed to have a great deal of magical power for love, healing, and protection. An Egyptian papyrus described an ointment of roses used to draw a woman to a man. This idea was still to be found in the English love spell that advises *Take three roses (white, pink, and red) and wear them next to your heart for three days. Give them to your lover and he will be yours forever.* In the West Country, a girl would pick a rose on Midsummer morn-ing and put it away wrapped in a piece of white paper. If it did not fade, she could wear it to church on Christmas morning and her lover would reveal himself by taking it from her.

Roses could also repel evil. In the National Library of Turin, a text against the power of evil has a series of protective spells to be used by a person who wishes to invoke the powers of the divine realm against malevolent forces by drawing four angels whilst wear-ing a wreath of roses. Another text recommends a person inflicted by a demon to have a

---

102   http://alchemyguild.memberlodge.org/page-311919.

prayer uttered over a flask of rosewater, which is then to be poured over the unfortunate victim.[103] Roses were grown in monastery gardens, and it was held that a person possessed by demons could not abide the scent of a rose.

Roses were employed in old country cures. In Britain children were passed through a wild rose arch three times on three successive mornings to cure whooping cough, and sometimes a piece of bread and butter was left beneath the arch so that any animal taking it would absorb the disease. The briar was sometimes made into a cross for the patient to wear.

The rose has long been valued for its healing abilities. The Roman Pliny described thirty-two medical cures that could be prepared from roses. The English herbalist Culpeper (1616–1654) said of rose remedies "to write at large of every one of these would swell my book too big." Gerard (1545–1612) commented that "the distilled water of roses is good for strengthening the heart and refreshing of the spirits and likewise for all things that require a gentle cooling...it mitigateth the pain of the eyes proceeding a hot cause, bringeth sleep, which also the fresh roses themselves provoke through their sweet and pleasant smell."[104]

The Greeks, Romans, and Egyptians all knew how to extract the rose's perfume by steeping the petals in oil, vinegar, or alcohol. From the Middle Ages, roses featured in many household recipes for perfumes, cosmetics, medicine, pomanders, toilet waters, pastilles, and potpourri.

As a symbol of luxury and extravagance, Roman emperors would shower their guests with rose petals, a tradition started by the emperor Nero (37–68 CE). However, the teenage emperor Heliogabalus (202–224 CE) got carried away and showered his guests with so many roses that several of them were suffocated.

MAGICAL USES

The rose is a symbol of the Goddess who is the mother of us all. The heart of the rose stands for that which is unknown, the hidden sacred world. In the folded structure of the rose, the flower seems to be concealing a secret inner core. To contemplate the mysteries of the rose is to meditate on mysteries of existence.

The white rose is purity, perfection, innocence, and virginity, while the red is earthly passion and fertility. The red and white rose wound together signify the union of opposites, symbolism we can use at Beltane to celebrate the sacred marriage of the God and Goddess,

---

103   Meyer and Smith, *Ancient Christian Magic*.
104   Gerard, *Gerard's Herbal*.

an act which reconciles male and female, summer and winter, life and death, flesh and spirit, and brings about all creation, driven by the most fundamental and powerful force in the universe: love. The priestess might wear a chaplet of white roses and the priest a chaplet of red roses, which are brought together as part of the ritual.

This symbolism can also be used for the Great Rite. As a symbol of the Mystical Marriage on a personal level, the red rose represents a special kind of love in which one "melts away" into the beauty of another, and the old identity is surrendered for that of the beloved or a higher identity within oneself. In this sense, the rose is a symbol of complete surrender to the divine and permanent transmutation.[105] Red and white rose petals can be added to the cup into which the athame is plunged in obvious symbolism. Rose oil can be used as the anointing oil.

During a handfasting ceremony, roses should play a part in chaplets, incense, decorations, bouquets, and the anointing oil, while rose petals may be scattered around the circle as a blessing. **Rose Petal Wine** would be a suitable drink for the chalice. Roses are used in love magic, spells, rituals, incense, oils, talismans, and charms.

At the Autumn Equinox, red rose petals represent the blood of the sacrificed god that fertilises the fields and brings us our harvest. The petals can be baked into the bread, which becomes the proxy sacrifice or scattered on the fields at the cutting of the grain. **Rose Hip Wine** would be a suitable drink. The hips may be included in garlands or altar decorations. The sacrifice of the God reminds us that unselfish sacrifice is an important aspect of divine love, and **Rose Oil** can be used to anoint the heart chakra to connect with it and develop this characteristic within.

At Midsummer roses are a symbol of the sun. Use roses in the decorations, chaplets, incense, and wine.

Like the sun, which dies each night and is reborn each day at sunrise, the rose is an emblem of renewal, resurrection, and eternal life. Use roses to make memorial offerings to dead loved ones.

Rose is a flower of peace and harmony, so to ensure a happy home, roses may be hung up around it and used in potpourri, charm bags, and flower arrangements. To ensure a peaceful night, rosewater can be used to wash the face and rinse bed linen, and rose petals may be scattered around the bedroom.

The rose is also a symbol of secrecy and suspended from the ceiling during meetings will ensure that none will break this trust. Because of its association with the workings of

---

105   http://alchemyguild.memberlodge.org/page-311919.

the heart, the rose in alchemy has come to symbolize secrets of the heart, things that cannot be spoken, or an oath of silence in general.

CULINARY USES

Rose hips are the flask-shaped fruits of the rose, and all rose hips are edible, though the hips of the dog rose have the best flavour.[106] They contain thirty times more vitamin C than oranges, as well as many other vitamins and minerals. During World War II, hundreds of tons of rose hips were collected from the wild each year in Britain and made into **Rose Hip Syrup** to prevent scurvy. **Rose Hip Tea** is a pleasant drink, as is **Rose Hip Wine**, and the hips can also be used in making jams, jellies, syrups, and soups. They can be cooked, dried, or frozen. **Rose Hip Vinegar** can be used for salad dressings. NB: In any rose hip recipes, the irritant hairs must be strained out as they can be highly irritating to your digestive tract.

Rose petals can be used fresh to makes **Rose Petal Tea**, **Rose Petal Jam**, **Rose Petal Wine**, crystallised for cake decorations or baked into cakes and cookies, and used to make **Rose Petal Vinegar** for salad dressings.

Rosewater (rose hydrosol) can be used to make sophisticated cocktails—add a few red rose petals for decoration.

COSMETIC USES

Roses and beauty go hand in hand, and they have been used in cosmetic preparations for millennia. Commercially, rose essential oil and rosewater (the by-product of making rose essential oil), also known as rose hydrosol, is added to products, although rose geranium oil or synthetic rose perfumes are often substituted.

Roses are astringent, toning, anti-inflammatory, and regenerative, promoting new cell growth. This makes roses excellent for rehydrating and smoothing aging, dry, inflamed, and sensitive skin.

Rose essential oil is incredibly expensive because of the number of roses it takes—10,000 roses to fill a single 5 ml (1 teaspoon) bottle. There are two different kinds of rose essential oil: **Rose Otto**, extracted through steam distillation, and **Rose Absolute**, obtained through solvent extraction. I've given instructions for both below, though it is much easier to make a **Macerated Rose Oil**.

---

106   The wild rose is called a dog rose (*Rosa canina*), possibly from the idea that it cured the bite of rabid dogs, a belief mentioned by Pliny the Elder in *Natural History*. Other possibilities are that "dog" is a corruption of "dagger," referring to the plant's jagged-edged leaves, or that "dog" is used in a derogatory sense because the flowers are not as showy as cultivated varieties.

Macerated Rose Oil is very good to use in massage; it's very soothing and is marvellous for the skin, moisturising and hydrating. It is especially good for dry, mature, and irritated skin, broken capillaries, redness, and eczema. You can incorporate it into homemade salves, creams, soaps, etc.

Rose petals make a good skin cleanser. Use **Rose Petal Tea** as a facial wash. Use rose petals in a facial steam. Rose petals can be added to a relaxing bath.

Rosewater (**Rose Hydrosol**) can be used as an antiseptic tonic for the skin. It is especially useful for dry and mature, inflamed and sensitive skins. It can be incorporated in lotions and creams. Use chilled rosewater in a compress to refresh tired and puffy eyes. Use diluted rosewater (50:50) as a final rinse for your hair.

Medicinal Uses

The dog rose (*Rosa canina*) is usually used for medicine, though all fragrant varieties can be used.

Rose Hip Syrup is high in vitamin C. It is good for colds and flu and excellent for children. The flavonoids in rose hips are anti-inflammatory and may help painful joints and arthritic conditions; take **Rose Hip Tea** or **Rose Hip Syrup**. The tannin content of rose hips makes them a useful treatment for diarrhoea, and they are helpful for stomach spasms and stomach irritation—try **Rose Hip Tea**.

Rose Petal Tea is mildly sedative, antidepressant, and anti-inflammatory. The petals support the nervous system, helping insomnia, nervousness, and mild depression. It may also relieve headaches and can be gargled for a sore throat. It can be used in a compress for sore eyes. In the digestive system, **Rose Petal Tea** cuts acidity in the stomach and reduces the spasms of diarrhoea, dysentery, and colitis. **Rose Petal Tea** makes a cooling tonic for the female reproductive system, reducing period pain and menopausal symptoms.

Rose Petal Vinegar can be helpful for headaches; pour some of the vinegar into a bowl, soak a clean washcloth in it, wring it out, and apply to the forehead. Repeat as necessary. You can also chill the bowl of vinegar in the fridge, which will help if your headaches are relieved by cold.

You can dry rose petals and put them in a grinder, then combine them with honey or agave syrup to make a paste. Take a spoonful for sore throats, upset tummies, and mild depression.

Caution: To prepare ripe rose hips for tea, wines, face masks, and liqueurs, etc., you will need to remove the irritant hairy seeds by straining through several layers of muslin. Rose hip is considered safe for adults when applied to the skin or taken by mouth. To be on the safe side, avoid if you are pregnant or breastfeeding, have a bleeding condition, and for two weeks before and after surgery.

Recipes

ROSE PETAL TEA

FRESH PETALS OF 1 LARGE FRAGRANT ROSE OR
2 TEASPOONS DRIED ROSE PETALS

250 ML OR 1 CUP BOILING WATER

Infuse, covered, for 5–10 minutes. Strain and drink for insomnia, nervousness, mild depression, headaches, period pain, and menopausal symptoms.

ROSE HIP TEA

25 GRAMS OR 1 OUNCE FRESH ROSE HIPS

250 ML OR 1 CUP WATER

Cut the rose hips open, put them in a pan with the water, and bring to boil. Turn off the heat and allow the rose hips to infuse for 15 minutes. Strain the liquid through a very fine sieve or several layers of muslin to remove the irritant hairs. Add honey, agave syrup, or a dash of lemon as desired. Take for colds and flu and to treat the symptoms of diarrhoea.

ROSE PETAL STEAM FOR MATURE SKIN

1 LITRE OR 4½ CUPS BOILING WATER

1 HANDFUL ROSE PETALS

Pour boiling water over the rose petals and allow to infuse for 5 minutes. Putting a towel over your head to keep the steam in, lower your face over the bowl and allow the steam to penetrate your pores for a few minutes. Rinse your face with cold water to seal the pores and finish with a moisturiser.

. . . .

Rose Petal Syrup

Place roses in a jar and fill the jar with water. Put a lid on the top and infuse for 8 hours. Then pour the roses and the water they are soaking in into a pan. Heat the water to boiling point. Filter off the liquid, squeezing the flowers. Return the liquid to the jar and add more flowers and repeat the operation. Then, to every 500 ml or 2 cups of the infusion, add 900 grams or 4½ cups of sugar and boil for 20 minutes. Pour into sterilised bottles. Store in the fridge. Pour over desserts. Take a spoonful before bed for insomnia.

. . . .

Rosehip Syrup

900 GRAMS OR 2 POUNDS HIPS

1700 ML OR 7 CUPS WATER

450 GRAMS OR 2¼ CUPS SUGAR

Pick red hips and mince in a food processor. Put them straight into the water, bring to boil, and then remove from the heat and allow the pan to stand for 15 minutes. Strain though very fine muslin (reserve the liquid) and return the hips to the pan with a fresh 850 ml or 3½ cups water. Boil, then stand for 10 minutes and strain. Reserve the liquid and combine it with the first batch of retained liquid and boil until the liquid is reduced to around 850 ml or 3½ cups. Add the sugar and stir until dissolved. Boil 5 minutes. Strain into bottles and seal immediately. Store in the fridge. Pour over desserts or take a spoonful as required for colds and flu, painful joints, and arthritic conditions.

. . . .

Rose Petal Vinegar

ROSE PETALS (RED OR PINK FRAGRANT TYPE)

WHITE VINEGAR OR CIDER VINEGAR

Fill a glass jar with the rose petals. Cover with the vinegar and leave on a sunny windowsill for 2 weeks until the vinegar has turned a good red. Strain into a clean dark bottle and seal. Use on salads or dab on the forehead to relieve headaches.

. . . . .

Rose Body Scrub

200 GRAMS OR 1 CUP SUGAR

15 GRAMS OR 3 TEASPOONS DRIED ROSE PETALS

10 DROPS ROSE ESSENTIAL OIL (OR ROSE GERANIUM OIL)

120 ML OR ½ CUP VEGETABLE OIL

1 TABLESPOON VEGETABLE GLYCERINE

Combine the ingredients in a jar. Use as a body scrub in the shower to exfoliate and remove dead skin cells.

Sweet Rosewater to Perfume Clothes
(BASED ON A RECIPE FROM 1594)

500 ML OR 1 CUP ROSEWATER (AVAILABLE COMMERCIALLY)

1 TABLESPOON FRESH LAVENDER FLOWERS

2 TABLESPOONS ORRIS ROOT POWDER

4 DROPS CLOVE ESSENTIAL OIL

Place in a large glass jar and leave on a sunny windowsill for 14 days. Strain into a clean jar and keep tightly stoppered. Add a teaspoonful to the final rinse water of your magical robes.

Rose Hip Vinegar

25-30 HIPS

WHITE VINEGAR OR CIDER VINEGAR

Slit the hips. Put them in a jar and cover them with vinegar. Sit the jar on a sunny windowsill for 30 days, shaking daily. Strain off the liquid (through several fine layers of muslin to remove the irritant hairs) into a clean jar. Mix with water and take for sore throats; gargle with it, then swallow the mixture. For colds, take 1 tablespoon in a mug of hot water. Use in salad dressings.

. . . .

Rose Petal Wine

4½ LITRES OR 19 CUPS BOILING WATER

2 LITRES OR 8 CUPS ROSE PETALS

900 GRAMS OR 4½ CUPS SUGAR

WHITE WINE YEAST (AVAILABLE ONLINE)

WINE YEAST NUTRIENT (AVAILABLE ONLINE)

Pour boiling water over the rose petals and allow to infuse until the water becomes scented. Strain and dissolve the sugar into the liquid. Transfer to a demijohn and add the yeast and nutrient according to manufacturer's instructions. Fit an airlock. Leave in a warm place until the wine has finished fermenting (until the bubbles stop in the airlock). Siphon into a clean demijohn and leave to settle for a few weeks. Siphon into sterilised bottles. Store as you would any other wine. The longer this wine is kept, the stronger the rose perfume becomes.

. . . .

Rose Hip Wine

900 GRAMS OR 2 POUNDS HIPS

900 GRAMS OR 4½ CUPS SUGAR

4½ LITRES OR 19 CUPS BOILING WATER

JUICE OF 1 LEMON

WINE YEAST (AVAILABLE ONLINE)

WINE NUTRIENT (AVAILABLE ONLINE)

Wash and crush the hips. Put the sugar in a brewing bin with the hips and cover with boiling water. Stir well and cool to lukewarm. Add the lemon juice, yeast, and nutrient according to manufacturer's instructions. Cover and leave for 14 days, stirring daily. Strain well, transfer to a demijohn, and fit an airlock. Leave in a warm place until it has finished fermenting (the bubbles in the airlock have stopped) and siphon into a clean demijohn. Leave to clear for several weeks, then siphon off into bottles. Store as you would any other wine.

. . . . .

ROSE PETAL JAM

100 GRAMS OR 4 OUNCES ROSE PETALS

680 GRAMS OR 3⅜ CUPS SUGAR

1 TABLESPOON LEMON JUICE

150 ML OR 10 TABLESPOONS WATER

150 ML OR 10 TABLESPOONS ROSEWATER

Put the rose petals in a heatproof bowl and set aside. Meanwhile, put the sugar, lemon juice, water, and rosewater in a pan and bring to boil. Reduce the heat and simmer 5 minutes, then pour over the rose petals. Stand overnight. Put the mixture into a pan and simmer gently for 30 minutes or so until it thickens.

ROSE HIP FRUIT CHEESE

1 KILO OR 2½ POUNDS APPLES

60 GRAMS OR 2 OUNCES ROSE HIPS

JUICE OF 4 ORANGES

140 ML OR 9½ TABLESPOONS WATER

900 GRAMS OR 4½ CUPS SUGAR

Wash the apples and chop, without removing the skin and cores. Slice the hips and put them in a muslin bag. Put the apples, hip bag, and orange juice into a pan with the water. Cook over a low heat until the apples are soft and pulpy. Remove the bag with the hips and discard them. Press the apples through a sieve and measure the resulting puree. For each 560 ml or 1 pint or 2⅓ cups, add 450 grams or 1 pound or 2 cups sugar. Put the sugar and pulp in a pan over a medium heat and cook until the mixture becomes very thick (this will take about 60 minutes), stirring frequently to prevent burning. Spoon this into jars. Serve with bread, hot buttered toast, scones, cheese, or meat dishes.

. . . .
ROSE HIP JELLY

Gather hips and cut them in half. Put them in a pan and cover them with water. Simmer until soft, which will take about an hour. Strain the pulp through muslin and collect the juice. Measure it and for each 560 ml or 1 pint or 2⅓ cups, add 450 grams or 1 pound or 2 cups sugar and the juice of one lemon. Return to the pan and simmer until the setting point is reached on a sugar thermometer. Spoon into jars.

. . . .
MACERATED ROSE OIL

If you want to make a rose oil, by far the simplest method is to make a macerated rose oil. Simply pack a clean glass jar with strongly scented, lightly crushed rose petals. Cover with a light oil, such as grapeseed or sunflower, and put in a dark place for a week, shaking daily. Strain the oil from the petals onto fresh petals and repeat. Keep repeating this process until the oil takes on the strength of scent you would like. Use directly on your skin or add to homemade cosmetics. It is good for dry, mature, irritated skin in particular.

. . . .
ROSE OTTO ESSENTIAL OIL AND ROSE HYDROSOL

To make a homemade distilled (rose otto) oil, use the homemade flower hydrosol method. Take a big saucepan and put a trivet on the bottom of it. Pack your rose petals around it and add just enough distilled water to cover them. Put a small heatproof bowl on top of the trivet. Bring the water to boil. Now place a large heatproof bowl on top of the big saucepan and fill it with ice cubes. This will cause the rising steam to condense back into water droplets and drop back down onto the smaller bowl. (Add more ice if it starts to warm up.) Simmer for a while before carefully removing the pan from the heat and taking out the small bowl—there will be some condensed liquid in it. Allow it to cool. As you tilt the bowl you might be lucky enough to find a few tiny drops of pure rose oil amongst the condensed rosewater. You might need a syringe to get these away from the rosewater, and you won't have very much at all. At least you will have some rose hydrosol (rosewater), the condensed water which is very useful. It may or may not smell very strongly.

. . . .

ROSE ABSOLUTE ESSENTIAL OIL AND BONUS ROSE VODKA

For an alcohol (rose absolute) extraction, take as many roses as you can and allow them to wilt and lose their water content. Fill a jar with the petals and cover them with the highest proof vodka you can find (at least 120 proof). Keep in a dark place for a week, shaking daily. Strain off the vodka. Add more dried roses to it and repeat. You can repeat this whole process several times, and you will have to repeat it many times to get a strong scent. Eventually, strain off the final batch and leave the sealed jar to stand for a day or two. You will see some separation of the vodka and plant oils. Place the jar upright in the freezer very carefully without agitating it and mixing them up again. Leave overnight. Vodka doesn't freeze, but the plant materials will. Remove the bottle from the freezer and quickly skim off the plant material onto some cheesecloth stretched over a bowl. Pick off the frozen bits before they melt and place them in a dark glass bottle. This is your essential oil. It may not smell very strong or be very pure, and you won't get much at all, but you will have made some! You can drink the rose vodka.

Sunflower

Helianthus annus

PLANETARY RULER: Sun

ELEMENT: Fire

ASSOCIATED DEITIES: Inti

MAGICAL VIRTUES: Sun, Midsummer,
happiness, blessings, fertility, abundance, strength,
courage, action, self-image, consecration

With their large heart-shaped leaves and giant flowers that look like bright rayed suns, I don't think any plant is more cheerful than a sunflower. These tall annual plants are native to North and Central America but now are widely cultivated throughout the world. And they are so easy to grow!

The botanical name is derived from the Greek words *helios* (sun) and *anthos* (flower). This also accounts for the plant's common name, a reference to the way in which the flowers turn to follow the path of the sun across the sky during the day. Sunflowers were unknown in ancient Greece, and despite what I keep reading on the internet, the flower that the god Apollo turned the nymph Clytie into was not helianthus, but the calendula marigold, which was also called sunflower from the way it responds to the sun.

Native Americans have grown sunflowers for at least 3,000 years and for food, fodder, fibre, and oil. In Central and South America the sunflower was a symbol of the sun. Aztec priestesses carried them during ceremonies and wore jewellery in the shape of sunflowers.

For the Incas, the sunflower was in the image of Inti, their sun god. The sunflower was introduced into Europe in the sixteenth century by Spanish explorers. It was grown for the first time in 1562 in Madrid from seeds that came from Mexico and Peru.

Sunflowers were widely employed in folk medicine. Native Americans used them as a remedy for snakebite and boiled the seeds to make an oil to dress their hair. Whole flowers were boiled by the Dakota for lung problems. Russians also used them for lung problems and preserved the stalks and leaves in vodka for gout. Sunflowers were smoked in the USA for hayfever. In Iran and Turkey, a tincture made from the seeds was used as a substitute for quinine to relieve fevers. Sunflower seeds were made into necklaces to protect the wearer from smallpox.

Magical Uses

Sunflowers represent joy, luck, and abundance. Plant them in your garden or have some cut flowers in your house for good fortune. Put some sunflowers on your dining table to invoke plenty or put the petals in potpourri.

They are plants of fertility. Eat sunflower seeds or sunflower oil. Use them in fertility spells and charms. Wear a necklace of sunflower seeds.

The sunflower is considered a flower of loyalty because day after day, it follows the sun from east to west. Use sunflowers in rituals and shared food to foster the loyalty of a group. Use it in charms and spells to ensure fidelity.

They are flowers of the sun and can be used to honour sun gods, in all solar rituals, and in magic, particularly for the summer solstice. Wear it in chaplets, use it in decorations, add sunflower seeds and oil to the food, drink **Sunflower Seed Tea**, or add the petals to incense. The flowers can be boiled to yield a yellow dye for robes and other ritual clothing for Midsummer.

The stems are fibrous and excellent for homemade paper making for ritual scrolls and books.

If you are feeling depressed, use the energy of sunflowers in a flower essence, take **Sunflower Seed Tea**, or soak in a bath to which sunflower petals have been added. Use in spells to improve your self-image.

Use sunflower oil to consecrate healing stones and gems.

Add the petals and seeds to charms designed for courage and action.

Culinary Uses

Sunflower seeds are a rich source of vitamin E, vitamin B1, manganese, selenium, phosphorus, magnesium, vitamin B6, folate, and niacin. They can be eaten raw or roasted, added to bread, cakes, and salads, or used as a coffee substitute. They can be ground into a powder for use as a gluten free flour; when mixed with cereal flours, it makes a nutritious bread.

Sunflower Seed Butter can be used as a sandwich filling and for dips and spreads. The sprouted seed can be eaten in salads and sandwiches. The young fresh flower buds can be steamed and served like globe artichokes. The petals can be made into tea, added to salads, used as a garnish, or added to soups, stews, and rice dishes.

Cosmetic Uses

Sunflower Petal Oil contains antioxidants and moisturising agents that help prevent aging and can help minimise wrinkles. It is suitable for all skin types. You can massage the oil directly into your face and body (be sparing). Add it to baths.

Add sunflower petals to soaps and bath bombs.

Medicinal Uses

Sunflower Seed Tea or **Sunflower Tincture** may be useful for bronchial, laryngeal, and pulmonary infections, coughs, colds, and for whooping cough.[107]

A tea made from the leaves or **Sunflower Tincture** is used to reduce high fevers. The crushed leaves can be used as a poultice on sores, swellings, and insect bites.

Caution: Sunflower is considered generally safe for oral and topical use. However, the plant can trigger asthma and skin allergies in some sensitive people. The growing plant can accumulate nitrates, especially when fed on artificial fertilizers.

---

107   S. Guo, Y. Ge, and K. Na Jom, "A Review of Phytochemistry, Metabolite Changes, and Medicinal Uses of the Common Sunflower Seed and Sprouts (*Helianthus annuus* L.)" in *Chemistry Central Journal* 11, 95 (2017), https://doi.org/10.1186/s13065-017-0328-7.

Recipes

SUNFLOWER SEED TEA

1 HANDFUL SUNFLOWER SEEDS, CRUSHED

600 ML OR 2 CUPS WATER

Boil the seeds in water for 20 minutes, strain, and sweeten with honey if desired. Drink for bronchial, laryngeal, and pulmonary infections, coughs, colds, and whooping cough.

SUNFLOWER PETAL OIL

250 ML OR 1 CUP PURCHASED SUNFLOWER OIL

HANDFUL SUNFLOWER PETALS

In a double boiler or slow cooker, combine the oil and petals and simmer very gently for 2 hours. Strain into a clean jar. Massage directly into your face and body to soothe the skin and minimise wrinkles.

SUNFLOWER LIP BALM

7 TABLESPOONS SUNFLOWER PETAL OIL (AS ABOVE)

2 TEASPOONS. RUNNY HONEY

6 TABLESPOONS BEESWAX, GRATED

In a double boiler or slow cooker, warm the oil and honey together (do not boil). Remove from the heat and stir in the wax until it has melted. Pour into small pots and seal.

. . . .

SUNFLOWER SKIN TONER

SUNFLOWER PETALS

WITCH HAZEL

Crush the flower petals and put them into a jar. Cover with the witch hazel. Leave overnight and strain the liquid into a clean bottle. Use in place of your usual skin toner and follow with a moisturiser.

. . . .

SUNFLOWER PETAL SALVE

SUNFLOWER PETAL OIL (AS ABOVE)

BEESWAX OR SOY WAX

Slightly warm your prepared oil and add the wax, allowing 1 tablespoon of grated beeswax to 250 ml or 1 cup macerated oil. As soon as the wax has melted, pour into jars. This will keep 1–2 years. Apply to sores, swellings, and insect bites.

. . . .

SUNFLOWER SEED BUTTER

Put a handful or two of sunflower seeds into your food processor and whizz them up. You are looking for a consistency like peanut butter. Be careful not to overheat the motor of your processor and stop now and again if necessary. It will take at least 10 minutes. Scrape it out, add salt to taste, and put into a clean jar. It will keep in the fridge for 2 weeks.

. . . .

SUNFLOWER TINCTURE

SUNFLOWER LEAVES, DRIED

VODKA

Put the crumbled leaves in a glass jar and cover with the vodka. Put a lid on the jar. Infuse 10 days in a cool, dark place. Strain. Take for bronchial, laryngeal, and pulmonary infections, coughs, colds, and whooping cough.

. . . . .

Violet

Viola odorata

. . . .

PLANETARY RULER: Venus

ELEMENT: Water

ASSOCIATED DEITIES: Aphrodite, Io,
Orpheus, Venus, Attis, Ares, Persephone

MAGICAL VIRTUES: Ostara, death, love, renewal

One of the first signs that spring is really here are the sweet violets blossoming beneath my trees. Violets are small hardy perennials, native to Europe and North Africa but now naturalised in North America and eastern Asia. They can often be found growing in fields, hedgerows, meadows, and on scrub or waste ground. The leaves are heart-shaped and the purple (or occasionally white) five-petalled flowers are borne on long stalks in early spring. There are more than 500 species; the pansy is a cultivated kind of violet.

Like other such early flowers, they carry with them the promise of the regeneration of the year and all the good things to come as the weather warms. In the Middle Ages, the appearance of the first violets were a cause for great celebration in Europe; Duke Leopold (1198–1230) sent his whole court out to scour the banks of the Danube for the first violet. In many places, it was believed that the very first violet of the year had special properties and would protect the finder from illness or the evil eye for a whole year.

For the ancient Greeks, they were dedicated to Persephone, who was both the goddess of spring and the queen of the dead. She was out collecting violets when she was abducted by Hades and stolen away to his chthonic realm. While she was there, the earth fell into a permanent winter while her mother, the goddess Demeter, searched for her. Eventually, all the gods agreed that Persephone should spend part of the year in the netherworld, ruling over the dead with her sombre husband, and part on earth with her mother. When she returns in the spring, the land is rejuvenated and flowers bloom, but when she goes back to the underworld, winter comes. This gives the violet its dual mythology as a happy flower of spring but also a flower of the dead. Strangely, one further association of the violet with the underworld is that they grow a second kind of flower that never sees the light of day but grows underground. These are called cleistogamous flowers (*cleistos* meaning "closed" and *gamos* meaning "marriage"), yet these flowers produce viable seeds.[108]

Violets were associated with another death and resurrection figure, the vegetation god Attis. When his mysteries were celebrated in Rome at the spring equinox, he was represented by a pine tree decorated with violets that were believed to have sprung from his blood. Attis was laid in his grave; in the morning the priest opened the tomb and declared that the god had risen and returned from the dead. The day was marked as the festival of joy, the Hilaria.

Because of its association with the underworld, its purple colour, and its drooping head, the violet was a symbol of death. On the day ancient Romans remembered their dead, violets were laid on graves. Even by the time of the Victorian language of flowers, violets signified death, so it was unlucky to bring them indoors. In England it was believed that picking violets with the dew still on them would result in the death of a loved one.

Conversely, with its sweet scent and heart-shaped leaves, for both the Greeks and Romans the violet was also associated with Aphrodite (Venus in Roman mythology), the goddess of love, though Aphrodite has her own aspects as the fertile regenerator of spring. Violets sprang up wherever she trod, while her attendants, the Three Graces, plaited her crown of violets.[109] Naturally, this meant that violet, with its heart-shaped leaves, was a frequent ingredient of love potions and spells. The association with love persisted. A sixteenth-century poem runs: "Violet is for faithfulnesse / Which in me shall abide / Hoping likewise that from your heart / You will not let it slide."[110] During the nineteenth century, violets were often used to decorate love tokens, porcelain, and treasure boxes. Napoleon

---

108   https://chestnutherbs.com/even-violets-need-a-plan-b/.

109   There is no ancient authority for Herrick's tale (in his *Hesperides*) that violets are the descendants of some unfortunate girls, who, having defeated Venus in a contest of sweetness, were beaten blue by the goddess in her jealous anger.

110   A. Cook, "Iostephanos," *The Journal of Hellenic Studies* 20 (November 1900), 1–13, doi:10.2307/623737.

was said to have given Josephine a violet nosegay on each wedding anniversary, and when he was banished to Elba, he vowed to return with the violets in the spring. Queen Victoria popularised posies of violets, and they were a traditional Mothering Sunday (the first Sunday of Lent) gift in the UK.

The genus name *Viola* comes from the Greek for the plant, *ione*. There are several legends as to how it got its name. In one, the god Zeus turned Io into a heifer so that his wife Hera would not suspect their affair; Io's tears turned into violets. Others say that certain nymphs from Ionia offered violets to Zeus, or that the hero Ion met water nymphs on his way to Attica who presented him with violets to show their favour, so he founded the city of Athens there. Violet was one of the emblems of ancient Athens, which was called the City of the Violet Crown.

Sweet violets are so-called because they are sweetly scented, though other types of violets do not share this property. In Bohemia it is said that violets lose their scent after the first clap of thunder, meaning that the later summer flowering varieties of violets are scentless. The strange thing is that if you inhale the perfume of sweet violets, they seem to quickly lose their perfume, hence the phrase "smell the smell out of violets." This is because they contain the chemical ionine, which supresses the sense of smell. The nineteenth-century French scientist de Panille claimed that the scent had a harmful effect on the voice, and it is said that the singer Marie Sass could not sing after smelling violets; even today, some singing teachers forbid the use of violet cologne. This is somewhat at odds with their connection with the ancient Greek legendary musician Orpheus, whose music was so beautiful that it could charm the birds from the trees. Violets were said to have bloomed where the lute of Orpheus fell when he was killed by drunken Maenads. Zeus took the lute and placed it in the stars, but the violets were the sweet embodiments of his music and dedicated to Orpheus.

The shy little violet, nestling half-hidden on the woodland floor, is a symbol of humility, purity, chastity, modesty, and discretion. In Christian lore they are a symbol of Christ's humility through incarnation and the Virgin Mary, whom St. Bernard of Clairvaux wrote of as the "sweet virgin of humility."[111] In a spurious piece of mythology, René Rapin (1621–1687) related that the flower was once a maid called Ianthis, one of Diana's nymphs, who was forced to run away from the unwanted attentions of Apollo in order to save her virginity, till Diana stained her face blue to put him off. Others say that Ia, a daughter of Midas, betrothed to Attis, was transformed by Diana into a violet so that she might be saved from

---

[111] de Cleene and Lejeune, *Compendium of Symbolic and Ritual Plants in Europe.*

Phoebus, the sun god. However, neither Ianthis nor Ia are genuine mythological characters.

The white violet is a symbol of innocence and openness.

Violets have long been used in cosmetic and healing preparations. They were believed to have the ability to moderate anger, strengthen and comfort the heart, and promote refreshing sleep. The Roman writer Pliny recommended that revellers wear chaplets of violet flowers to prevent hangovers. The ancient Greeks wore them to induce sleep and to prevent headaches. According to the ninth century Codex Sangellensis, to cure a headache, rub the forehead with violets. The sixteenth-century herbalist Ascham said that "for them that may not sleep for a sickness seethe violets in water and at even let him soke well his temples, and he shall sleepe well by the grace of God."[112]

The leaves should be collected during the early spring and dried. The flowers should be harvested when available and dried slowly in the shade to retain their colour. The flowers can be dried and used for potpourri or for decorating homemade Valentine's cards, and you can even make a DIY soil tester from them—an infusion of violets will turn red if something acidic is added to it (such as a few grains of acid soil) and green if something alkaline is added.

Magical Uses

The power of violets concerns the return of life, the energy of green shoots emerging from the underworld in spring, and new life coming from death. Use violet flowers in your Ostara decorations and chaplets or use **Violet Wine** for your ritual drink. Dried violet flowers and leaves may be added to incenses for the spring equinox and any incenses designed to invoke springtime death and resurrection deities or vegetation deities. Keep the first violet you find in spring as a protective amulet; place it in a small cloth pouch and carry it with you.

You can use the power of violet when you need to emerge from a personal dark time too, when you have been shaken by major changes and transitions. Working with the plant, perhaps in the form of **Violet Tea** or **Violet Flower Essence**, will help you to accept yourself, recognise your own self-worth, overcome your timidity, and find a place of balance and stillness that will prepare you to emerge into a time of happiness.

Use violets in funeral flowers and funeral incenses or plant violets on a grave to signify that from death, rebirth will come.

---

112   Quoted in Watts, *Elsevier's Dictionary of Plant Lore.*

Violets are sacred to goddesses of love and may be employed in incenses to invoke and honour them, as well as employed in love spells, rituals, charm bags, and amulets. To attract a new love, carry a sachet of violet and lavender flowers. When you invoke the goddess of love, you may use violet decorations in your temple or circle. Give violets to your beloved or place them in the wedding bouquet/handfasting flowers. Share **Violet Wine** with your lover or use it in the handfasting ritual.

Violets are sacred to the god of music, so use them in incense and spells when invoking him or drink **Violet Tea** or **Violet Wine** when looking for musical inspiration.

Lastly, violets are associated with the twilight, a magical "time between times," when the otherworld is closer and it is easier to slip into. **Violet Wine** or **Violet Tea** may be taken at twilight to facilitate passage into the otherworld and make contact with the fairy folk. This is especially effective on Midsummer's Eve.

CULINARY USES

All the members of the true Viola family (violets and pansies) are edible, though sweet violets have the best flavour and in the past were commonly consumed. The Greeks and Romans made wine (*Vinum Violatum*) from violets, the buds were eaten in salads in Elizabethan times, and Mon Amy, a pudding made with violets, was popular in the Middle Ages.

They are rich in vitamins A and C. The young leaves, which taste faintly of celery, can be eaten in salads, crystallised, or added to soufflés. The flowers can be made into a soothing **Violet Tea**, **Candied Violet Flowers** used for cake decorations, or the petals used fresh as an edible garnish for soups, salads, and cocktails, or freeze them into ice cubes and drop them into drinks. The flowers can be made into **Violet Wine**—if you can harvest enough (please don't take them from the wild). A **Violet Syrup** can be added to cocktails or poured over desserts and ice cream.

COSMETIC USES

Violet flowers are good for aging skin, acne, and large pores. The natural properties of violets include saponins (soap), which makes them an excellent cleanser. Our great-grandmothers used **Violet Milk** for this, or you can use **Violet Tea** as a facial wash.

Add **Violet Bath Salt** to the bath for a soothing and relaxing soak.

Violet salve makes a good moisturiser if you have very dry or irritated skin—the vitamin C in them brightens the look of the skin, the vitamin A improves the appearance of fine lines and wrinkles, while the natural oils and mucilage in the plant plump up the skin. **Macerated Violet Oil** can be used to soften hard skin and callouses on the feet and hands.

Macerated **Violet Oil** is also great for your hair. The mucilage in violets helps smooth frizz. Massage the oil into your hair, wrap your hair in a warm towel, leave for 2–3 hours, and wash out.

MEDICINAL USES

Sweet violet is naturally anti-inflammatory and soothing so can be helpful for those with eczema, rashes, insect bites, chafed skin, and dry skin conditions, applied directly in the form of violet salve or **Macerated Violet Oil**.

Violet Tea or **Violet Syrup** can be useful for treating coughs, chest colds, and catarrh. A teaspoon of **Violet Syrup** or **Violet and Rose Lozenges** will soothe sore throats.

Violet Infusion is used internally in the treatment of gout, headaches, rheumatism in the small joints, heartburn, gas, and urinary infections. It is also beneficial in cases of poor nerves, hysteria, insomnia, irritability, mild depression, and menopausal symptoms, including hot flushes. Add **Violet Infusion** to your bath, where its anti-inflammatory properties can help with muscular aches and joint pains.

Violet Infusion can be used as a gargle for the treatment of mouth inflammations and externally as a wash for eye inflammations and skin disorders such as eczema and psoriasis.

Use a violet poultice for bruises, wounds, abscesses, and skin rashes.

The leaves and flowers of sweet violet are slightly laxative. Take a cup of **Violet Infusion** or a spoonful of **Violet Syrup** for constipation.

Caution: *All of the true viola (including pansies) species are edible, but note that other flowers may be called violet, such as the African violet, and these are toxic and should not be consumed. No side effects or contraindications of violas have been reported except for individuals with the rare inherited disorder G6PD (glucose-6-phosphate dehydrogenase) deficiency, because it can aggravate haemolytic anaemia, and for those allergic to aspirin (salicylic acid). However, to be on the safe side, avoid medicinal amounts if you are pregnant or breastfeeding.*

Recipes

Violet Tea

250 ML OR 1 CUP BOILING WATER

1 TEASPOON VIOLET FLOWERS AND LEAVES

Pour the water over herb and infuse for 15 minutes. Strain and drink. You can add a little honey or agave syrup. Drink for coughs, chest colds, and catarrh.

Violet Infusion

600 ML OR 2½ CUPS BOILING WATER

60 GRAMS OR 2 OUNCES VIOLET LEAVES AND FLOWERS

Pour boiling water over the leaves, cover, and leave overnight or at least 8 hours. Strain. Will keep 24 hours in the fridge. Use internally in the treatment of gout, headaches, rheumatism in the small joints, heartburn, gas, urinary infections, insomnia, irritability, mild depression, and menopausal symptoms. Add it to the bath for muscular aches and joint pains. Gargle for the treatment of mouth inflammations. Use as a wash for eye inflammations and skin disorders such as eczema and psoriasis.

Great Grandma's Violet Milk

250 ML OR 1 CUP MILK, OATMILK, OR YOGHURT, WARMED

HANDFUL OF VIOLET FLOWERS

Pour the warmed milk over the violets. Steep for 4 hours. Strain and refrigerate when cool. Using cotton buds, dab this over your face and neck. Rinse with clean water and moisturise. Keeps 2 days in the fridge.

. . . .

Macerated Violet Oil

Pack the flowers and leaves into a clean glass jar. Cover them with oil. Put on the lid and place on a sunny windowsill for 2 weeks, shaking daily. Strain the macerated oil into a sterilised jar, fit the lid, and label. Will keep 8–12 months. Apply to eczema, rashes, insect bites, chafed skin, and dry skin conditions.

. . . .

Violet Syrup

1 LITRE OR 2 CUPS WATER

50 VIOLET FLOWERS

50 GRAMS OR ½ CUP SUGAR

Pour the water over the violets and stand overnight. Strain, discarding the flowers, then add the sugar to the retained liquid. Heat gently for 20 minutes (do not boil), then strain again into a clean jar. Keep refrigerated. Pour over desserts or take a spoonful as required for coughs and constipation.

. . . .

Candied Violet Flowers

2 TABLESPOONS ICING SUGAR (CONFECTIONERS' SUGAR)

1 LARGE EGG WHITE

25 VIOLET FLOWERS (LEAVE A BIT OF STEM ON
    TO MAKE THEM EASIER TO HANDLE)

Sift the sugar into a bowl. Beat the egg white until frothy. One by one, dip the flowers into the egg white, then hold them over the sugar, and sprinkle it over the flowers, trying to get an even coating. Place the coated flowers on a tray covered in greaseproof paper to dry. Pop them in the fridge for 24 hours. Remove and leave in a warm place for 24 hours. Cut off the stems and store in an airtight container for up to 2 months.

. . . .

Violet and Rose Lozenges

1½ TEASPOONS VIOLET FLOWERS, POWDERED

1 TEASPOON DRIED ROSE PETALS, POWDERED

1 TEASPOON MALLOW ROOT, POWDERED

HONEY OR MAPLE SYRUP

ICING SUGAR (CONFECTIONERS' SUGAR)

Combine the flower powders with the mallow root powder. Mix these with enough honey to enable you to form them into pea-sized balls—you might need to add a little sugar to help this along and keep the shape. Roll them in the sugar. Leave to harden for 24 hours. Store in an airtight container. Suck a lozenge as required to ease a sore throat and cough.

. . . .

Violet Flower Essence

To help you recognise your own self-worth and find a place of balance that will prepare you to emerge into a time of happiness, gather a few mature violet flowers. Float them on the surface of 150 ml spring water in a bowl and leave in the sun for 3–4 hours. Make sure that they are not shadowed in any way. Remove the flowers. Pour the water into a bottle and top up with 150 ml brandy or vodka to preserve it. This is your mother essence. To make up your flower essences for use, put 7 drops from this into a 10 ml dropper bottle, and top that up with brandy or vodka. This is your dosage bottle. The usual dose is 4 drops of this in a glass of water four times a day. When making flower essences, it is important not to handle the flowers—it is the vibrational imprint of the flowers you want to be held by the water, not your own imprint.

. . . .

Violet Bath Salt

2 TABLESPOONS FRESH VIOLET FLOWERS

4 TABLESPOONS COARSE SEA SALT

1½ TABLESPOONS EPSOM SALTS

Pound the violet flowers into the sea salt in a pestle and mortar or just put both in a food processor and give it a quick whizz. Spread on a tray and leave to dry for 24 hours. Then add the Epsom salts and put into a pretty jar. To use, just drop a handful or two into your bath and swirl around.

. . . .

Violet Rum

750 ML OR 3 CUPS DARK RUM

5 CM OR 2-INCH PIECE CINNAMON STICK

PETALS FROM 80 VIOLETS

15 CLOVES

2 STAR ANISE

JUICE AND ZEST OF 2 ORANGES

1 VANILLA POD

Put the rum in a jar and add the rest of the ingredients. Leave in a cool, dark place for one month. Strain into a clean bottle. This will keep around 5 years.

. . . .

Violet Sweet Creams

450 GRAMS OR 2¼ CUPS SUGAR

200 ML OR 13½ TABLESPOONS WATER

½ TEASPOON CREAM OF TARTAR

½ TEASPOON VANILLA ESSENCE

CANDIED VIOLET FLOWERS (SEE ABOVE)

. . . . .

Put the sugar and water in a pan and heat slowly until the sugar has dissolved. Increase the heat and bring to boil. Do not stir. Add the cream of tartar and continue boiling until a drop of the mixture forms a soft ball when dropped into cold water. Remove from the heat and add the vanilla essence. Sprinkle a board with cold water and put the fondant mixture onto it. Cool for a few minutes, then work the fondant with a palette knife until it is white and opaque. Knead with your hands until it is smooth. Shape small pieces into balls and press a crystallised violet on top of each one. The sweets will harden in about an hour and can be kept in an airtight tin.

VIOLET ICE CREAM

425 ML OR 1¾ CUPS SINGLE CREAM

140 ML OR 9½ TABLESPOONS MILK

60 GRAMS OR ⅝ CUP SUGAR

1 HEAPED TABLESPOON VIOLET FLOWERS

YOLKS OF 3 EGGS

Place the cream, milk, sugar and flowers in a pan and bring almost to boiling point. Remove from the heat. Cover the pan and leave it to stand for 1 hour. Strain the contents through a sieve or jam bag, pressing the flowers to obtain their flavour. Reheat the liquid to near boiling point. Remove from the heat. In a bowl, beat the eggs. Beat in some of the hot cream mixture, then add this to the cream in the pan. Heat gently until the mixture is thick enough to coat the back of a spoon. Pour into a container and leave to cool before placing it in the freezer (or into an ice cream maker if you have one—if you do, follow the manufacturer's instructions and disregard the following steps). When half frozen, whisk the ice cream thoroughly and return to the freezer. After 1 hour, whisk again. Leave a further hour and repeat the process. Freeze until ready to serve.

APPENDIX

Other Garden Plants for Magic

ACONITE (*Aconitum napellus*)—Ruled by the planet of Saturn and the element of water. Sacred to gods and goddesses of death and the underworld. NB: poisonous.

AGAPANTHUS (*Agapanthus* spp.)—Ruled by the planet Mars. Use in spells of fertility and love. NB: Poisonous.

AGRIMONY (*Agrimonia eupatoria*)—Ruled by the planet Jupiter and the element of air. Use for emotional healing, protection, psychic work, as a smudge, and in counter magic.

ALECOST (*Crysanthemum balsamita* syn. *Tanacetum balsamita*)—Ruled by the moon and the element of air. Use for women's rituals and rites of mother goddesses.

ALYSSUM (*Alyssum* spp.)—Ruled by the planet Mercury and the element of air. Use for balance, calm, peace, and protection. NB: Poisonous.

AMARANTH (*Amaranthus* spp.)—Ruled by the planet Saturn and the element of fire. Sacred to Artemis and Demeter. Use for rituals of death and funerals and for healing, immortality, and protection.

ANEMONE (*Anemone* spp.)—Ruled by the planet Mars and the element of fire. Sacred to Aphrodite, Tammuz, and Adonis. Use for rituals of Ostara, healing, hope, and renewal. NB: Some types of anemones are poisonous.

ANGELICA (*Angelica archangelica* syn. *Angelica officinalis*)—Ruled by the sun and the element of fire. Sacred to sun gods and Venus. Use in rituals of Beltane, Midsummer, healing, protection, cleansing, exorcism, purification, banishing, blessing, clairvoyance, visions, warding, and peace.

ARNICA (*Arnica montana*)—Ruled by the sun and the element of fire. Sacred to Apollo, Helios, Freya, and Ra. Use in spells of fertility and protection. NB: Poisonous when taken by mouth.

ASPHODEL (*Asphodelus albus*)—Ruled by the planets Saturn/Venus and the element of water. Sacred to Aphrodite, Venus, Hecate, Persephone, Pluto, Saturn, Hades, and Saturn. Use for spells of fertility, peace, and love. NB: poisonous if ingested.

ASTER (*Aster* spp.)—Ruled by the planet Venus and the element of water. Sacred to Venus and Aphrodite. Use for rites of calming, astral projection, and love. NB: poisonous.

AVENS (*Guem urbanum*)—Ruled by Jupiter and the element of fire. Sacred to Thor, Zeus, and Jupiter. Use for exorcism and purification.

BAMBOO (*Bambuseae* spp.)—Use in rites of protection, luck, hex breaking, and banishing.

BERGAMOT, MONARDA (*Monarda didyma*)—Ruled by the planet Mercury and the element of air. Use for protection and meditation.

BINDWEED (*Convolvulus* spp.)—Ruled by Saturn and the element of water. Use for spells of binding.

BLUEBELL (*Hyacinthoides non-scripta* / *Endymion non-scriptus* / *Scilla non-scriptus*)—Ruled by the moon/Saturn and the element of air. Sacred to Pan, fairies, Endymion, and Diana. Use for spells of constancy, fairy contact, joy, love, death, funerals, and at Beltane. NB: poisonous.

BURDOCK (*Arctium lappa*, greater dock, and *Arctium minus*, lesser dock)—Ruled by the planet Venus and the element of water. Sacred to Blodeuwedd. Use for counter magic and healing.

CALAMUS AKA SWEET FLAG (*Acorus calamus / Calamus Aromaticus*)—Use for spells of compelling, luck, healing, money, and protection.

CATNIP (*Nepeta cataria*)—Ruled by the planet Venus and the element of water. Sacred to Bast and Sekhmet. Use for trance and shapeshifting work.

CELANDINE, GREATER (*Chelidonium majus*)—Ruled by the sun and the element of fire. Sacred to sun gods. Use for protection, happiness, Ostara, and Beltane. NB: Poisonous.

CELANDINE, LESSER (*Ranunculus ficaria*)—Ruled by the sun and the element of fire. Sacred to Artemis, Hecate, Diana, and sun gods. Use for visions, cleansing crystal balls and scrying tools, and at Ostara. NB: Poisonous.

CHICKWEED (*Stellaria media*)—Ruled by the planet Venus and the element of earth. Sacred to Brigantia. Use for fertility and love and at Imbolc.

CHRYSANTHEMUM (*Chrysanthemum* spp.)—Ruled by the sun and the element of fire. Use in rites of the ancestors, funerals, home, strength, protection, and cheerfulness.

CLEAVERS (*Gallium aparine*)—Ruled by the moon and the element of water. Use in rites of renewal, Ostara, and purification.

COLUMBINE (*Aquilegia vulgaris*)—Ruled by the planet Venus and the element of water. Use in rites of healing, childbirth, gifts of the spirit, courage, love, spiritual warrior, second-degree initiation, and otherworld journeys. NB: Poisonous.

COMFREY (*Symphylum officinale*)—Ruled by the planet Saturn and the element of air. Sacred to Hecate. Use for cleansing, divination, luck, healing, love, safety whilst travelling, and protection.

CORNFLOWER (*Centaurea cyanus*)—Ruled by the planet Saturn and the element of water. Sacred to Flora, Chiron, and gods and goddesses of the harvest. Use to open the third eye chakra and clairvoyance or at the Autumn Equinox and Lughnasa.

CROCUS (*Crocus* spp.)—Ruled by the planets Mercury/Venus and the element of water. Sacred to Aphrodite, Venus, Eros, Cupid, and Persephone. Use for friendship, love, peace, or at Imbolc and Ostara. NB: Poisonous.

CUCKOO PINT (*Arum maculatum*)—Ruled by the planet Mars and the element of fire. Use at Beltane to mark the sacred marriage of the Lord and Lady. NB: poisonous.

CYCLAMEN (*Cyclamen* spp.)—Ruled by the planet Mars and the element of water. Sacred to Hecate. Use for banishing, fertility, protection, happiness, and lust. NB: poisonous.

DAFFODIL (*Narcissus pseudonarcissus*)—Ruled by the planet Mars. Use for love, luck, fertility, and death. NB: poisonous.

DATURA (*Datura stramonium*)—Use for sleep, protection, astral projection, and hex breaking. NB: poisonous.

ECHINACEA (*Echinacea* spp.)—Ruled by the planet Mars. Use for healing, prosperity, and protection.

ELECAMPANE (*Inula helenium*)—Ruled by the planet Mercury and the element of air. Use in rites of love, protection against magic, psychic powers, Midsummer, connection with nature spirits, and luck.

EVENING PRIMROSE (*Oenothera biennis*)—Ruled by the moon. Sacred to Diana. Use in spells of beauty, success, and friendship.

FEVERFEW (*Tanacetum parthenium* syn. *Chrysanthemum parthenium*)—Ruled by the planet Venus and the element of water. Use for protection, Midsummer, meditation, and healing.

FERN, MALE (*Dryopeteris felix-mas*) –Ruled by the planet Mars and the element of air. Sacred to dawn/sun gods and goddesses, sky gods of thunder and lightning, Hades, Pluto, Kupala, and Kupalo. Use for home protection, divination, and fairy contact.

FORGET ME NOT (*Myosotis sylvatica*)—Ruled by the planet Venus and the element of water. Sacred to Persephone. Use for love, memory, the underworld, shamanic initiation, spring, remembrance, and the dead.

FOXGLOVE (*Digitalis* spp.)—Ruled by the planet Venus and the element of water. Sacred to fairies. Use for protection, fairy contact, and third-degree initiation. NB: Poisonous.

GOLDENROD (*Solidago* spp.)—Ruled by the planet Venus and the element of air. Use for divination, love, luck, money, and prosperity.

HELIOTROPE (*Heliotropium arborescens*)—Ruled by the sun and the element of fire. Sacred to Clytie, Apollo, and Helios. Use for protection, wealth, devotion, prophetic dreams, and banishing. NB: poisonous.

HELLEBORE (*Helleborus niger*)—Ruled by the planet Saturn and the element of water. Sacred to Athene and Hecate. Use for astral projection, exorcism, and banishing. NB: poisonous.

HOLLYHOCK (*Althea rosea* syn. *Alcea rosea*)—Ruled by the planet Venus and the element of earth. Sacred to plant devas. Use for healing, success, money, protection, and meditation.

IRIS (*Iris* spp.)—Ruled by the planets Venus/moon and the element of water. Sacred to Aphrodite, Hera, Iris, Isis, Juno, Osiris, Venus, Demeter, and Persephone, and used to placate the Furies.

LARKSPUR (*Delphinium Consolida*)—Ruled by the planet Venus and the element of water. Use for joy and protection. NB: poisonous.

LILY (*Lilium* spp.)—Ruled by the moon and the element of water. Sacred to Adonis, Attis, Athene, Ceres, Astarte, Isis, Jupiter, Kundalini, Lakshmi, maiden goddesses, moon goddesses, Osiris, Psyche, Venus, and Sophia. Use in rites of the new moon, purity, and Imbolc. NB: Some types of lily are poisonous.

MIMOSA (*Mimosa pudica*)—Ruled by the planet Saturn and the element of water. Use for prophetic dreams, joy, love, healing, and protection.

MULLEIN (*Verbascum thapsus*)—Ruled by the planet Saturn and the element of water. Sacred to Circe, Jupiter, and crone goddesses. Use for protection, courage, attraction, Samhain, and ancestor contact. The powdered root is known as "graveyard dust."

NARCISSUS (*Narcissus* sp.)—Ruled by the planet Venus and the element of water. Use for beginnings, hope, peace, fertility, love, death, and renewal. NB: poisonous.

NICOTIANA (*Nicotiana* spp.)—Use for cleansing and purification. NB: poisonous.

ORRIS (IRIS) ROOT—May be added as a fixative to incense and used for spiritual protection and to connect with the higher self. NB: poisonous.

PHLOX (*Phlox* spp.)—Use for love, healing, weddings and handfastings, bonding, and harmony.

SNOWDROP (*Galanthus nivalis*)—Ruled by the moon and water. Sacred to Adonis, Attis, Ceres, Brigantia, Brighid, Isis, and the Virgin Mary. Use in rites of Imbolc, purity, and cleansing. NB: poisonous.

SOLOMON'S SEAL (*Polygonatum multiflorum*)—Ruled by the planet Saturn and the element of water. Use for banishing negativity and evil spirits, and to bring about change. NB: poisonous.

SWEET PEA (*Lathyrus odoratus*)—Ruled by the element of air and the planet Venus. Attracts loyalty and affection. NB: poisonous.

THISTLE (all)—Ruled by the planet Mars, the element of fire, and the star sign Aries. Sacred to Bacchus, Pan, Priapus, Thor, and Vesta. Use for spells of endurance and at Samhain.

VALERIAN (*Valeriana officinalis*)—Ruled by the planet Mercury and the element of water. Use for healing, love, soothing quarrels, protection from lightning, and working with cat familiars. The powdered root is called "graveyard dust."

WATER LILY (*Nymphaeaceae* spp.)—Ruled by the planets Neptune / moon and the element of water. Use at Yule, funerals, and moon rituals. NB: Some water lilies are poisonous.

WISTERIA (*Wisteria* spp.)—Use for good fortune and prosperity. NB: poisonous.

YARROW (*Achillea millefolium*)—Ruled by the planet Venus and the element of water. Sacred to Cernunnos, Herne, and Pan. Use at Midsummer and for healing, divination, clairvoyance, aura cleansing, and protection.

BIBLIOGRAPHY

Aristotle. *Nicomachean Ethics.* Loeb Classical Library, Harvard University Press, 1989.

Arnold, James. *Country Crafts.* London: John Baker Ltd., 1968.

Baker, Margaret. *Folklore and Customs of Rural England.* David and Charles, Newton Abbot, 1974

Barcroft, Alasdair. *Aloe Vera: Nature's Silent Healer.* London: BAAM Publishing, 2003.

Beyerl, Paul. *The Master Book of Herbalism.* Washington: Phoenix Publishing, 1984.

Bloom, William. *Working with Angels, Fairies and Nature Spirits.* London: Piatkus Ltd., 1998.

Blunt, Wilfred. *Flowers Drawn from Nature.* Sharpethorne: Leslie Urquhart Press, 1957.

Boxer, Arabella, and Philippa Back. *The Herb Book.* London: Octopus Books, 1980.

Brink, Laurie, and Deborah Green. *Commemorating the Dead: Texts and Artifacts in Context; Studies of Roman, Jewish, and Christian Burials.* Berlin: de Gruyter, 2008.

Brown, Deni. *Encyclopedia of Herbs and Their Uses.* New York: Dorling Kindersley, 1995.

Bruton-Seal, Julie, and Matthew Seal. *Hedgerow Medicine.* Ludlow: Merlin Unwin Books, 2008.

Buhner, Stephen Harrod. *Sacred and Herbal Healing Beers.* Boulder: Siris Books, 1998.

Castleman, Michael. *The Healing Herbs.* Emmaus: Rodale Press, 1991.

Chaucer, Geoffrey. *The Canterbury Tales* (1387). London: Penguin Classics, 2005.

Chevalier, Andrew. *The Encyclopaedia of Medicinal Plants.* London: Dorling Kindersley, 1996.

Culpeper, Nicholas. *Culpeper's Herbal* (1652). London: W. Foulsham & Co., n/d.

De Bray, Lys. *The Wild Garden*. London: Weidenfeld and Nicholson, 1978.

De Cleene, Marcel, and Marie Claire Lejeune. *Compendium of Symbolic and Ritual Plants in Europe*. Ghent, Belgium: Man & Culture Publishers, 2003.

De Menezes, Patricia. *Crafts from the Countryside*. London: Hamlyn, 1981.

Dietz, S. Theresa. *The Complete Language of Flowers: A Definitive and Illustrated History*. New York: Wellfleet Press, 2020.

Diodorus Siculus. *The Library of History*. Loeb Classical Library edition, 1933.

Down, Deni. *The Royal Horticultural Society Encyclopaedia of Herbs and Their Uses*. London: Dorling Kindersley, 1997.

Evans, Alex. *The Myth Gap*. London: Penguin Random House, 2017.

Evelyn, John. *Acetaria: A Discourse of Sallets* (1699). London: Marion Boyars Publishers, 2005.

Faber, Lee. *Aloe Vera*. Wigston: Abbeydale Press, 2008.

Fogel, Edwin Miller. *Beliefs and Superstitions of the Pennsylvania Germans*. America Germanica Press, 1915.

Franklin, Anna, and Sue Lavender. *Herb Craft*. Chieveley: Capall Bann, 1995.

Franklin, Anna. *Hearth Witch*. Earl Shilton: Lear Books, 2004.

———. *The Illustrated Encyclopaedia of Fairies*. London: Vega, 2003.

———. *Working with Fairies*. Career Press, 2005.

Frazer, J. G. *The Golden Bough: A Study in Magic and Religion*. London: Macmillan Press, 1976.

Genders, Roy. *Natural Beauty*. Lucerne: EMB-Services, 1992.

Gerard, John. *Gerard's Herbal* (1597). Senate Edition. London: Senate, 1994.

Gill, W. W. *A Manx Scrapbook*. London: Arrowsmith, 1963.

———. *A Second Manx Scrapbook*. London: Arrowsmith, 1932.

Gledhill, David. *The Names of Plants*. Cambridge University Press, 2002.

Gordon, Lesley. *A Country Herbal*. London: Peerage Books, 1980.

Green, James. *The Herbal Medicine Maker's Handbook*. Berkeley: Crossing Press, 2002.

Green, Miranda. *Gods of the Celts*. Gloucester: Allan Sutton, 1986.

Grieve, Maud. *A Modern Herbal*. New York: Dover Publications, 1981.

· · · · ·

Griffith, F. L., and H. Thompson, ed. *The Leiden Papyrus*. New York: Dover, 1974.

Griggs, Barbara. *Green Pharmacy: A History of Herbal Medicine*. New York: Viking Press, 1982.

Grigson, Geoffrey. *A Herball of All Sorts*. London: Phoenix House, 1959.

———. *The Englishman's Flora*. London: Phoenix House, 1955.

Guyton, Anita. *The Book of Natural Beauty*. London: Stanley Paul & Co., 1981.

Hemphill, Rosemary. *Herbs for All Seasons*. London: Penguin, 1975.

Henderson, Lizanne, and Edward J. Cowan. *Scottish Fairy Belief: A History from the Fifteenth to the Nineteenth Century*. Glasgow: Tuckwell Press, 2001.

Hoffman, David. *The Holistic Herbal*. Shaftsbury: Element Books, 1986.

Holmes, Peter. *The Energetics of Western Herbs*. Boulder: Artemis Press, 1989.

Hunt, Robert. *Popular Romances of the West of England*. London: Chatto and Windus, 1930 [first pub. 1881].

Jung, Carl. *The Practice of Psychotherapy* (Second Edition; Collected Works of C. G. Jung). Routledge, 1993.

Krauss, Helen K. *Begonias for American Homes and Gardens*. New York: Macmillan & Co., 1947.

Lawless, Julia. *The Illustrated Encyclopaedia of Essential Oils*. Shaftsbury: Element Books, 1995.

Leyel, Mrs C. F. *Herbal Delights*. London: Faber, 1937.

Little, Kitty. *Kitty Little's Book of Herbal Beauty*. Harmondsworth: Penguin Books, 1981.

Lust, John. *The Herb Book*. New York: Bantam Books, 1974.

Mabey, Richard. *Flora Britannica*. London: Sinclair-Stevenson, 1996.

———. *Food for Free*. Glasgow: William Collins, 1972.

———. *Plants with a Purpose*. London: Fontana, 1979.

MacLean, Dorothy. *To Hear the Angels Sing: An Odyssey of Co-Creation with the Devic Kingdom*. Lindisfarne Press, 1994.

McGrath, Sheena. *The Sun Goddess*. London: Blandford, 1997.

Mercatante, Anthony S. *The Magic Garden: The Myth and Folklore of Flowers, Plants, Trees, and Herbs*. New York: Harper & Row, 1976.

Meyer, Marvin W., and Richard Smith. *Ancient Christian Magic*. HarperSanFrancisco, 1994.

Murray, Liz, and Colin Murray. *The Celtic Tree Oracle*. London: Rider, 1988.

Nahmad, Claire. *Garden Spells: The Magic of Herbs, Trees and Flowers*. London: Pavilion Books, 1994.

Newdick, Jane. *Sloe Gin and Beeswax*. London: Charles Letts & Co., 1993.

Ody, Penelope. *The Complete Medicinal Herbal*. London: Dorling Kindersley, 1993.

Opie, Iona, and Moira Tatem, eds. A *Dictionary of Superstitions*. Oxford University Press, 1989.

Passebecq, Andre. *Aromatherapy*. Wellingborough: Thorsons, 1979.

Pennick, Nigel. *Secrets of East Anglian Magic*. Milverton: Capall Bann, 2004.

Phillips, Roger, and Martyn Rix. *The Ultimate Guide to Roses*. London: Macmillan, 2004.

Pliny the Elder. *Natural History*. Penguin Classics. London: Random House, 1991.

Raven, J. E. *Plants and Plant Lore in Ancient Greece*. Oxford: Leopard's Head Press, 2000.

Rhind, Jennifer Peace. *Fragrance & Wellbeing: Plant Aromatics and Their Influence on the Psyche*. London: Singing Dragon, 2013.

Rorie, David. *Folk Tradition and Folk Medicine in Scotland*. Edinburgh: Canongate Academic, 1994.

Ruck, Carl, and Danny Staples. *The World of Classical Myth*. Carolina Academic Press, 1994.

Seymour, John, and Sally Seymour. *Self Sufficiency*. London: Faber and Faber, 1973.

Simpson, Jaqueline, and Steve Roud. A *Dictionary of English Folklore*. Oxford University Press, 2000.

Spangler, David. *Subtle Worlds*. Issaquah: Lorian Press, 2010.

Spector Platt, Ellen. *Lavender: How to Grow and Use the Fragrant Herb*. Mechanicsburg: Stackpole Books, 2009.

Stapley, Christina. *Herbcraft Naturally*. Chichester: Heartsease Books, 1994.

Staub, Jack. *75 Exceptional Herbs for Your Garden*. Kaysville: Gibbs M. Smith Inc., 2008.

Steel, Susannah, ed. *Neal's Yard Remedies*. London: Dorling Kindersley, 2011.

Strauss, Rachelle. *Household Cleaning*. London: New Holland Publishers, 2009.

Summer Deer, Thea. *Wisdom of the Plant Devas: Herbal Medicine for a New Earth*. Vermont: Bear & Company, 2011.

Sumner, Judith. *Plants Go to War: A Botanical History of World War II*. Jefferson, NC: McFarland & Co., 2019.

Thiselton-Dyer, Thomas Firminger. *The Folk-lore of Plants* (1889). Echo Library, 2008.

Tisserand, Robert B. *The Art of Aromatherapy*. Rochester: Healing Arts Press, 1977.

Tongue, Ruth. *Somerset Folklore: County Series* VIII. Folk Lore Society, 1965.

Trevelyan, Marie. *Folk Lore and Folk Stories of Wales*. London: Elliot Stock, 1909.

Vickery, Roy. *Oxford Dictionary of Plant Lore*. Oxford University Press, 1995.

Walsh, Penny. *Spinning, Dyeing and Weaving*. London: New Holland Publishers, 2009.

Waring, Phillipa. A *Dictionary of Omens and Superstitions*. London: Souvenir Press, 1978.

Watts, D. C. *Elsevier's Dictionary of Plant Lore*. San Diego: Elsevier, 2007.

Wilde, Lady. *Ancient Cures, Charms and Usages of Ireland*. London: Ward & Downey, 1890.

———. *Ancient Legends, Mystic Charms and Superstitions of Ireland*. London: Ward & Downey, 1887.

Wong, James. *Grow Your Own Drugs*. London: Collins, 2009.

To Write to the Author

If you wish to contact the author or would like more information about this book, please write to the author in care of Llewellyn Worldwide and we will forward your request. Both the author and the publisher appreciate hearing from you and learning of your enjoyment of this book and how it has helped you. Llewellyn Worldwide cannot guarantee that every letter written to the author can be answered, but all will be forwarded. Please write to:

Anna Franklin
℅ Llewellyn Worldwide
2143 Wooddale Drive
Woodbury, MN 55125-2989

Please enclose a self-addressed stamped envelope for reply
or $1.00 to cover costs. If outside the USA, enclose
an international postal reply coupon.

Many of Llewellyn's authors have websites with additional information and resources. For more information, please visit our website:

WWW.LLEWELLYN.COM